FROM

THE

SANDS

OF

KANDAHAR

DAVID
WISEMAN

From the Sands of Kandahar

Copyright © 2025 by David Wiseman

Paperback: 978-1-963732-27-6

Hardcover: 978-1-963732-28-3

Published by

The Publishing Pad
www.thepublishingpad.com

To my two daughters
I love you to the moon and back.

To the animals
Every single one offered me the kind of love humans never could.

Anderson, Cooper, Maddie, Seven, Spencer, Austin, Steward, Tommy, Claw, Chewie, Thor, and Sheppie: I carry you all. You made life on this planet feel less like exile.

Praise for
From the Sands of Kandahar

"For anyone who has ever served, and especially all the veterans and their families impacted by the horror of Mefloquine, this book is a must-read. My hope is that as he shares so honestly about his life, other families who do not understand the veteran who returned home after Mefloquine just might find this book a window to understanding."
—**Marj Matchee,** Founder of The Annual Veterans Mefloquine Rally/Conference

"This is a must-read book and a great gift anytime for anyone who is struggling in life."
—**Mr. Glenn Roil,** Executive Chairman, Senior Advisor, and Co-Founder, Mental Health Foundation of Canada

From the Sands of Kandahar is not only a gripping account of military service in Afghanistan—it's a profound exploration of trauma, healing, and the invisible burdens carried across generations. In sharing his story, Wiseman has created more than a memoir—he's offered a road map for healing, a call for compassion, and a reminder that the scars of war are not always visible."
—**David Muise,** Director of Business Development, Nuvista Psychedelic Medicine

"From the Sands of Kandahar is not just a war memoir—it's a testimonial of survival and transformation. It exposes the hidden costs of military service, the silence of trauma, and the courage it takes to rebuild a soul. Wiseman's story ends not in despair but in reclamation."
—**Simon B. MacInnis,** Ocdt. Retired

"By relaying his experiences in the military at multiple levels, crossing continents and commands, Wiseman illuminates a broken link within the chain of currency unspent in the care of our injured soldiers who are suffering and enduring hardships despite the systems meant to support them. A read worth sharing. Spread the awareness! Pro Patria!"
—**Bruce Given,** CD, Sgt. Retired, Fellow RCR, Author, and Veterans' Advocate

"With refreshing candor, David Wiseman immerses the reader in his remarkable triumph over unimaginable adversity. Abused and neglected in the most malevolent ways in childhood, he had no blueprint to navigate relationships. In the military, obedience, hardship, and survival were well-known protagonists. His six-month tour in Afghanistan was his final descent into hell. From deadly Taliban ambushes to unnerving patrols in bazaars where even children were potential threats, fear was his constant companion. The same fear that permeated his childhood met him on the sands of Kandahar. Unwavering fortitude has since guided him in his ascent to healing body, mind, and spirit."
—**Dr. Sandra T. de Blois,** PhD., Professional Counsellor and Trauma Expert

Table of Contents

Part 3 The Aftermath

Part 4 Healing

Preface

I did not join the military to be a hero.

I joined to escape.

People say basic training breaks you down to rebuild you, but breaking was not anything new to me. By the time I donned the Canadian military CADPAT uniform, I had already survived a war no one talked about—a war fought in the hallways of my home, with blood and silence as its weapons.

In battle, I thrived.

Killing was what I was trained for.

Fear? I had known it my whole life.

It was the silence that followed that cut the deepest. The silence after a mission. The silence after friends died. The same silence that used to fall over our house after my father hurled furnitur e down the hallway while I, counting his footsteps, prayed they would not stop at my door.

In Afghanistan, the adrenaline was familiar. My body had already learned long before how to freeze, how to scan for danger, how to make myself invisible.

Combat did not scare me.

Coming home did.

This is not just a story about war.

This is the story of surviving one war before ever being deployed and learning how to live again after both.

Acknowledgement

To My Ancestors

To those whose names were never written down,
Whose pain echoed through blood and bone,
Whose survival carved the path beneath my feet—

I carry your stories in my marrow.
The wars you fought, the silences you endured,
The prayers whispered into cracked ceilings—
They live on in me.

You endured what should have broken you.
I write to remember.
I write to heal.
I write to break the cycle.

This memoir is not just mine.
It is ours.
A resurrection of the voices buried beneath duty,
Beneath shame,
Beneath history.

May this offering reach back through time
And forward through generations
As proof that we did not suffer in vain.

I am a survivor, a truth bearer, a builder of sacred ground from the depths of trauma. I have risen, not as who I once was, but as who I was always meant to become. My path is forged in pain alchemized into purpose, silence transmuted into voice, and darkness transformed into light. I walk the line between Protector and Healer, Warrior and Mystic, anchored by lived truth, guided by spirit, and committed to breaking the cycle that once bound me. I do this not just for myself, but for others still finding their way home. This is my vow to live with fierce compassion, create with soul integrity, and serve as a light in places where hope once flickered.

Part 1

Childhood

CHAPTER 1

Inheritance of Ash

Where It Started

I was born on March 24, 1985. My mother once told me I was a difficult birth, that I seemed unwilling to enter this world. While she struggled through more than thirty-six hours of labor, all she could think about was having a cigarette. In the end, they cut me out of her body by C-section. That was my welcome: hesitation, exhaustion, and craving.

I entered a family already thick with silence and conflict, shaped by wounds my parents never named: survival, addiction, and the programming of the Canadian Armed Forces. Their injuries became mine before I could even speak.

My parents had inherited those patterns from their own families and, later, from the institution that shaped them. The complex PTSD that followed was a current I was destined to repeat.

Their story had begun in Lahr, Germany, in the 1980s during the Cold War. My father was a Canadian soldier; my mother, a local girl desperate to escape an alcoholic father and a mother buried beneath hoarded silence. Their union was not romance but refuge, two wounded people colliding, mistaking escape for love.

My father spent his youth partying across Europe, drinking away his paycheques, showing up at home only in fragments. A few crumpled bills pressed into my mother's hand, a fleeting gesture of guilt, and then he was gone again. With us, he was mostly silent. His charm was reserved for strangers.

He cut us off from my mother's side of the family—the only ones who had ever tried to love us. It felt like a kidnapping, though I had no words for it then. In that isolation, he rewrote our story. Fed us lies until love itself became suspect, until distance felt safer than closeness, until fear was the air we breathed.

The Move to Canada

That fear deepened when we left Germany. In 1987, we boarded a Canadian Forces transport plane bound for Calgary, like so many other military families.

I remember flashes more than moments. The roar of engines. My mother's tight grip on my hand. The way the air smelled different when we stepped off the plane—dry, sharp, and strange. In Germany, the world had been soft and green. Here, it felt bigger, emptier, like the sky could swallow me. Boxes were piled around us like walls. My father's voice cut through everything, loud and final. I didn't understand the words, only the feeling—something ending, something gone.

In Canada, the abuse only sharpened. My father, a functioning alcoholic, deployed to Iraq to "save" strangers, yet he could not provide the basics for his own child. When he left, the rent went unpaid. My mother later told me she had to march into his workplace and beg his commanding officer for help. An elderly Italian couple down the hall kept us from eviction, offering food and ensuring we had shelter when he would not. My father excused it as the chaos of short-notice deployment orders, but neglect had been the pattern since my first breath.

Hunger marked those early years. Hunger for food. Hunger for safety. Hunger for someone to take responsibility. My mother, an immigrant, isolated in a foreign country, was left with nothing but bills and a child to carry.

The Fire

I remember the afternoon the candle almost burned us alive. Sunlight spilled through the window, warm on my skin, while the air inside hung heavy. My mother was passed out on the couch, her breathing slow, uneven. On the coffee table, a candle burned low, its flame small and harmless-looking, until it wasn't.

At first, it was just a faint smell, sharp and strange—not like the sweet wax I was used to, but something darker, more bitter. I rubbed my eyes and sat up, confused. Then I saw it. The flame had leaned too far, stretching tall and wild, licking at the edge of the table. The wood had started to blacken, thin trails of smoke curling upward like warning signs.

My heart jumped so hard it hurt. I wanted to call for her, but my voice got stuck. My throat felt like it was closing. All I could think was *We're going to die here, and no one will come in time.* I was small, so small, and the fire looked bigger every second.

I pushed at her shoulder, first softly, then harder. "Mom," I whispered, my voice breaking. Nothing. I shook her again, harder, panic spilling out as tears blurred the edges of everything. My hands were clumsy, shaking. I could hear the faint crackle of the wood, see the way the flame's shadow flickered against the wall, stretching tall and cruel in the afternoon light.

Finally she stirred, groggy and slow, as if swimming up from deep water. By then I was sobbing, my body trembling so hard I thought my bones might splinter. She waved the smoke away as if the fire had not almost swallowed us. But the smell hung thick in the air, choking me. That day, I learned how closely safety and danger live together, and how quickly someone can dismiss the flames.

Levels of Abuse

Some nights, we tried to pretend at being a family. Fast food was a treat, a small joy. I remember especially the smell of fries filling the room one night as my father set McDonald's bags on the table. But he'd brought nothing for her. He smirked when she asked, his cruelty casual, deliberate. The fight erupted in seconds. I sat frozen, clutching my Happy Meal, then broke my nuggets in half and slid pieces across to her. She took them with shaking hands, tears streaking her face.

Later, she and I sat in the corner with what was left. A cigarette burned between her lips, the ash trembling as if it might collapse at any second. She exhaled smoke and told me quietly that she was going to leave him one day. I nodded, too young to know what to do with her secret. What should have been joy became a battlefield, and her whispered confessions became mine to carry.

Through the blur of tears, I watched the smoke rise and twist, fragile patterns dissolving into the air. I did not know it then, but those patterns were already etching themselves into me: lessons of love and danger, hunger and ash.

In Calgary, things started to feel different. My dad said I had to shower with him. I didn't like it, but he said it was what families did. The water was hot; the room smelled like soap and fear. He told me it was love. He told me not to tell. I was four, and I wanted to believe him. I wanted to be good.

As he molested me, I would turn inward, back to those nights in the corner with my mother. I could still see the cigarette smoke drifting through the house, fragile patterns dissolving above us. That smoke became my escape, the only thing I could hold on to when there was nothing safe left to touch.

I had two sisters, both born into chaos. My first sister was born in 1989, a small baby with a mother still starved by my father's control. My second sister followed in 1990—a so-called mistake whose birth almost killed both her and our mother. I remember both arrivals not as celebrations but as times of confusion, the house thrown into chaos while I was left alone with my abuser. No adult stepped in. My sisters came wrapped in danger, deprivation, and silence.

My mother's pain spilled into me through late-night cigarettes and whispered promises. His shadow haunted our house. And then, in 1992, we left Calgary and moved across the country to Newfoundland.

The Move to St. John's, Newfoundland

We rode in a haze of exhaustion. My dad didn't stop often, and when he did, it was only for a few hours, all of us still trapped in the car. One memory of crossing the island of Newfoundland still haunts me. He pulled the van over to sleep in the dark woods, headlights switched off, the world outside swallowed by blackness. The trees pressed close, their branches clawing at the night sky, and the only light came from a scattering of cold, faraway stars.

Inside, the minivan was its own storm. Every child was screaming, our voices ricocheting against the windows, the air thick with sweat and tears from the long drive. His frustration erupted everywhere, sharp and unpredictable, striking out at anyone within reach. The night outside was vast and silent. Inside, it was chaos. For him, it was rest. For the rest of us, it was terror.

By the time the van carried us into St. John's, we arrived not as a family starting fresh but as survivors dragged into another chapter. The shadows from Calgary had followed us east, pressed into our lungs like the smoke we could never escape.

Thirty-seven years later, in the fall of 2023, I returned to the same German town where our story had begun. In an Airbnb, over coffee with relatives I hadn't seen since childhood, the unspoken finally surfaced. Their stories filled the gaps I had carried like unanswered prayers. One truth struck hardest: my father had not wanted me. A high-school friend of my mother's told me gently, her voice carrying sorrow instead of malice, as if she had been holding the secret too long. Her words confirmed what I had always felt: I was never wanted, only endured.

Canadian Forces Station, St. John's: Stars Through the Shelter's Window

I was just a kid, running down the streets pretending to be a Ninja Turtle. Leonardo, Michelangelo, Donatello, Raphael: They weren't just cartoon characters. They were my escape. On the nights when my parents screamed until the walls shook, when my mother's sobs filled the air, I prayed the Teenage Mutant Ninja Turtles would crash through the windows and rescue me and my sisters. But no one came. Just the noise. Just the fear. Just the bruises hidden behind closed doors.

That chaos followed something darker: a sex party in my bed. Four adults, including my mother, lay in the same place where I had once curled up under Ninja Turtle sheets, dreaming of rescue. I hid in my usual spot, a cabinet built into the wall, clutching the silence. In the morning, I crawled out and found strangers naked in my bed. I climbed back into the cupboard, needing the dark, needing the quiet. Later, a babysitter took us out and I pretended things were normal. But that evening, everything exploded.

My father's army friends stormed the house, convinced by the lies he'd told at work that he was the one being abused. Loyalty ran deep among soldiers; questioning a brother was unthinkable. They showed up like they were answering a call for backup, not visiting a family home. Their boots thudded against the floor, their voices sharp and commanding, barking orders as if we were prisoners instead of children frozen in fear.

At a neighbour's house, I tried to sleep, but the screaming still poured through the thin walls. Then red and blue lights flickered through the window as RCMP cruisers pulled up outside. The smells of cold vinyl and diesel filled the back seat as we huddled inside. I was only a child, but I had already seen too much.

That night, my mother, my sisters, and I were taken to a women's shelter.

What shocked me most was that my mother had finally made a move to save herself. My father, away in uniform, told me over the phone, "Do what the police tell you. Everything will be fine." But nothing was fine. That short drive to the shelter felt like the longest of my life.

We arrived after midnight. Clothes were scattered across the floor. Children's cries echoed down the hallways. This was not safety. It was survival. That star-filled night, I stayed awake, watching the sky shift from black to violet to orange. The stars were the only thing that had never lied to me. In their light, I made a silent promise: *I will never trust another human being again.*

The next morning, my immigrant mother did what she always did. She tried to carry on. She bundled us onto a city bus so I could get to school. I still hear the squelch of the brakes as we pulled up outside the building, a sound carved into memory. Years later, she told me she had begged the school not to release me to my father. But no one told me. As always, the adults made decisions in secret and left me to carry the cost.

A Fateful Choice

That afternoon, out of habit, I rode home with a friend's family. It seemed harmless at the time. I didn't know that choice would change everything.

When I stepped through the door, the chaos of the night before had been erased. Everything was spotless and staged as if nothing had ever happened. A babysitter stood watch until my father returned.

When he came through the door, there was no hug, only orders. That morning at the shelter was the last time I was alone with my mother for three years. My sisters arrived a few days later under the supervision of a youth worker.

My father threw her belongings to the curb like garbage and taught us to see her that way. One afternoon, as she drove past, I raised my middle finger at her from the window. I was nine years old—already weaponized. That image still haunts me. Not because I was angry, but because I believed it was right.

Only later did I understand what had really happened—that a child's love had been twisted into loyalty, that my gesture wasn't hatred but survival. I had been taught to mirror his contempt. I did it to stay safe, to earn belonging. It wasn't rebellion. It was obedience. And in that obedience, something innocent in me quietly died.

Another Move

That summer we moved again, just like we had a few years earlier. Pack up, shut up, and move on: that was the unspoken rule. While our world crumbled under lies and denial, the Canadian Forces packed up what was left of our house, the shattered remnants of a life already breaking apart. We got in our car and headed down the long highway toward our new house in Nova Scotia, putting all my memories, both good and bad, in the rearview mirror.

From then on, I turned inward. Imagination became my hiding place. Silence became my escape. Outwardly, I became the parent. I fed my sisters, bathed them, and dressed them. By the time I was eleven, it had become routine—especially during visits with my mother, who often lay paralyzed by depression. I was no longer just a child. I was a caretaker.

CHAPTER 2

Learning the Script

Canadian Forces Base, Debert, Nova Scotia: The Children in Transit

I was nine years old. Another move. Another school. Another set of strangers I was expected to call friends. By then, I had already learned how to pack up a life in silence, how to smile through goodbyes, how to disappear and start again. I was nine and already tired of starting over.

Confusion clung to me like a shadow. Nothing felt steady: home, family, even my own body. And when I stepped into that classroom, the chaos I had absorbed at home spilled out. I was reactive, quick to anger, quick to lash out. I had watched my father abuse my mother so many times that violence had already carved itself into me. His violence became my script, my default response, before I even understood what I was doing.

The schools didn't want to hear what I was going through. In the mid-1990s, it all felt so common. Kids like me weren't listened to; we were just labeled *difficult*. No one looked beneath the behavior. No one asked why.

I was always sick back then, worn down by the constant lack of food. Those early days in Debert were when I first began to realize how much my mother had done for us. Suddenly, I was making my own meals, patching together whatever I could find. My father worked long, erratic hours and couldn't afford babysitters, so we were often left on our own.

Most days, I dragged myself through school, fighting crushing fatigue. My body was already weakened by nights filled with his rage and mornings without proper nourishment. I was a child, but I felt hollow, depleted, carrying the exhaustion of a grown man before I even knew what childhood was supposed to feel like. I kept telling myself to stay awake, to keep going, as if survival was something you could will into being.

The Red-Haired Woman

When the red-haired woman first came to Debert in the summer of 1995, I let myself hope. Maybe he had chosen someone kind. I was wrong. I remember her smiling as if she belonged, but to me it felt like an invasion.

It was surreal watching him act affectionate, even romantic, after everything he had done to my mother and sisters—the beatings, the screaming, the psychological warfare. Now he was gentle and playful, talking about champagne and bear rugs, treating this woman like a prize. On the drive home from the Halifax airport, I sat in silence, terrified. My mother had been cut so completely out of our lives that for the first year, I half-believed he had killed her.

At first, his new girlfriend tried to buy our love with toys and treats, gifts instead of presence. They worked for a moment, but the warmth never lasted. Her own wounds surfaced, and his abuse seeped into her, too. Sarcasm replaced tenderness. Jokes covered pain. The cruelty continued, sharper now, more hidden.

I carried it into school without knowing. When I pushed a girl on the playground, I wasn't just acting out. I was replaying the only script of manhood I had been given: men hurt women. That was what I thought men did. When the school sent a note home, the red-haired woman read it aloud and looked at me coldly.

"Your father is going to kill you. Just like he killed your mother."

Her words hollowed me out. We hadn't seen or heard from my mother in months. Silence filled the space where she should have been, and I filled that silence with nightmares.

One night, I finally broke. Something inside me split open, something I had been holding down. I asked where my mother was. My father's voice was flat, cruel.

"She's where she wants to be."

I cried harder. He barked at me to stop. I wasn't asking for much, only to know if my mother was alive.

Our mother was erased like a chapter he was ashamed of, as if she had never existed. When the new woman arrived, we were suddenly expected to forget everything that had come before her. The message was unspoken but absolute: conform or be crushed.

A Season With Our Paternal Grandparents

We visited my father's parents in those early days of his separation from my mother. He needed someone to dump us three kids on while he deployed with the Canadian Forces. I saw it there, too: the same control, the same manipulation. His mother, his father, his sister—all part of the same machine that had taken us from our mother. It was never about love. It was about ownership. He didn't seek custody to raise us. He sought it to prove he could take us.

What was supposed to be a short visit stretched into six months. We spent the 1996 school year in Labrador, tucked into my grandparents' rigid world. These were people who had already raised two traumatized children, my father and his sister, and now those same unhealed wounds fell to us. To my father, it was logistics. To me, it was exile.

I remember the smell of my grandmother's cooking: boiled dinners heavy with salt, bread fresh from the oven, molasses cookies cooling on the counter. Those smells should have meant comfort, but they were always shadowed by my grandfather's presence. His belt hung like a threat; his voice carried sharp enough to split the air. The warmth of her kitchen never quite reached us, because his anger seeped into everything. The food filled our stomachs, but the fear hollowed us out. I wondered if other kids ever felt this way at dinner tables, if their stomachs clenched with dread instead of hunger.

By the summer of 1996, the cracks in that house were impossible to ignore. I remember sitting at the kitchen table while my grandfather complained about how much my father owed him for everything he had done, especially raising his three children. His bitterness filled the room as he went on about the cost of the flight and how his son was nothing but a deadbeat. My grandmother finally screamed at him to shut up, her voice cutting through his tirade. He stormed off into the next room and slammed the door. The rest of us sat in silence.

We ate my grandmother's sweet-and-sour meatballs, pretending nothing had happened. A few hours later, we climbed into my grandparents' old red van for the drive to the airport.

The terminal felt enormous, buzzing with strangers rushing in every direction. My grandfather muttered about money the whole way, as if each step toward the gate cost him something. Then, without ceremony, we were handed over to the airline staff, three kids standing in line with tickets in our hands, no adults beside us.

On the plane, we were scattered, each of us placed next to strangers. I remember the weight of the seat belt, the smell of recycled air, the way I pressed my forehead to the window to hide the fear that knotted my stomach. My sisters looked small and lost in their separate rows, and I fought the urge to cry, knowing no one was coming to reassure us. I told myself to be strong, that I was the one who had to hold it together. If I broke, we all would.

We carried more than our small bags onto that flight. We carried silence, exhaustion, and the kind of fear children aren't supposed to know.

And then, Newfoundland. Rain streaked down the windows as the plane jolted onto the runway. My youngest sister's face was pale with fear, and I reached over to comfort her, pretending I wasn't also afraid. When we finally taxied to the gate, we were the last passengers off. A flight attendant walked us down the brightly lit corridor.

And there she was. My mother. Bright red lipstick cutting through the fluorescent glow. I ran to her, desperate for her arms, and the familiar smells hit me—cigarette smoke and perfume—scents etched into memory. Beside her stood a man I didn't recognize, almost twenty years older than her, liquor heavy on his breath.

We piled into the car and began the two-hour drive into rural Newfoundland.

Winter 1996

When we finally arrived in Port Blandford, the car pulled into a driveway where a house stood frozen in time, stuck somewhere in the 1980s and never finished. Inside, the air hit me like a wall—the stench of mold, cigarettes, and stale beer was thick enough to taste. Garbage and empty bottles were scattered everywhere, stacked in corners like part of the décor.

My mother led us through the clutter, showing me the room where I would sleep. There were no doors, just sheets tacked up for privacy and boxes pushed against the walls. As we climbed the unfinished stairs, the boards creaked under our weight, and the cold seeped into my bones. The wood stove had long before gone out, leaving the house icy and damp.

I stood there shivering, my body vibrating, unsure if this place was safe or if I had just stepped into another kind of danger. My mother was depressed and couldn't manage two small children. During those visits, she leaned on me the way she had when I was little, relying on me to bathe and feed my sisters while she chain-smoked and complained about my father. I whispered to myself that at least she was alive, and that being here was better than nothing. It was the only way I could make the smell of mold and cigarettes feel bearable.

I remember the cigarette butts floating in the toilet, staining the water with ash and tar. I stared at them and saw myself, adrift, limp, caught between two sick parents. Part of me wanted to flush it all away, but part of me knew I was stuck floating there, too.

The visit lasted only a week. By the time I returned to Debert, I reeked of smoke and neglect, my mouth quick and sharp in ways my father didn't tolerate. He punished me for it. In my head, I cursed myself for slipping, for bringing her smell back with me like evidence. Soon after, he began recording our phone calls with her, turning every conversation into evidence, every word another weapon.

I remember those nights in Debert, the stereo set up to record every court-ordered call. He pumped us up beforehand, filling our heads with lies, stories about how abusive our mother had been. It was all scripted. He gave us questions to ask and lines to repeat while he sat in the background like a puppeteer pulling strings. Afterward, he replayed the tapes, coaching us on how to refine the performance next time.

He didn't care about the three children he had stolen. What he cared about, obsessively, was control. Hurting her was the goal. That was the ritual. And the red-haired stranger, barely out of her twenties, joined him in it. Every call became a stage where they fed off the performance, playing savior to three confused, heartbroken children.

In that house, if you were sensitive, you became the problem. Tenderness was weakness. My sensitivity wasn't nurtured. It was mocked, criticized, weaponized against me. There was no space to feel. Only to survive.

Memories With Our Mother

We children would visit our mother one more time before my father remarried. That visit is etched into my memory. She and her alcoholic boyfriend were always losing jobs. We were left alone a lot, drifting through days with little structure and few rules. Beer and cigarettes were easy to find.

I spent most of my time by the ocean or with the local kids, riding ATVs along the coast until the sun went down. In the evenings, my mother would drag us to her friends' houses, determined to keep up her social life. We'd sit for hours as she complained about money, about how my father had been abusive, sharing it all openly in front of her friends as if we kids weren't even there.

Sometimes we stopped by her boyfriend's mother's house down the road. The air there always felt heavy, filled with the same stale sadness that seemed to follow us everywhere.

One afternoon, her boyfriend decided to take us for a ride. He hitched a small trailer to the back of his ATV. The ball was too small for the hitch; it wouldn't lock. He grabbed a piece of yellow rope and tied it off anyway, muttering something about it being "good enough." We climbed in—three kids, barefoot and giggling, and he gunned the engine.

We bounced up the dirt road, dust rising around us like smoke. Then, in an instant, the world tilted. The rope snapped. The trailer jerked free. For a heartbeat, we were airborne, weightless, before crashing back to Earth in a blur of metal, dirt, and screams.

I saw panic fill his face as the ATV skidded to a stop. He took a quick sip from his flask, hands shaking, eyes darting between us and the broken trailer. We were screaming, three kids tangled in the chaos. Dust and fear were thick in the air.

When everything finally went still, he stumbled over and pulled us out, muttering curses under his breath. No one was seriously hurt, just bruised and shaken. The house was only a few minutes away, so we walked back, accompanied by the clattering of the loose hitch.

Inside, my mother's face went pale when she saw us. They told us not to fall asleep, saying they didn't know if we had concussions. Mostly, they didn't want my father to find out. They knew his anger and tried to get our silence.

Losing Her Again

When the visit was over, we were picked up at a gas station off the highway—a strange and lonely meeting place. My mother had driven us up on her ATV, her hair whipped by the wind, her face tight with worry. We waited together by the pumps, laughing and crying in turns, knowing somehow that this goodbye would be different.

When my grandparents' red van finally pulled in, I felt my stomach clench. The moment they stepped out, the air shifted. Their faces were sharp with anger, their voices already raised. They didn't see children standing with their mother. They saw possessions to be reclaimed.

"Stop crying. Get in the van," they barked. "No hugs."

I was old enough now to understand what was happening. They didn't want us to belong to her. They wanted control, the same control they had always clung to. My mother tried to hold on, tried to kiss us, but they commanded her to step back. Then, with a force that is burned into me forever, they ripped my youngest sister from her arms.

Our mother asked for a photo, just one picture to remember us by. My grandparents refused. "We must drive. We have places to be."

It all happened in moments, but it felt like hours. My mother stood there, empty-armed, as we were shoved into the van. Her face blurred through my tears as the door slammed.

She was sobbing in the bright summer air, and that sound followed me down the highway. It haunted me for the rest of the drive. Eventually I numbed it out, the only way I knew how to survive.

The next summer, my father remarried. And in that house, love became something rehearsed, controlled, and weaponized. Whatever genuine affection I had known before was gone.

Return to Newfoundland

By the summer of 1999, we left Nova Scotia and moved back to Newfoundland. Rumors spread that the Canadian government would soon shut down the base. One afternoon, I came home from school, and my father told me directly: the base was closing. With it, I knew that another chapter of our lives would be forced closed. With his retirement approaching, he had chosen for us to move back to St. John's, where my stepmother's family lived.

By then, I was used to moving. We had stayed in Debert longer than most of my father's other postings, but as the school year ended, the signs were everywhere. Moving trucks rumbled down the narrow streets; tailgates slammed shut like punctuation marks. Families stood on front lawns, exchanging forced goodbyes as their children tried to mask both excitement and dread. Cardboard boxes stacked in windows became the landscape of the town.

I watched it all with strange detachment. Moving had never meant freedom for me; it only meant being uprooted, pulled from one cage and dropped into another. The fists pounding on bedroom doors, the silence of being locked away, the basement secrets—those did not disappear just because we were packing boxes. They came with us, sealed inside.

I was not angry. I was not even surprised. Just numb. Beneath that numbness, though, was the quiet throb of fear. High school was about to begin in a new city with new faces, and I would be stepping into it carrying scars no one could see and with no friends to help me hide them.

And yet, strangely, some of my fondest memories still come from those years in Debert. I remember playing in the woods, flying gliders with the air cadets, doing anything that gave me a break from the constant pressure inside our house. Those moments of play felt like a breath of air in a suffocating world. But joy never lasted. My father, my abuser, always found a way to steal it.

We were off to our next destination the very next day. Debert was behind us, but Newfoundland would not bring freedom, only the next chapter of survival.

CHAPTER 3

Return to the Rock

Canadian Forces Station, St. John's

That summer of 1999, just before I was set to start high school, we left quiet Debert, Nova Scotia, and returned to St. John's, Newfoundland. The shift was violent. Debert had been contained, almost innocent. Eight of my closest friends were there; we still call those years the days of innocence. But innocence does not last. By the time we returned to the Rock, it was gone.

We ended up living across the street from the house where everything had collapsed in 1994. I was nine when my parents finally split. Now, years later, we were back, pretending none of it had ever happened.

Walking into that neighbourhood felt like stepping back into a crime scene. The chalk outlines had faded, but the memories still haunted the streets.

The move was not a fresh start. It was my father's retirement posting. The Debert base was shutting down, another casualty of federal cutbacks. The new house was big, but it was not home. Cold rooms, sagging mattresses, nothing to soften the edges. Even the air felt suffocating, as if there was nowhere left to hide.

That August, my stepmother brought me to her old high school. She spoke of it like it was sacred. "Back in my day," she said, smiling, "this was the best school in the city." She wanted her nostalgia to cover what we lacked.

The principal looked at me over his glasses. "What language do you want to take? French? Spanish? German?"

"I was not good at French," I said.

"Why not?"

I shrugged. How could I explain that abuse had filled the space where learning should have been? That survival had always mattered more than schoolwork? Instead, I offered what I could: "I like science. And history."

History always made sense to me, maybe because mine refused to leave me alone.

Back at home, the old patterns returned. My father still blamed my mother for everything, labelling her as unstable, abusive, addicted. Anything to keep himself the victim. His new wife played along. They bought big-screen TVs and new beds for themselves while we kids went without glasses, without dental work, without care. I slept on a sagging mattress while their new bed frame gleamed like a reminder: you do not matter.

Retirement gutted my father. He sat on the couch, glued to the news that fed his fears. His wife grew bitter, watching as the promises he had made her dissolved into nothing. He did not know how to be a man outside the Forces. He did not know how to be a father.

Tears were not welcome in that house. They made him uncomfortable. So, I learned to swallow them. Over time, silence became the only way to survive.

By the time I turned fifteen, escape was no longer an option. Responsibility was handed to me like a sentence. On my birthday, my father told me to get a job. "Man up," he said. "Your mother is not paying enough. If you want to live here, you contribute."

I could never imagine doing that to my own kids, making them pay to exist and carry the weight of a war they did not start.

9/11/2001

I was sixteen, in grade eleven—body at the desk, mind elsewhere, always scanning survival scenarios. Would there be food at home? Peace, or another storm? Then the whispers started. Planes. Towers. Smoke. Something terrible in New York.

For a moment, the whole class fell silent. But inside me, silence like that was already familiar. The world was just catching up to the fear I'd been living in for years.

They sent us home early. I walked in a daze, but the collapse haunting me was not on the TV. It was waiting at home.

My father was pacing, the news blaring. He had just retired, and I could see him unraveling.

"The world's on fire," he said. "We're going to war." He did not know where or when, but he was sure.

He sat by the phone as if it might ring and call him back into service. What no one else could see was that the war had already started in our house. His PTSD from Iraq had followed him home, and now it lived with me.

For the next two years, his rage and fear were aimed at me. He became obsessed with pushing me into the military, convinced it was my only path to worth. I was just trying to finish high school, but his moods dictated everything: when I slept, when I ate, whether I could breathe without consequence.

Math nearly broke me. One afternoon, my teacher pulled me aside. His voice was steady. "I'll give you a 50 this time. But that's it." He knew. They all knew. Failing was not just an academic problem. It was dangerous. That June, I passed math by grace, not merit.

At home, food was rationed like contraband: every bite watched, every plate measured. Hunger gnawed at us constantly. My teeth broke from neglect. My vision blurred without glasses. My mother had once taken us to appointments, but after she left, no one cared.

He did not want to raise us. He wanted to break her. That was the mission.

Even as I turned from boy to man, I saw clearly the man he was: a kind of man I could never allow myself to become. But, at sixteen, I was still trapped.

One night I skipped work for a party. My stepmother's sister offered me a ride. I refused, grabbed a cab instead, and tried to disappear into laughter, into forgetting.

But the phone would not stop. Buzz after buzz. Voicemail after rage-filled voicemail. By morning, he had called the police. I was ordered to report in, then interrogated like a criminal by one of his old army buddies.

The bus ride home was two hours of dread. When I walked in, my room had been stripped bare. A prison cell. He screamed in my face, spit flying, chest heaving until he could not breathe.

I stumbled into what was left of my room, grabbed a bottle of Tylenol, and stared at it, wondering how many it would take. Wondering if this could finally be the end.

By 2003, I was finishing high school at Holy Heart of Mary. Around me, classmates spoke of universities and futures. My marks were decent, but math had always been a war I could not win.

I remembered the multiplication tables taped to the basement wall. "You'll sit here until you know them," he would yell, breath hot with frustration. Numbers never stuck. Shame did.

Now I was ready to join the family business. But the truth was simple: I was not chasing a career. I was running. The military was an escape, the only door left open.

Graduation that spring smelled of cheap cologne and plastic chairs. Balloons arched over a stage while CNN's footage of "shock and awe" in Baghdad played on the lobby screens. Fireworks over sand and blood. The war felt both far away and close, like a storm only I could smell.

When I shook the principal's hand, it did not feel like a beginning. It felt like a countdown. I was already hardened, already trained in silence. Ready to leave.

I never earned my driver's license in high school. I failed a few times and gave up until my father dangled one of his promises: the military owed him money, and he would use it for my driving course.

Like most of his promises, it never came to pass.

When I pressed, he screamed, punished, grounded me. So, I stopped asking. Eventually, I scraped together the money for a weekend class. The instructor was a Korean War vet with a hook for an arm. I used to imagine he had lost it in combat. Eventually, he told us the truth: he had spilled a pot of boiling coffee and tripped over his cat, and the burns took his arm. I thought it would be a cool war story, but it turned out not to be.

After a few sessions, my father pulled me out anyway. "The money didn't show up," he said. Another excuse. Another door slammed.

That was his gift to me: promises as hollow as the house we lived in. If I wanted a way forward, I would have to build it myself.

My First Introduction to the Army

Many times, my father had used his military service to put me down, saying I could never make it as a soldier, that the military wouldn't even want me. As my graduation neared, he kept saying it. But then his attitude changed.

I had barely finished high school when my father drove me into St. John's, steering the car straight to the military recruiting office. He was eager, almost restless, his words tumbling out the whole drive.

"The army made a man out of me," he said again, pounding the steering wheel like it was a drumbeat. "It'll make a man out of you, too."

I sat in the passenger seat, saying nothing. I had seen what the military had made of him. The rages. The silence. The bruised kind of pride that never softened into love. But I didn't have the courage to argue. I just followed him inside.

The office smelled of old coffee and floor polish. Lining the walls were posters of soldiers in pressed uniforms, smiling under banners about pride and honour. I filled out the forms, nodded at the right times, and answered the recruiter's questions. My father loomed behind me, watching as though he were reliving something.

Then came the silence. The recruiter's eyes flicked toward my father and lingered just a second too long. A stiffness entered the room, sharp as barbed wire. The conversation ended abruptly. We shook hands, and that was it.

I waited for the next step—for a call, a letter, anything. Nothing came. Days became weeks. Then months. I asked my father once or twice what was supposed to happen next. He only shrugged, changed the subject, and poured another drink.

Almost twenty-one years later, I learned the truth. Someone told me, offhand, that back in Debert, Nova Scotia, my father had been court-martialled for stealing. In an instant, the memory of that office returned. The recruiter's glance. The tension in the air. The way my father had avoided the subject afterward. It all made sense. He had carried his shame in silence, and he passed that silence down to me.

My father's dream of me joining the military ended there. With that door closed, I drifted into whatever work I could find: odd jobs that barely paid the bills, shifts that blurred into each other. University became the next dream he tried to push onto me. He wanted me to have the education he never had, the legitimacy of a degree. But his dream wasn't mine. I went through the motions—applying, trying to make it work but inside I was already breaking away.

A few years later, I realized I couldn't keep living under his roof. The walls of that house were too thick with unspoken orders and old anger. Moving out wasn't just about independence. It was survival.

May Long Weekend, 2004

I met my girlfriend on the May 24th long weekend at a cabin in the middle of nowhere—one of those tucked-away places owned by a mutual friend. Off-grid, damp, and soaked in that strange early-adulthood energy where every moment feels like a test of who you're becoming.

From the moment I saw her, something was off—different. Not bad, just unpredictable. Dangerous in ways I couldn't yet name. I had a gut feeling she might sleep with me that night, so I leaned in hard. Tried to impress her. I masked nerves with bravado, acting like I knew what I was doing. That was my shield.

We stayed up most of the night, catching only a few winks in the cold May morning—the kind of chill that bites your fingers even though it's technically spring. The next day, still buzzing from booze and weed, I lit the Coleman stove and tried to cook bacon in beer while joking around with people I barely knew. I was desperate to be seen as competent, funny, useful—anything but vulnerable.

But I was already cracking. My stepmother and my sister used to dig through my things and pull out condoms just to mock me. "I'm glad I found these. We thought you were gay." Every corner of my world was subject to judgment.

She became my first real relationship, but it turned toxic fast. She sneered at the no-name food I bought, as if poverty were a character flaw. That pain still lives in me. I thought love might be my way out, but even that relationship couldn't escape the shadow of parental control.

Trying to Find Stability

I wanted to move to Banff. A hotel job had come up, and I applied. But when I sat in the office of my father's first civilian job, watching him behind his desk as a spa manager, and told him of my plans, he said I wasn't ready.

I had been ready for a long time. Underneath it all, I think he was the one who wasn't ready to let me go.

I hated Newfoundland and Labrador. Everyone seemed angry, and if I showed emotion, my father called me a "pussy," weak for even feeling. After his retirement from the Canadian Armed Forces, we left military housing and crammed into a small apartment. It was hell. He was drowning in his own trauma, still desperate for the approval of a father who had never given it, and he poured all of that pain onto me. He couldn't stand the fact that I was beginning to make it on my own.

That house was less a home than a prison. Growth was forbidden. Every time I tried to stretch into myself, they crushed it.

I was already plotting my escape. My "room" was a utility closet in the basement, shared with a freezer and a laundry machine. I spent that winter shivering down there, my breath hanging in the air while the walls sweated with damp. One night, after months of cold silence, I finally snapped. I shoved clothes into my old camping pack, slung it over my shoulder, and walked down the road. For a moment, I felt free.

But guilt hit harder than the cold. I knew if I left, my sisters would pay the price. I knew he would turn physical on them once I was gone. So, I turned around and walked back into the cage.

If I couldn't escape my father, maybe I could escape into someone else.

November 2004: The Bloom Room, St. John's

I met my first serious girlfriend at a Mardi Gras–themed party at a downtown pool hall called the Bloom Room—exclusive access, shoulder to shoulder, music thumping, beads swinging, alcohol flowing. I weighed 115 pounds soaking wet. As we stood around talking, a friend from high school cracked a joke about me having a "huge German sausage," and, for whatever reason, she was hooked.

She had spent her whole life being shamed for a speech impediment. I didn't mock her. I knew what it was like to be different. I was scrawny, anxious, half-feral, and already well on my way to alcoholism, having learned from the finest.

After that night, we started chatting on MSN Messenger. I was clawing my way out of my parents' house, and she latched on quickly—like every woman who came after her. We had sex constantly. She was studying baking, and between classes she'd pick me up so we could drive somewhere and fool around. She was chasing pleasure. I was starving for companionship. I had been used, violated in one form or another, since I was five years old. So, when someone held me, I mistook it for safety.

Once she had me, she didn't want to let go. And, truthfully, I couldn't let go of her parents' house. It was warm. It had food. Her mother cooked and cleaned, then erupted in rages when she didn't feel appreciated but I could handle that. At least there was heat. At least there was dinner.

CHAPTER 4

Trauma Echoes

Winter 2005: The House of Control

The winter of 2005 was my private hell. For a decade, I had endured the same cycle—chaos, control, relocation, confinement—until my soul was threadbare. I was twenty, yet my parents demanded to know every move I made, as though I were still a child smuggling secrets in my backpack.

I worked over sixty hours a week, went to night school to claw my way toward university, and came home only to collapse. Exhaustion was my constant companion, yet they still found ways to break me. That Christmas, the trigger came disguised as cheesecake.

I was walking through the entryway toward my basement room when my father blocked the way. His voice was tight, rehearsed. My stepmother had accused me of stealing Costco cheesecakes from the freezer.

I didn't even know they existed. But that wasn't the point. The point was control. Even dessert had become a weapon.

He spat in my face as he yelled. Confused and humiliated, I snapped, "You can tell that whore I never touched her precious cheesecakes!"

I stormed into my room, heart racing. It wasn't about the cakes. It was about power. It always had been.

Ultimatum in the Entryway

Weeks later, he confronted me again. If I wasn't joining the military or in school full-time, he said, he would charge me five hundred dollars a month in rent.

I knew where the money would go: not to bills, but into bottles. His thumb and forefinger worked at his nose, a nervous habit I had watched all my life, the tell of his stress.

In that moment, watching him burrow into his own skin, I realized I was done. Twenty years of being stripped of agency. Twenty years of silence pressed into me like a brand. I could not survive much longer in that house.

Ghost in My Own Home

By March, I had vanished in spirit. I moved through the house like a ghost, careful not to rattle chains. When my father picked me up from night school, he would ask about my day. For years, I thought such questions were a sign of his interest in me. Now I understood they were surveillance, and I gave him nothing.

My silence unsettled him more than my rage ever had.

Then came the message. A text from my stepmother: *If you don't talk to him soon, he'll throw your stuff on the curb like he did your mother's.*

The words were a blade. Memories surfaced of my mother's belongings thrown into the street as punishment. Seeing it spelled out stripped away the last veil. I knew then: if I stayed, I would be next.

Escape Under Rain and Snow

At work, on break, I made the call. My girlfriend and a coworker whose mother owned a truck would help. We would move in the dark, unseen.

I packed in secret. Heart pounding. Belongings in garbage bags. The futon dragged across the floor. The 300-pound TV heaved one inch at a time. Every sound felt like a siren. I was terrified they would catch me, that my father would block the door, that my stepmother's warning would come true—that everything I owned would end up tossed on the lawn as the neighbours watched.

I closed the door softer than I wanted to. No slam. No final word. Just the screen door clicking shut behind me as it always had, followed by the sound of my heartbeat in my ears as I carried the weight of everything unsaid.

I still see the night I last spoke to you.

"Hey, Dad, look at me . . ."

The words echoed in my head for years, long before I even knew I was moving.

I had been begging without words, bleeding effort into silence, hoping he would see me—not the person he wanted me to be, not the disappointment, but just me.

"I'm sorry I can't be perfect."

God, how many times did I whisper that to the ceiling at night?

How many chores, early mornings, and shut mouths had I offered up like burnt sacrifices, hoping he would just . . . soften?

But the love never came the way I needed it. Not once.

When I finally left, I did not take much. Just a few garbage bags, clothes, memories, and pieces of myself I hadn't yet learned to hold gently.

I looked back only once, expecting maybe a wave, a look, a "You did your best."

But the porch light was on as the freezing rain poured down. My coworker and my girlfriend helped me flee, just as my mom had that night in 1994. There were no RCMP lights flashing this time, only the cold confusion as I sat in the back of the tiny pickup truck, crying for myself and for my sisters, who I had to leave behind. My body left that night, but their shadows stayed with me.

It was then that I realized: I was not leaving home.

I was leaving the house I had survived in.

A war zone in denim and drywall, where love came with conditions and silence filled the cracks like insulation.

"It's just too late, and we can't go back . . ."

He had his version of me.

But I was walking into mine. And for the first time in my life, I could say it without shame: "I'm okay with not being perfect."

My phone rang repeatedly. His voice came through the phone sharp and hateful, like a dull knife pressed into an old wound. Still, the five-minute drive felt like resurrection. My first taste of freedom.

When we arrived at my new apartment, snow began to fall. Slow at first, then harder, as though the sky itself was erasing my tracks, blessing my escape. The storm washed the old life clean, even as the phone kept ringing.

Reduced to a Remote

When I finally answered, my father's voice was ragged and furious. He threatened to call police, screamed about betrayal. My chest tightened until I realized what he wanted.

The remote control for his satellite receiver.

That was all. Not me. Not my future. Not even a fight for reconciliation. Just a plastic object with batteries and buttons.

That was how quickly he compartmentalized me. His son, reduced to a missing device.

And in that moment, shivering in a bare apartment as snow piled at the window, I understood the truth: leaving wasn't betrayal. Staying would have been.

Freedom Is Slower Than Leaving

I thought leaving home meant freedom. But the chaos followed me.

When I moved out, all I had was a jar of applesauce and a box of baby crackers. My girlfriend's mom slipped me pots, pans, bedsheets, and grocery cards. Things a boy should not have needed if his parents loved him.

The first nights in Mount Pearl were quiet but not peaceful. The silence pressed in, thick and unnatural. One afternoon, my cat slipped into a hole in the wall and got stuck. I panicked, not because I thought I would lose the cat, but because my body betrayed me. My chest tightened, skin burned, and suddenly I was back in 1995, cornered in my father's house with no way out. The drywall was not just drywall anymore. It was every wall I had ever wanted to escape.

Freedom does not come when you close the door behind you. It is slower. Harder. The past waits in the body, waits in the walls. And it takes years to learn how to stop being trapped in houses you no longer live in.

CHAPTER 5

Proof of Love That Never Came

Seeing My Mother Through Adult Eyes

I reunited with my mother as I was moving out of my father's house. A brief phone call that winter stirred something dangerous inside me, a hunger I could not name. Maybe it was desperation. Maybe it was the little boy inside me, still begging for proof that one parent, just one, could love me.

The calls were short at first, but every word burned. My childhood trauma was everywhere, coiled amid her sentences. After nearly a decade apart, just hearing her voice made my chest tighten. I could not bring myself to call her "Mom." The word felt foreign, poisonous on my tongue. I had never known a mother as comfort, as shelter. Only as chaos.

And she delivered. She filled the silence with bile, talking about how my father had raped her, about wanting to kill herself. I sat there, frozen, wondering what role I was supposed to play. Her son. Her caretaker. Her confessor. I hated her for making me hold those words. I hated myself for listening.

Her boyfriend was a man of fifty-five, another drunk. When his mother died, they invited me to the funeral in a rural town, the same one I had been dragged to as a boy in 1997. I told myself it would only be a weekend. But deep down, I knew better. My body already knew.

When she pulled up to the bus stop in her ATV, it was like no time had passed. The stale reek of smoke hit me as I climbed on My stomach clenched. My hands shook. I was no longer a grown man. I was the child she had abandoned, trapped again in her world of filth and need.

The drive down those roads was suffocating. Every tree, every ditch, a memory was waiting to ambush me. I tried to force conversation, but underneath, I was screaming. I wanted to jump off and run.

Her house came into view like a curse. Broken siding. Grass waist-high. The deck sagging like it might collapse under its own weight. My chest ached. I wanted to cry before we even stepped inside.

The stairs groaned as we climbed. The door opened. The smell slammed into me: old smoke, damp mildew, rot. My eyes watered. Inside, it was the same nightmare preserved in dust. Blankets draped over furniture. Doors hanging loose on their hinges. Garbage piles pressing into the corners.

Empty bottles clinked underfoot. Photographs of "good times" were scattered across the floor, lies frozen in glossy paper. My knees buckled. Rage surged. I wanted to rip the fridge door off its hinges. Burn the house down.

I opened that fridge, searching for something normal. Instead, I found hell. Rotting food stacked and dripping, a sour stench that made my throat close. It wasn't just neglect. It was a monument to everything I had been denied as a child. Hunger. Shame. Now rotting in front of me.

We sat together, trying to talk, but it was pointless. She chain-smoked, filling the room with a choking haze. My head throbbed. My chest burned. I swallowed every word I wanted to say. Rage. Grief. Hatred. The truth that she had never been a mother to me.

I wandered the house, each step heavier than the last, the floorboards creaking as if they remembered me. The walls pressed in. The past clawed at me. No matter what wars I had survived, this house and its weight had never changed. And, standing there, neither had I.

I woke up in a panic the next day, nose full of sour air. The walls were stained, the plumbing shot—just as it had been years earlier. I wanted to cry. Instead, I hardened. My father's words about her echoed in my head. That morning, I realized he had been right. I swallowed the grief, forced the tears back, and walked down the cold wooden stairs into her chaos.

We ate something barely edible in silence. Then, we left for the funeral.

The church was orderly, clean, almost sterile. Wooden pews lined in rows. Hymns rising in practiced harmony. Outside, winter sunlight filtered through stained glass. Inside, the air carried grief that felt different from hers—structured, dignified, almost bearable. And it broke me.

The tears I had been holding finally fell, not for the woman we buried that day, but for the mother I never had.

Before the Uniform

In 2006, I enrolled in carpentry school in St. John's, Newfoundland. Thirty-two weeks later, I had a certificate in my hands—a trade, a chance, maybe even a way out. Everyone around me talked about Alberta as if it were the land of gold. Oil money, union wages, a life built instead of one scraped together.

So, I went. I boarded a plane west, imagining a future where I could finally prove myself. The shock came fast. Rent prices chewed through every dollar I thought I'd earn. Just existing felt impossible. Within weeks, I was unraveling, already plotting my escape. I flew back to Newfoundland, broke and ashamed, my girlfriend's disappointment heavy on me like a sentence. She didn't need words. Her silence, her looks, said it all: I hadn't made it.

What I didn't understand then was that the shame wasn't only about Alberta. As I'd walked those unfamiliar streets, counting coins for groceries, panic had crawled through my chest. The same panic I'd felt as a boy in my father's house. The body doesn't forget. Every slammed door, every accusation, every night without safety rushed back in waves. I didn't know the term CPTSD (complex post-traumatic stress disorder) then. All I knew was that fear was choking me, burning my skin, scattering my thoughts like trapped birds. Alberta wasn't just a failed trip west. It was a return to the battlefield inside me.

Back home, I was already defeated, and my girlfriend made sure I felt it. Her shame pressed down in every sigh, every sideways glance. I rented a small apartment in St. John's, but it never felt like mine. At first, the clutter seemed harmless, just scraps of a young man starting out. But the piles grew. Receipts, tools I might one day need, clothes I never wore. The rooms closed in, dust rising, cardboard smelling faintly of mildew. I couldn't throw anything away. I couldn't say no to her, either. If she wanted something, I gave it. If she asked me to change, I bent. My voice, my will, my space, all of it eroded until I barely recognized myself inside those four walls.

Still, I worked when I could. Construction jobs came and went, paycheques gone before I could catch them. One layoff cut deeper than the rest. I hadn't been fired for poor work. The owner had an old feud with my girlfriend's parents, and I was collateral. Standing there, tool belt still heavy on my hips, humiliation burned through me.

It was then that I began to see her family differently. On the surface, they were polished—firm handshakes at church, easy smiles for neighbours. But their kindness had edges, sharp ones that cut when you got too close. Behind their doors lived grudges, manipulation, and control. Their approval was never free; it came at a price, and I was already paying it.

I thought Alberta had broken me. But defeat doesn't always mean leaving. Sometimes, it looks like staying, burying yourself in clutter and compromise, trying to build a life out of pieces that don't fit.

By winter, I was back on unemployment. I told myself I was catching my breath, but the stillness only suffocated. The apartment air was cold and heavy with dust. Outside, Christmas lights blinked against the snow, cheerful in a way that deepened the hollow inside me. My one escape was the cats. I'd toss crumpled balls of paper across the floor or let them curl in my lap as I stroked their fur. Their purring anchored me when nothing else could. For those moments, I wasn't a failure. I was just breathing in sync with another living creature that asked for nothing but presence.

But moments pass. The benefits were running out, and the shame sharpened under my girlfriend's ridicule. Every sigh, every look reminded me of what I wasn't providing.

A Second Attempt

On New Year's Eve, after a night out with her friends, we came back to her mother's house. While she talked in the kitchen, I sat at the computer. The glow of the screen lit the dark. Restless, half-numb, I filled out an application for the Canadian Armed Forces. I didn't think much of it. Hit submit. Shut the screen. Walked away. By the time the holiday ended, I'd almost forgotten I'd applied.

Then, late in January, the phone rang. An unknown number flashed. A recruiter's voice on the other end: They'd received my application. All I needed was a medical. For a second, I thought it must be a mistake. Then the rush hit, shock and joy and fear tangled together, cutting through the frozen silence of that winter.

Within weeks, I was at the recruitment center. I ran the physical test, sat for the interview, and handed in my medical questionnaire. By early February, the paperwork was done. I raised my hand and swore the oath, already a soldier in words before I'd ever worn the uniform.

By March 2007, I was on a plane bound for Canadian Forces Leadership and Recruit School (CFLRS), Saint-Jean-sur-Richelieu, Quebec, to start basic training. At the time, it felt like salvation: discipline, structure, belonging, a steady paycheque, proof I wasn't the failure everyone believed. I didn't yet see the toll the military would take on my body, my mind, my years. All I knew was that I was leaving. For the first time in a long time, there was a way out.

Part 2

The Canadian Armed Forces

CHAPTER 6

Becoming Someone Else

2007

I entered the military chasing a dream to become a protector, something I had never seen. But the truth came quickly: the military does not train you to help. It trains you to harden, to hate.

Integrity. Honesty. Duty. Loyalty. Those words were carved into us through sweat and suffering at CFLRS Saint-Jean. But before we could live them, we had to be broken.

Basic Training, Canadian Forces Leadership and Recruit School

I left Newfoundland and Labrador believing the military would save me. That it could deliver me from the war zone of my childhood. Instead, I simply traded one battlefield for another.

The journey began in the cramped seat of an Air Canada flight, lifting off from St. John's on a grey March morning. The engines roared, pressing me into the upholstered seat as the rock of Newfoundland fell away beneath the wings. Through the window, I watched the coastline dissolve into the Atlantic, jagged cliffs swallowed by cloud. It felt like a severing. Every memory, every scar, shrinking into the distance.

The cabin smelled of burnt coffee and recycled air. I sat rigid, knees jammed against the seat in front of me, fingers locked to my armrests as if they could anchor me. My thoughts circled: *Who will I be when I land? Will this turn me into someone new, or will I still be the same boy I am running from?*

For two hours, I floated between worlds, the old life behind me, the unknown waiting in Montréal. It felt like a one-way trip, a baptism in jet fuel and clouds. There was no turning back.

By the time the taxi carried me the last stretch to Saint-Jean on March 7, 2007, the weight of that flight was still on my chest. The cab's vinyl seat was cold under my legs, the silence thicker than the glass separating me from the driver. My heart pounded. I was scared, but I was ready. Ready to shed the skin of the boy who had been beaten, belittled, and broken by the people who were supposed to love him. Ready to become someone else.

In the window's reflection, I caught sight of him—the ghost I carried. Long hair. Hollow eyes. Shaped by violence and nights watching war shows with a father I could never reach. He had left me no legacy but discipline and silence. Yet here I was, carrying his story forward, even as I swore I would not become the same kind of soldier.

"The Mega," the megacomplex at Saint-Jean Garrison, rose ahead, a fortress of brick and fluorescent light. Inside, the air smelled of floor wax and sweat. My boots scraped against hard tile, and as I stepped across the threshold, something dissolved—my name, my ego, the last fragile illusion of safety.

The halls swarmed with bodies moving in formation, ants in a colony. Then the storm hit.

"CUNT! FUCK! JESUS TAP-DANCING CHRIST!"

A five-foot Airborne sergeant from the Princess Patricia's Canadian Light Infantry tore into a recruit with a fury that shook the corridor. His voice filled every corner, towering far larger than his frame. Strangely, it felt familiar. Raw. Brutal. Like home.

Structure had always been key to my survival. My father, himself a soldier, had ruled our house with the same cadence of terror. I had been trained for this long before I ever wore a uniform.

Within minutes, my hair, my clothes, even the way I stood were stripped away. We were lined up, shouted at, reduced to numbers. Instructors prowled the rows like predators sniffing out weakness. I tried to hold steady, but sweat slicked my palms and my stomach twisted tight.

That night in the barracks, I lay in the dark, listening to the silence between snores and coughs of strangers. The blanket itched against my skin, the mattress thin as plywood. My chest rose and fell in rhythm with those of men I didn't know, yet somehow already belonged to. The fear didn't leave; it burrowed deeper.

The army wasn't only building soldiers. It was unmaking boys.

The Pointed End

Our platoon was stacked with future combat arms: infantry, artillery, and recce (reconnaissance). No soft spots. No mercy.

The instructors were all sharp-edged veterans—infantry sergeants back from Afghanistan, artillery master corporals, and a salty navy guy who had worked the Swissair crash. They were there to carve us into warfighters.

From day one, the message was clear: We are going to break you.

Hesitation gets you killed.

Doubt gets your brothers killed.

I lay prone on the cold tile floor of the Mega as I drilled the five principles of effective fire.

Elbows grinding against tile.

Stock pressed hard against my cheek.

Fluorescents buzzing overhead.

A thick-accented RCR (Royal Canadian Regiment) sergeant from Quebec paced behind us like a lion.

"Squeeze the trigger like you're playing with a woman's nipple. Not a pinch. Roll. Gentle. Controlled."

We clenched our jaws. Tried not to laugh.

But it burned in.

Deep.

Years later, in bed with a girlfriend, I would hear his voice echo in my head. And I would laugh again, realizing how deep that imprint went.

Then came Easter weekend. News broke: soldiers from the 2nd Battalion of the RCR had been killed by an IED (improvised explosive device) in Panjwaii, Kandahar Province, Afghanistan.

Something in me cracked.

Before that, I had gone to the Saint-Jean Garrison chapel on Sundays, searching for centre. But that Easter, the hymns fell flat. The stained glass seemed drained of colour.

Compassion went dark.

Ghosts in the Glass

That night, after the news from Panjwaii, I walked into the barracks bathroom with another private. We hadn't arranged it, but we both ended up there, standing in front of the mirror. No words. Just two reflections, young and unsure, staring back like ghosts waiting to be claimed.

I pulled a cheap orange BIC razor from my kit. The first stroke dragged across my scalp, scraping hair away with a sound like tearing cloth. Dark strands clung to the blade, then swirled down the drain.

Beside me, the other private did the same, his head bowed over the sink, jaw locked tight. The smell of soap and iron filled the air. Nicks dotted our scalps like red beads of initiation.

When it was done, we stood side by side, scalps gleaming under the fluorescent light.

The next morning, the two of us stood out like sore thumbs. The instructors clocked us instantly. For a moment, there was silence—then they pounced.

"You think you're soldiers now? You think shaving your heads makes you ready for war?" they screamed, spit flying. Boots stomped. Fists slammed against doorframes. "You are nothing. You haven't earned shit."

The words landed like blows, but under the noise there was something else—a recognition, almost a challenge. They would break us harder now.

We were soldiers, but only in the way they would allow.

CHAPTER 7

Devoured by the Machine

Early-Morning Physical Training

Those first weeks at the Canadian Forces Leadership and Recruit School were a blur of sweat, frost, and fear. Brotherhood wasn't forged in trust but in the ache of lungs, the sting of razors, the throb of legs forced past their limit.

Mornings detonated without warning. Doors crashed open. Staff voices tore down the hall. My hands shook as I dragged a razor across half-asleep skin, each scrape leaving raw tracks that burned in the icy air. Water from the sink was so cold it stabbed the roots of my teeth. My stomach churned from the rush, from the sour taste of nerves, from not enough food to fuel the punishment that was coming.

The grey tracksuit clung roughly against my body, still damp from the day before. My socks never seemed dry. Pulling on the boots felt like binding shackles around my ankles, heavy and unyielding.

We hurled ourselves down seven flights of concrete stairs, skipping steps until shins rattled and knees screamed. The smell of disinfectant hung in the stairwell, failing to mask the reek of sweat, fear, and adrenaline that was trapped in the cinder block walls. Boots slapped in a frantic rhythm as a hundred heartbeats pounded in unison.

Outside, winter struck like a fist. Air so sharp it sliced the throat. Each breath stabbed the lungs and left a bitter, metallic tang, as if we were inhaling iron. Fingers numbed instantly; toes pressed into damp socks stiffened with cold. My calves burned, and my thighs felt carved open with each sprint.

"Ten minutes early, or you're late." The staff's mantra lived in our guts. We didn't jog; we sprinted, the square echoing with footfalls and the ragged pull of air through clenched teeth. A side stitch jabbed my ribs like a knife, sweat turned to ice down the curve of my spine, my throat grew raw from gasping. Every stumble threatened collapse. Worse, it threatened someone else. The words still rang: *If you screw up, your fire team partner dies.*

The square filled with steam from our bodies, a fog of exertion. Vision blurred with sweat; lashes iced over. The burn in my muscles mixed with the sour churn of hunger. It wasn't just exercise. It was erasure—a daily ritual of being scraped down to the bone, each of us filed into the same shape.

We weren't training our bodies. We were being devoured by the machine.

The Soldier Emerging

When I'd first stepped through the doors of the Canadian Forces Leadership and Recruit School, my body was already a record of neglect. I hadn't seen a doctor or a dentist in years. The front tooth I'd cracked while building a bed with my father still split my smile. He blamed my mother and drank away any money that might have fixed it. By the time I arrived in Saint-Jean, the crack felt permanent, like part of my face. Only after basic training would the Canadian Forces repair it. That was my inheritance: shame, scarcity, and scapegoats.

I was scared, hungry, tired, yet somehow still upright. Each day, I expected someone to pull me aside, say there had been a mistake, and ship me back to Newfoundland and Labrador to rot in the place I had crawled out of. But no one came.

What came instead was food. More food than I knew how to look at, let alone eat. Trays piled high with meat and bread, endless potatoes, milk in cold metal pitchers. I stood in the mess hall line with a kind of dread, as if I were stealing. As if any second someone would snatch it away and tell me I didn't belong here, either. I ate until my stomach ached, but even then I couldn't shake the fear that it was temporary. My body, trained on scraps and silence, didn't believe in plenty. Eating felt like trespassing. Every bite carried guilt.

Lying in the barracks, I barely recognized myself. My stomach was stretched tight, a dull ache pressing against my ribs. I shifted side to side on the thin mattress, searching for relief, but the food inside me felt heavy, foreign, and shameful. Every swallow sat like regret.

My broken rib throbbed with each breath, a private reminder of what I'd hidden from the instructors. I closed my eyes, remembering the obstacle course in Quebec where I had fallen and injured my ribs. The sheets smelled faintly of detergent, unfamiliar and too clean, while the air buzzed with fluorescent light leaking under the door. Around me, other recruits snored, their bellies rising and falling with the rhythm of ordinary sleep. For me, sleep refused to come.

I had never gone to bed with a full stomach. Hunger had always curled up with me, sharp as bone, familiar as breath. Now, fullness pressed against me like an intruder. My body didn't trust it. My skin prickled, my heart raced, my mouth kept tasting salt and grease long after the meal was gone. It felt unreal, as though I had slipped into someone else's life, borrowed for one night only. I lay there waiting for the food to be taken back, for the punishment, for the catch that always came.

And still, I trained. I ran with a broken rib, never letting it show. I mouthed off to the instructors, calling their PT (physical training) soft. It wasn't bravado. It was survival. I had been raised on cortisol and chaos, taught that suffering was the only constant. Pain didn't frighten me. Pain was familiar, even comforting. Pain was proof I was still alive.

The Language of Cruelty

During our first exercises in the CFLRS Saint-Jean training area, we were not performing up to the staff's expectations, and we knew it. They drilled us relentlessly, like it was personal.

Punishment came without pattern, the same way it had at home. A sharp word. A sudden hand. Instructors circled us like my father once did, scanning for weakness, waiting for the smallest mistake. A missed step, a crooked elbow, and I was flat on the tile floor, palms burning, lungs tearing themselves apart. Their voices cut sharper than belts ever had—*faster, harder, again.*

I recognized the language of cruelty. It was fluent in my body long before I put on a uniform.

Group Punishment

The calendar said it was spring, but the weather had not caught up. The cold clung to us, our uniforms soaked through from days of relentless rain. We formed up in two ranks and marched. Rain pattered gently on my glasses, slowly fogging them up. I squinted through the blur, silently whining to myself about how I just wanted to be warm. The sergeant's voice cut through my thoughts like a blade.

"You're not working as a team!" he roared.

And we all knew what came next: group punishment, the military's favourite teaching tool. My stomach dropped. At least it was not another weekend locked in the barracks. We had already been confined for the first four weekends.

As the rain kept falling, I muttered inside my head, *It isn't training if it isn't raining.* The sergeant started pacing in front of us, scanning for weakness. The rest of the staff circled around like sharks smelling blood.

"We're going to do some team-building this afternoon," the sergeant said, his voice soaked with sarcasm.

The course senior fell in, and the sergeant bellowed again.

"Platoon! By the right, quick march!"

We moved as one, boots squelching through soft mud. Left, right, left, right. In the distance, I saw it, a bog, or just a giant puddle pretending to be a lake. A lump formed in my throat as we marched closer. Surely, they were not serious . . . but I knew better than to hope.

We halted. I could feel the soft ground give beneath my boots, the edge of the bog kissing my soles. He lined us up in an extended line. I felt like I was about to sell my soul. Everyone was tense. No one spoke. What the fuck was about to happen? I clenched up instinctively. The wind cut through me, cold on my cheeks and louder than the sergeant's voice in my ears.

"We're going to learn how to pepper-pot!" he announced. This is a tactic used by infantry advancing under fire. We had been doing this since March.

The instructor screams, "Up, he sees me! Down!"

We all drop and pop up in rhythm.

"Only expose yourself for a few seconds at a time! Again, up, he sees me! Down!"

I cannot believe this is real. I chuckle dryly, already bracing for what is next.

"Prone position!" he shouts.

I hit the dirt, or rather, the water. My chest slapped down into the cold brown muck. My breath was knocked out of me. Hyperventilating, I lowered my body, face brushing water. My testicles retreated into my stomach. I gasped and caught flashes of the world through fogged-up glasses.

"On my order, you will pepper-pot across this field. Three hundred meters!"

It might as well have been three thousand. I closed my eyes, adjusted my helmet, and waited for the signal.

A whistle screamed.

Chaos erupted.

Water splashed. People grunted and yelled. I heard the staff repeating, "Up, he sees me! Down!" as we scrambled through the swamp. I could barely keep my footing. My boots slipped beneath me.

Please do not screw this up, I begged myself. *Do not fall. Do not make a scene. Do not draw attention.*

It would be easier to just swim through it, I thought as I dragged my body like a sack of meat. My voice joined the noise around me, loud and primal. A war cry, something we had practiced for weeks.

Then, suddenly, I was not fully there anymore.

I flashed back to my first traumatic brain injury (TBI). On the obstacle course in Quebec, I had slipped on an icy bridge. Slammed face-first into the ground. My ribs took the first hit, then whiplash, my head spinning. Nothing was the same after that. My heart rate jacked. Brain scrambled.

Then I came back to the present, sort of.

I was soaked. Water, sweat, piss, even tears. I tried to keep pace with the others, dissociating in and out like some twisted game of Red Light, Green Light. We pepper-potted for what felt like hours, though it was closer to only one.

Finally, the whistle sounded. The yelling stopped.

We formed up again. Two ranks.

I made it. I did not quit. I fucking made it.

Adrenaline still pulsed through my 120-pound frame. Sensitive. Soaked. But standing.

Fuck, yes!

Rifle Range, 2007

We marched to the C7 range in Saint-Jean. The sun beat down. Heat shimmered off the gravel. The rifle dug into my palm. Heavy. Cold. Too much for one man.

Don't screw this up. Don't be him.

"PRONE!"

I dropped. Dust in my throat. Gravel under my elbows. Vest pinching ribs until each breath burned. Cheek pressed to stock. Cold. Then warm with sweat.

Boots scraped closer. A shadow.

Smack. His hand on my vest.

"WISEMAN!"

The name cracked me open. My heart was hammering. Blood rushed in my ears.

"I served with your father."

My stomach fell. I was no longer on the range. I was back in the living room. His glare. His contempt. The bayonet of his voice still inside me.

I forced out a laugh. Thin. Breakable. "Don't judge me on him," I said.

A flicker of softness. Then, steel again.

"FIRING ORDERS INCOMING!"

The line erupted. Bolts clacked. Voices barked. Rifles snapped. I pulled the bolt. Metallic and final. Sweat burned my eyes. Breath broke.

"FIRE!"

The rifles roared. My weapon kicked. Casings rattled across stone. Smoke and oil clung to my tongue. I shook. I gasped. Inhale. Exhale. Squeeze.

But he was still there, crouched at my side. Waiting for me to fail.

Every shot was not at the target. It was at him.

Cease fire. Silence. I stayed prone, cheek in grit, ribs on stone.

It was not about shooting. It was about shadows.

And I still did not know who hit whom.

Years later, lying in a ditch in Afghanistan with my cheek pressed into foreign dust, the memory returned. The sound of rifles, the bite of gravel, the ghost crouched beside me. I carried him across oceans and into war. Sometimes, I wondered if I was fighting the enemy at all, or if I had only ever been fighting him.

Blood Makes the Grass Grow

They handed me a bayonet and told me to scream.

The steel glinted in the sun, dark from oil and worn fingers. My palms were already blistered from weeks of drills and the endless rhythms of parade-square punishment, but pain did not matter anymore. We were being stripped down to instinct. The uniform was only the outer layer.

"WHAT MAKES THE GREEN GRASS GROW?"

The master corporal's voice shook the air around us.

"BLOOD! BLOOD! BRIGHT RED BLOOD!"

We roared it, all of us, like possessed boys pretending to be men. I tasted copper in my mouth, though I had not been hit.

We were marched to the bayonet assault course, and that is when I saw them—the targets. Plywood silhouettes of German soldiers. Stahlhelms. Black crosses. Some bore crudely painted swastikas, symbols scrawled carelessly by instructors long dead or too far removed to understand the weight of what they resurrected.

It was supposed to fuel our rage.

But for me, it did something else.

My ancestors fought under those helmets. My blood traces back to the same soil those plywood ghosts had been painted to represent. They did not look like the Taliban. They did not even look like modern enemies. They looked like my people. And now I was being trained to slaughter them, repeatedly, with every shout, every stab, every twisted thrust of steel into wood.

No one else hesitated.

But I did.

Just long enough to feel it crack something in my chest.

"THRUST!"

"BUTTSTROKE!"

"FINISH HIM!"

I moved on command. I shouted on command. I killed on command. And with each bayonet drill, each scream of violence forced from my mouth, I could feel my soul retreat further into the back of my skull. Like it could not bear to watch what I was becoming.

"HE'S NOT DEAD! HIT HIM AGAIN!"

So, I did. Until my arms were jelly and my heart felt poisoned.

The others were grinning afterward, fired up on adrenaline and ego. But I stayed quiet. My uniform was wet with sweat and my rifle was still warm from use, but the only thing I felt was grief. Not for the plywood, not for the training but for what it cost to keep going.

That night, I lay in my bunk and stared at the ceiling, trying not to cry.

No one talks about what it does to a man to be taught to kill his own reflection.

I did not tell anyone. Not my section mates, not the padre, not the mirror.

But I carried it. That silent betrayal of blood and bone.

Bayonet training was meant to awaken the warrior.

Instead, it taught me how to kill my own soul.

Captured

We were on a raid, everything moving too fast. One moment, we were holding the line, whistles shrieking, artillery pounding. The next, I was grabbed. Cuffed. An empty sandbag yanked over my head. Darkness.

The smell hit first: sweat, mildew, damp canvas. My own breath bounced back, hot and metallic. Panic filled my lungs.

They threw me into the back of a pickup. I landed shoulder-first on cold steel, knees twisted beneath me. Diesel fumes mixed with the dust in my mouth. When they hauled me out, they shoved me onto crushed gravel. Sharp rocks tore through the thin fabric of my uniform. My cuffs rattled with every shift. Then they left me there, blindfolded, bound, kneeling in the cold.

At first, I reminded myself it was training. I was fine.

But my body knew better.

The wind cut through my sleeves, raising gooseflesh. My wrists swelled into the cuffs, fingers tingling, slipping toward numbness. My legs shook. My jaw locked until it ached. Beneath the sandbag, the world was muffled: boots crunching away, voices fading, my own heartbeat hammering in my ears.

Then, the past came back.

I was a boy again, locked in my room. The door bolted from the outside. No food. No escape. My father's voice echoing through the wall: "You stay there until you *learn*." Hours stretched into days. Punished for things I could never control.

My knees remembered the hard floor.

My stomach remembered the hunger.

My throat remembered swallowing tears until they burned.

Now my body carried it all into the gravel. Into the cold. Into the cuffs that cut deeper the more I struggled.

Here I was again, blindfolded, cuffed, freezing. The exercise field had become that locked room. The weight of my past pressed through the stones into my bones.

They called it training.

But it lit a fuse I carried for years.

The Hardening

I had entered the military chasing an image of strength, the kind I had only ever seen from a distance. What I became was something else entirely.

We were not just trained but transformed. Hardened in ways I did not yet understand. Somewhere in that process, I began to wake up.

By June 2007, I had clawed my way through fourteen weeks that felt like a lifetime of hell. The crucible burned away the boy and left behind someone new. Someone harder. Sharper. Addicted to suffering.

At night, twitching on the thin mattress, I carried the ghosts of both battlefields: the one I had left behind in my father's house and the one I was being initiated into now. Muscles locked in phantom drills, jaw clenched tight as if waiting for the door to burst open. For the first time in my life, I was full, yet I was also emptier than I had ever been.

That was the rhythm of transformation. Not the growth I had once dreamed of, but a stripping. Every day, something fell away—comfort, softness, illusion. Until all that was left was a soldier. Me, and not me.

CHAPTER 8

The Furnace Before the Fire

The Man I Was Becoming

After graduation leave and before battle school, my girlfriend and I drove around Conception Bay North to visit her family. The air was heavy with salt; the roads were lined with spruce trees and clapboard houses leaning into the wind. On the way back, a car in front of us lurched into an illegal U-turn. My girlfriend yanked the wheel, tires shrieking, her Pontiac Sunfire clipping hard against the other vehicle. The impact snapped my teeth together and rattled my spine.

Before I could think, I was out of the car. Barefoot on gravel. The stones dug in like nails, but the heat in my chest burned louder than pain. My pulse hammered in my ears. The slam of the door cracked like a rifle shot. I stormed forward, breath ragged. My shadow stretched long across the hood of the other car. Fists coiled, forearms buzzing like live wires.

"Fuck . . . cunt . . ."

The words tore free before I even knew they were there. My throat burned raw, the taste of metal on my tongue. Old words. Childhood words. Words pounded into me by fists on tables or spat in my face as the stink of beer choked the air. Now the same words came back like muscle memory. Automatic. As natural as breathing. My jaw locked, every muscle primed to strike.

I leaned down into the window. An older woman stared back, knuckles bone-white on the wheel, lips trembling. In the reflection of the glass, I saw my own face, red, hard, almost unrecognizable. The same face I had seen in my father when his rage took him.

And then my voice shifted. Lower. Hoarse. Almost calm. "Did you hear anything I said on the way over here?"

She blinked. Shook her head. "No."

The fuse went out. My fists loosened, my shoulders sagged. A long hiss of breath escaped me; my chest was still raw from the aftershocks of rage. My heartbeat slowed, heavy in my ribs, as if it had fought a war of its own. The anger was still there, coiled tight in my gut, but different now. Contained. A warning light instead of a blast.

For the first time, I realized military training had changed me. The boy who had once erupted without thought was gone. In his place stood someone else. Someone harder. Different. Someone who could stand in fire without being consumed. My childhood had wired me one way; the military was rewiring me again.

On the drive back to my apartment in St. John's, silence pressed thick between my girlfriend and me. Her hands gripped the wheel; her eyes were locked on the dark road. My own hands would not stop trembling. Tiny quakes ran through my fingers as I pressed them flat against my thighs. My jaw ached from clenching. Sweat cooled against my spine, leaving me clammy, hollowed out. Streetlights slid across the windshield, washing her face in alternating light and shadow. The radio crackled faintly, a pop song bleeding through static, absurd against the storm inside me.

I pretended the rage was gone. But it wasn't. It had only gone underground, waiting for the next time it would be called up.

A week later, I was back on a plane. The rock of Newfoundland slipped away beneath the wings, cliffs dissolving into cloud. The cabin smelled of burnt coffee and jet fuel. A baby cried somewhere up the aisle, its thin wail cutting through the drone of the engines. Flight attendants moved with brittle smiles, offering soda and pretzels as if the world were normal. The seatbelt light blinked overhead, followed by a cheerful chime. People shifted in their seats, flipped through magazines, dozed against windows.

It all felt absurd against the storm inside me. My reflection wavered in the glass: haunted eyes, jaw tight, body still humming with the residue of that night on the roadside. I gripped the armrest until my knuckles whitened, as if I could hold myself together through sheer force.

When the plane touched down in Ontario, the heat hit like a wall. The air was thick, suffocating, a furnace rising off the tarmac. My clothes were clinging to me before I even reached the bus. Sweat gathered under my collar, rolling down my back in rivulets. It felt less like arrival than initiation, as if the land itself meant to strip me bare before the first order was ever shouted.

Ahead, at Meaford, lay the real test. Another crucible. Another fire, waiting to consume what was left of the boy and shape what would come after.

2007—Battle School: Becoming a Weapon

I arrived at Land Forces Central Area Training Center, Meaford, Ontario, for infantry qualification. Stories said this phase broke even the toughest recruits. I half-expected screaming sergeants at the bus steps, *Tigerland* and *Jarhead* made real. Instead, the night was still, the only sounds the hiss of the bus brakes and the crunch of boots on gravel.

We had driven in from Saint-Jean, Quebec, in late June 2007. Our white Government of Canada charter bus pulled under floodlights. The *LFTC Meaford* sign glared stark against the dark. My stomach sank like a stone.

The duty sergeant met us with calm efficiency. No yelling, no theatrics. Just clipped orders. His voice echoed off the brick as we marched into a tired three-story building. Inside, the pale buzzing fluorescents washed everything in a sickly glow. The air carried the stale tang of sweat and disinfectant.

We bunked six to a room, strangers from every corner of Canada: hipsters from BC, roughnecks from Alberta, indigenous brothers from Ontario, and the familiar crew from the East Coast. Boots thudded on linoleum; gear clattered as it hit the floor. The air filled with a mix of deodorant, damp socks, and nervous silence.

We waited from June to August for the course to start. They said the delay was because too many infantry courses were running at once—there weren't enough instructors to go around. So we waited.

Days blurred together, unmarked by anything except the hum of fluorescent lights and the crunch of gravel under boots. We lived in limbo, killing time with busywork: sweeping the same hallways, polishing boots for inspections that never came, pretending there was still purpose in the waiting.

The waiting carved itself into fragments:

- Cards slapped on plastic footlockers, laughter covering nerves.
- Sandbags turned into dumbbells, push-up contests ending in sweat and jeers.
- Letters written hunched over desks, ink smudged with sweat or tears.
- A fight breaking out, fists flashing before NCOs pulled them apart.
- Cheap beer smuggled in: bottles hidden under kits and cracked open in whispers.

Nights were worse. The barracks hummed with snores, murmurs, the scrape of someone turning on a squeaky bunk. We traded stories in the dark: towns we had fled, families we could not face, dead-end jobs we had left behind. The laughter was real, but fear ran under it. Who would make it? Who would wash out?

For me, the silence pressed hardest. Lying on my back, looking up at ceiling tiles that faintly glowed with light from the hall, I felt the same dread I had felt as a boy waiting for my father's footsteps. The barracks were not violent like home, but they carried the same charge: any mistake, and chaos could erupt.

Small comforts kept us afloat: A chocolate bar passed in secret. Music smuggled in, listened to on headphones. Jokes whispered across bunks. Thin threads of brotherhood against the drag of time.

Most of us were not here because we'd had choices. We were here because we had not. And in those months of waiting, caught between who we had been and who we were about to become, we felt that lack of choices more than ever.

* * *

We were confined to barracks for the first four weeks. Testosterone thick in the air. Posturing. Egos. The instructors chipped away at us daily, carving us into something sharper, meaner, more obedient, and slipping us deeper into the program of sanctioned destruction. A few of us still clung to old rituals. On Sundays, those of us who believed, or at least wanted to believe, would ask to go into town for church services. When we came back, the mockery began. Quiet jeers from the rest: Bible-thumpers. Weak. Dreamers.

I stopped going after a few weeks. I was just too tired. By the time our weekends were returned to us, all I wanted was silence. Sleep. Food. Maybe a few movies on my little portable DVD player. My girlfriend's sister's boyfriend—himself a military brat—would burn me discs and send them in the mail. He understood the grind, the hollow spaces it carved inside you. His care packages felt like small acts of rescue.

Meaford was a ghost town on weekends if you were not on course. The rest of the guys would flood the bars, chasing numbness or trouble. I had already played that game. I drank enough in my teenage years to know where that road ended. The parties in St. John's, the blackouts. I remember falling down a staircase on my stomach once, coins spilling out of my pockets like I was paying some kind of toll. Or the night I got drunk at a friend's house and came home late, stumbling through the door as my father's and stepmother's family watched the hockey game in silence.

He knew. He could smell it on me before I even spoke.

"You're drunk," he said.

I shook my head, tried to steady myself. "No, I'm not."

But I was. The floor tilted. My words slurred. He made good on the threat he always kept in his back pocket. The police were called. Everything was stripped from my room—just like Debert. That same old punishment: take everything, erase the evidence of who you are, leave you with nothing but shame.

Funny how the army felt familiar after that.

CHAPTER 9

Battle School—Meaford

Ancre Heights

Each infantry course carried the name of a Royal Canadian Regiment battle honour. Ours, pulled from the First World War, was Ancre Heights, where boys drowned in mud and machine-gun fire before ever reaching their objective. The name gave shape to the weeks ahead, a reminder that suffering was the currency of this trade.

At LFCA Meaford, days fell into a relentless pattern. Morning PT began in darkness. Boots struck gravel in a steady rhythm as we pushed through ten kilometres before the sun cleared the trees. By breakfast, our uniforms were soaked, our faces streaked with salt. The body broke down and hardened at once, reshaped by repetition.

Weapons training broke the grind. The first time they laid out the C7s, the room went still. Rifles gleamed under fluorescent lights, each one spotless, waiting. The smell of oil clung sharply in the air. Instructors circled like hawks, voices clipped and unforgiving.

"Pick it up. Know it. This is your lifeline."

The weight surprised me. Heavier than I imagined. Solid in a way that made it feel alive. We stripped them piece by piece, bolts and pins clicking onto the tables. Every mistake drew a barked order or the slap of steel against wood. Magazines followed, green blanks rattling like teeth when we slammed them home. The bolts snapping forward echoed until the feeling lived in muscle memory.

At the range, theory turned into fire. We lay prone in gravel pits, sun burning our necks, rifles pressed into raw shoulders. The command rang out. The line came alive. The crack of C7s rolled down the berm, casings flying, the air thick with gunpowder. Instructors stalked behind us, boots crunching, and shouted corrections. Hours passed in bursts of noise and silence until every movement felt carved into us.

One section commander, a young master corporal fresh from Kandahar, carried himself like wire pulled tight. Sweat darkened the brim of his beret when he told us:

"Your job is to close with and destroy the enemy. That's it. Don't make it more complicated than that."

The words landed heavier than any manual. They sat in my chest like a stone, blunt and immovable. Part of me felt a jolt of pride, as if this was the doorway into the brotherhood I had come seeking. Another part went quiet, uneasy at how easily the act of killing had been named as our reason for being.

Evenings stretched long in the barracks. Rifles leaned against lockers. Boots dried in corners. Soldiers sprawled on bunks with the news on at low volume. The air held a permanent mix of gun oil, sweat, and cheap detergent, a smell that clung to skin and sheets. On television, Operation Medusa dominated the broadcasts. Canadians pushing into Panjwaii. Artillery hammering orchards. Firefights in grape fields. We traded rumours about casualties, about villages we could not pronounce: Zhari, Pashmul, Sperwan Ghar.

On the surface, it looked like downtime. Card games. Laughter. Someone sneaking a dip of Copenhagen. But under it ran a current none of us could name. I lay on my bunk, staring at the ceiling tiles while the static of the TV bled into chatter. It felt like waiting for a train I knew would hit me. Part of me wanted it to come, wanted to prove myself, step into the story. Another part braced for impact, just as I had braced for storms at home.

Meaford was only the platform. The train was already coming, and it did not stop in Ontario.

Every day began the same: wake up to Tupac blaring—*Dear Mama* bouncing off concrete walls—then rush to prep our bed spaces for inspection. Boots hammered the floors above, lockers slammed shut, rifles clattered like chains on steel. No matter how tight the corners, how clean the floor, it was never enough. The drill instructors would find a flaw. Always. And I would stand there, jaw clenched, asshole puckered, glasses fogging as spit from their screaming mouths landed on my face.

I knew the sting of spit on my face long before the Army. My father's breath, sour with beer, had taught me that lesson first. He used to corner me just like this, scream until I shrank, strip me of dignity. This was not new. This was familiar.

And in that familiarity, something hollow opened in my chest. Was this strength? Or proof that the world was only cruelty, dressed up in new colours and new ranks? The Army did not feel like escape—it felt like confirmation.

We did section attacks under the punishing sun of Grey County, heat shimmering off gravel roads. Mosquitoes swarmed in the Simcoe backwoods, whining in our ears as we patrolled. The earth smelled of rot and pine where we dug trenches, sweat dripping onto the rifle stocks that became extensions of our bodies. The tactics drilled into us were simple: Find. Fix. Destroy. Learn to kill the enemy until it lived in your marrow.

By then, the line between training and survival was starting to blur. I was no longer learning war. I was becoming it.

Soldier Qualifications

Weapons training—Soldier Qualifications, or SQ, they called it—was the part everyone talked about. From the C9 light machine gun to the

C6 general-purpose machine gun and all the way up to the 84mm Carl Gustaf recoilless rifle. The bigger the explosion, the better. That was the mentality.

There was nothing more freeing than squeezing off a ten-round burst from the C6, the earth warm beneath your body as you lay prone under the blistering Meaford sun. The hot brass clinking beside you, the smell of gunpowder lingering at your nostrils, a rush of adrenaline in your chest. Your number two confirming you had locked on target—it felt like power. Pure, controlled violence in a world that had given you none before.

2007 Infantry Training

During infantry training in 2007, I fired the 84mm Carl Gustaf recoilless rifle about ten times. Each shot cracked the air like thunder, the blast wave slamming into me hard enough to make the gravel jump at my boots. Heat and smoke washed over me, the metallic tang of propellant burning my throat.

The foam earplugs we were provided might as well have been nothing. The shock punched through my chest, ribs thrumming, lungs clamped. My skull rang, vision shivered. My ears screamed with needles of sound. Balance slipped, the ground rolling under me before it steadied. My teeth buzzed in their sockets. Smoke coated my tongue, thick and bitter. My spine wound tighter with every round.

We laughed it off. Called it toughness. But every blast etched itself deeper, the kind of mark no one else could see.

The final fighting withdrawal exercise left me stumbling, knees buckling under the crushing weight of my kit. Sleep deprivation clawed at my skull, turned my hands to lead and my legs to rubber. My mouth tasted of copper, thick and bitter, and my vision tunneled until the edges of the world blurred. I moved forward without thinking, every step a negotiation between instinct and collapse.

A shallow gully yawned ahead, gravel and jagged roots waiting like teeth. I fell in, hands scraping across sharp stones. Pain fired up my arms, and my body screamed *Stay down.* But I remembered my father's voice, sharp and sour: *You're soft. You'll never last.* It surged through me, automatic, like a reflex older than the Army.

Somewhere behind me, boots pounded, radios crackled, shouted orders ripped through the air. The platoon moved like shadows, bodies heaving, gear snagging on branches. No one slowed. No one cared. That was Meaford.

I got back up. Shook it off. Wounded dog.

Every step dragged me through memory and dirt. The taste of copper reminded me of broken teeth in a kitchen that never felt safe, the sting of my mother's fear, the sharp orders of a father who measured love in punishment. My body remembered every scrape, every bruise, every cut-down lesson from childhood. But there was no room for reflection here. Only motion. Only survival.

Ahead, a squad-mate tripped over a root, cursed, and kept moving. Behind, someone vomited on the dirt. The instructors circled like hawks. One barked, "Keep moving, Wiseman." His words cut sharper than gravel.

I weaved between fallen logs and shallow ditches, dragging exhaustion, pain, shame, and muscle memory behind me. The world narrowed to boots pounding dirt, blood in my mouth, my pulse hammering in my ears, and the echo of voices. *You'll never make it. You're soft.*

By the time we reached the final rally point, my body shook, muscles trembling like a marionette cut loose. I collapsed into mud and sun-warmed gravel, chest heaving, every nerve alight.

There was no sympathy in Meaford. And there never had been.

Gas Hut Baptism and Emotional Programming

Ontario's heat that summer climbed above forty degrees, pressing down like a hand over the whole camp. The NBC (nuclear, biological, and chemical) suit clung like a second skin. The smells of rubber and sweat filled my helmet before I even moved.

They ordered us to the ground. Push-ups. Hands slipping inside dirt-darkened gloves, arms straining against the weight of the suits. Each descent drove my chest into the rubber chest plate. Sweat poured off my face until it pooled beneath me. The hood stuck to my skin like glue. Breathing was already a battle.

Then, up. Jumping jacks. Arms pumping, boots thudding, legs dragging as heat built inside the sealed shell. Sweat ran down my back, soaked my socks, squelched in my boots with every landing. By the end, I felt half-drowned in my own body. The burn started before the gas ever touched us.

Next came the hut—a squat, windowless concrete box. Masks on, canisters cracked. CS gas spread, invisible and merciless. My eyes streamed, mucus flooded, my lungs clawed for air.

"Break the seal. Clear. Reseal."

I pulled the mask, fire rushing in. My chest seized, vision blurred. Every nerve begged me to run, to rip the mask off, to escape. But you did not run. Running meant weakness. Running meant death.

So, I forced my hands through the drill, trembling fingers slipping on rubber, body convulsing. Somewhere inside the haze, my father's voice rose: *Stop crying, or I'll give you something to cry about.* Childhood punishment braided into military programming. My nervous system could not tell the difference.

When it ended, we stumbled into sunlight, retching, coughing, some laughing like lunatics. My body hummed with pain, and underneath it was a weight I could not shake: the certainty that I had been changed.

Back in the barracks, the air reeked of sweat and chemicals. Shirts stuck to our skin as we stripped down, eyes red, faces raw. Some guys tried to laugh it off, cracking jokes between coughing fits, voices hoarse like we had swallowed gravel. Others stayed quiet, staring at the floor or their boots. The room buzzed with something unspoken. We had all been broken open and rewired, but no one wanted to admit it out loud.

That night, as the lights flicked off and the barracks fell into silence, I lay on my bunk, still tasting the gas in the back of my throat. The laughter, the bravado, it all faded in the dark. What stayed was the truth: The gas hut baptized us, but not into resilience. It baptized us into obedience.

The air was thick, heavy with the smell of hot asphalt and cut grass. Heat clung to my skin, trapped beneath the stiff polyester of my uniform. It dragged me back to CFB Greenwood—to the cadet camps I'd been forced into, sweating through wool for a father's approval I would never earn.

Meaford wasn't hell. It was purgatory.

By the end of hell week, time had lost its shape. Days bled into each other—dust, sweat, shouted orders that stopped sounding like words. My world shrank to blisters, rifle, rucksack. We were ghosts in green, stumbling through Meaford's hills with packs that dug into bone.

Sleep came in fragments, stolen between fire pickets and field drills. When it came, it was shallow and cruel. I'd wake to my name screamed through the heat, heart pounding before my mind caught up. The instructors circled like vultures, sniffing for weakness. They called it discipline. It felt like erasure.

During navigation, the air burned thick with heat, sweat stinging the cuts on my hands. The compass trembled between my fingers. I couldn't tell if the shaking came from exhaustion or from the fear of failing—of being sent home, of proving my father right. That I'd never be enough.

When dusk fell, the sky glowed dull red over the ridgelines. The air hung heavy, thick as a held breath. Just the sound of boots grinding through dirt. No applause. No praise. Only the quiet knowing that I was still standing. Barely.

I told myself it was just training, that once I earned the cap badge, it would all make sense. But something in me shifted out there in the heat—something small and human burned away. The harder they pushed, the more I disappeared. Every insult, every order, every sleepless march taught me to swallow pain before it had a name. I thought I was becoming stronger. In truth, I was learning how to vanish.

When the course finally ended, we stood on the parade square in pressed uniforms and sunburned skin, pretending pride was enough to fill the hollow inside. The instructors handed out badges, shook our hands for the cameras. The music of ceremony played, but I couldn't feel it. Only the hum of exhaustion, the ache in my shoulders, the echo of their voices still barking in my head.

The Fall

During the final defensive exercise before graduation, we were ordered into a fighting withdrawal. Dawn was just breaking—that pale blue hour when breath hangs in the air and every sound seems louder. The mist hadn't lifted yet; it pooled low across the training ground, clinging to the grass and our boots. The smell of damp soil and gun oil mixed with the faint sweetness of crushed pine.

Morning dew clung to the tall grass, turning every step slick. My uniform was already soaked from the knees down. I was carrying a full rucksack, a C9 light machine gun, and a pickaxe when my boot caught on a root. The world flipped.

I hit the ground hard, face first into a ditch filled with cold water. The rucksack drove the air from my lungs. The C9 twisted under me; the pickaxe slammed against my ribs. For a second, I couldn't move—just the taste of mud and the ringing in my ears.

Then came the voice. "Get the fuck up, Wiseman! You want to die down there?" The sergeant's scream tore through the fog, his silhouette cutting against the pale sky. "You're slowing down the whole section! Move your ass!"

I tried to stand, slipping in the muck, water streaming from my helmet. He was still shouting—every word a reminder that weakness had no place here. I swallowed whatever pain I felt and climbed out of the gully, dripping, trembling, pretending it was nothing.

No one looked back. That was the way of it. Reporting an injury meant questions, paperwork, and the risk of being recycled—sent back to start again. I couldn't bear that. Not after coming this far.

So I stayed quiet. Kept moving. The bruise deepened, the ache settled into my spine, but silence felt safer than shame. I told myself it was discipline. Later, I'd understand it was fear.

Graduation and Ghosts

November 2007

Nine months earlier, I'd been a scared kid. Now I had a pair, or so our course warrant barked as he drove us up and down the square.

"March like you've got a fucking pair! You are now Royals. Pro Patria!"

The parade square gleamed with frost. Each step hammered through my boots, sending cold shards up my spine. My calves ached, tight and burning from hours of marching in formation. Rifles pressed against my shoulder blades, biting into raw skin. Wool uniforms chafed my neck and wrists. My breath came in clouds, thick and hot, stinging my eyes. I counted each step left-right-left, trying to drown out the tremor still hiding in my stomach.

From the bleachers came the ripple of applause. Families braved the cold, bundled in scarves and coats, cameras flashing like stuttering stars.

Mothers waved, cheeks wet with pride. Fathers stood stiff, hands buried in pockets, their sons' reflections in pressed brass buttons.

I scanned the faces and found no one. My space in the stands was empty, just strangers filling the gap where blood should have been.

The roar of the crowd did not touch me. My shadows were louder. The boy who had flinched under my father's drunken spit. The teenager who had stared at the ceiling of his bedroom, wondering if he would ever escape. The hollow-eyed kid who showed up at Saint-Jean with nothing but hunger and shame. They marched beside me, step for step, stitched into every seam of my uniform.

The band played on, trumpets and drums rolling like cannon fire, drowning out thought, pushing us forward. My chin lifted, my spine locked, every boot strike sent vibration through my bones. For a moment, the scared kid inside me tried to keep up. But the soldier had already taken his place.

We wheeled as one body past the dais. The course warrant's eyes raked us. He was not just checking our lines or posture. He was measuring what was left of us. Had we been burned clean of hesitation? Had we been forged hard enough for war?

I saluted. My arm snapped down, fingers stinging in the cold. Cheers rose behind me. But in my chest, something else stirred, a silence heavier than any anthem.

When it ended, the crowd spilled onto the square, parents hugging their sons, girlfriends kissing polished brass. I stood apart, rifle slung, hands aching for somewhere to go. No one was waiting for me.

That night, we did what soldiers always do when there is nothing else. We got drunk.

Uniforms came off, socks and shirts clinging damp to skin. Bottles cracked and foamed, spilling bitter liquid over sticky tables. Beer burned my tongue, sharp and sour, hammering my stomach. Voices rose over music, rattling the drywall. The bass vibrated my ribs, my teeth, even my skull.

Somebody puked into the sink. Somebody else swung fists over nothing. I laughed until my jaw cramped, slamming glass after glass. My hands shook from cold, adrenaline, and alcohol. My throat burned, my eyes stung. Each swallow tasted of metal. Each laugh rang hollow.

By morning, the barracks reeked of stale beer and bile. My head throbbed like artillery fire, my stomach churned, my tongue felt raw. My legs ached from frost and falls. My body remembered the parade square in every pounding heartbeat and bruised muscle. And still, the shadows were there, sober as ever.

The next day, I boarded a jet back to Newfoundland. The engines droned in my skull, rattling the metal of the cabin and every nerve ending. Through the small oval window, Ontario shrank, a frostbitten patchwork fading beneath cloud. The coastline appeared as we descended: jagged rocks jutting into grey water, salt tang on the air already creeping into my nose. The city smelled faintly of diesel and wet pavement. My belongings sat in a duffel at my feet, everything I owned packed into nylon and canvas, ready for another chapter I was not sure I wanted.

I tried to sleep, but the hum of the engines, the memory of the square, and the shadows pressed me into the thin seat. My stomach churned again, not from the plane, but from the anticipation of home, of packing, of facing the life I had left behind, the people I had left behind.

The apartment smelled of damp carpet and old walls, the same as I had left it months before. My body remembered hunger, shame, and fear as easily as it remembered cold boots and brass buttons.

Graduation was supposed to be an ending. A reward. But even drunk, even hung over, even strapped into a jet bound for Newfoundland, I knew the truth. My body and my shadows knew the truth. It was only the beginning.

Packing Up—November 2007

As I packed up my life in Newfoundland that grey November, rain poured sideways and wind howled as if trying to talk me out of leaving. Movers hauled box after box from the U-Haul storage locker off Kenmount Road while I stood there, soaked through, supervising but barely present.

I could not believe I had made it. I had survived everything the military had thrown at me. From basic to battle school, from field exercises to gut checks, I had endured it all. Not just endured. I had passed. A hundred pounds soaking wet. Bones sharp against my skin. Forged into something new. A soldier.

My father's voice echoed in my head: *You'll never amount to anything.* He screamed it when I was a boy, spit flying, fists clenched, breath sour with rage. And yet, here I was. Loading up for the next chapter. Still broken in places. But also hardened.

The rain did not ease. It mirrored the grief and awe pooling in my chest. I was not just leaving a place. I was leaving an entire history. I did not know what awaited me on the other side.

We celebrated Christmas a month early. My girlfriend was moving with me to Gagetown, New Brunswick, to the home of my infantry regiment. We tried to make the best of it, but the mood was already souring. She was furious, certain I had forced her to leave her mother. She would carry that blame for years. Even as we lit the tree and exchanged gifts, pretending to build something hopeful, tension clung to the air.

The real storm hit when we loaded the silver Sunfire. Four cats yowling in their carriers. Snacks spilling from crumpled bags. Clothes still damp from the rain. She exploded when she realized I still did not have my license. Fists gripped the wheel as if she could crush the road itself. I sat there, chest tight. Shoulders heavy but steady. Hands curling into fists of my own. My body remembered how to endure. Years of field exercises.

Wet nights in mud. The weight of a hundred-pound pack. Each instinct kicked in now, keeping me upright in the middle of a domestic battlefield.

The car became a pressure cooker. Every sigh. Every clipped word. Every sharp glance was a fuse. The cats hissed, paws scrabbling against carriers, ears flattened. Wet clothes clung to my skin. Cold pressed against my spine. The storm outside seemed tame compared to the one we carried inside.

Finally, we eased onto the highway. Newfoundland receded in rain-streaked mirrors. Grey houses and twisted spruce faded into mist. The car jolted over potholes. A bump. A lurch. Every jolt reminded me how unsteady everything was.

Her jaw was tight. Knuckles white on the wheel. Eyes flicking to the road, she muttered under her breath, lips pressed thin. I could see her muscles coiled, ready to snap at the next word. I kept my hands folded in my lap. Focusing on breathing. Slow and deliberate. Soldier breathing.

The cats hissed. One carrier slid slightly. Snacks rattled in the back. Crumpled bags scratched against the upholstery. I ignored it all. Every sound. Every movement. Part of the rhythm. A rehearsal for the discipline I would need in Gagetown.

The highway stretched ahead. Endless wet asphalt reflected the stormy sky. I glanced at her profile. Rigid concentration. A flicker of frustration crossed her eyes. She tapped her fingers against the wheel, a small restless rhythm betraying the tension she did not voice. I let the silence hang between us, tight and charged.

Newfoundland slipped completely away. Ahead lay Gagetown. The regiment. Unknown drills. Tests of endurance. Every instinct I had honed in mud, sweat, and frost settled in. My chest ached. Heart thudding. But I sat taller. Forged. Hardened. Broken yet whole.

And for the first time in a long time, I felt ready. A flash of something in my stomach. A memory of leaving the old apartment, the smell of rain on asphalt. The quiet pride of knowing I had survived. The weight of my history. I exhaled. Let it sit. Let it flow forward.

CHAPTER 10

Royal Canadian Regiment

"Almighty God, we humbly implore Thy blessing on The Royal Canadian Regiment and all of us who serve therein. Help us to prove worthy to accept the high ideals and traditions of the past; to honor and revere the memory of those who have gone before us; to face our responsibilities in the future, in both peace and war, with courage, justice, love, honesty, and faithfulness. Remove all greed, hatred, selfishness, and envy from our thoughts that we may make true service to the Regiment and for Thee, our God; for our fellow man, and 'For Country.' Amen."

(THE REGIMENTAL PRAYER)

* * *

Between Two Wars

After our move to Canadian Forces Base Gagetown in New Brunswick, it didn't take long for me to realize that my girlfriend had never been taught how to manage life on her own. Her mother had done everything for her—folded her clothes, put them away, smoothed every wrinkle of her existence. So, when we arrived, she withdrew. Hid in the bedroom, overwhelmed. Blamed me for taking her from her family.

Her mother filled the gap with gifts, material comfort. I recognized the pattern immediately. Shame flared in me, the old ache of being beneath, less than, broken. But it also sparked something else. Competition. The need to prove myself. The hunger to rise above the wreckage I had come from.

Even as my body endured the rigors of training—lungs burning, muscles trembling, ribs aching, underweight, and disciplined—the moment I stepped through the door, a different battle began. She bought a thirteen-hundred-dollar camera we could not afford. Image mattered more than survival. The expectation was clear: like her father, I was expected to shut down, disappear, and absorb the same rageful, contemptuous dynamic she had grown up with.

But I did not disappear. I tried. God, I tried. I cooked. I cleaned. I trained to be a warfighter. I did what society said a man should do: be the breadwinner. Yet, we scraped by. Her taste for luxury always came first.

I pushed my body to exhaustion during training. Sweat matting my hair. Legs trembling. Skin raw under the sun. Then, I came home. My uniform damp. Every fiber of me sore. And the house greeted me with cold linoleum underfoot and a sterile bleach-and-fabric-softener smell that made my chest tighten. Relief never came.

Pain was forbidden. If I winced, faltered, if my ribs ached too visibly, she mocked me, called me dramatic, called me sensitive, then walked away. Silence became punishment. Any sign of weakness invited control.

I tried to speak, throat tight, words trembling. My chest clenched. Nerve endings alight with frustration. I clenched my jaw until it ached. Curled my toes against the cold floor. My body burned with unacknowledged pain.

First, she abused my mind. Then, she abused my body. Home was supposed to mean safety, recovery, peace. Instead, violence followed me into the kitchen, the bedroom, every space where I should have been a partner. I was raped repeatedly. Told to lie still. Told to be a man. I cried myself to sleep countless nights. The abuse seeped into my bones, into the chill of the floors, the stiffness of chairs, the tension in my shoulders, spine, and hands.

Her self-treatment plan unfolded like clockwork. Pills to numb. Days locked in her room. A self-imposed isolation that mirrored that of her mother. The pattern was not new. It had been drilled into her. I could see it echo in every gesture, every avoidance.

Suppression became a uniform stitched into daily life. I carried that lesson with me. Another armour of silence pressed against my body and mind. Endurance was required. Strength became a quiet rebellion, waged in the tightness of my chest, the tremor of my hands, the chill that never left my skin.

Every day, every night, I lived between two worlds. The rigor of training. The impossible demand to disappear at home. Every muscle learned discipline. Every nerve learned to hide. My body endured what my home would not allow me to show.

2008—Rage Beneath the Ice

The Medium Logistics Vehicle, Wheeled sat waiting like a beast, ancient and unwilling. Its engine coughed. Metal groaned. The heater squealed uselessly. Ice glazed the windshield. Wipers thrashed at nothing. Snow fell sideways, carried by a wind sharp enough to slice skin. Diesel smoke curled through the cab, choking and acrid, hugging my hair, pressing my helmet tighter into my skull.

"7-Alpha, engines running? Eyes on your instruments. Let's move!"

The instructor's voice snapped over the radio. My pulse spiked before I even touched the wheel. I stomped the pedals. The engine roared. The cab shook. Snow slapped the side like a drumline. My teeth clenched. My hands burned. Every childhood fall, every slammed door, every word I was never allowed to speak rose up in a thrum of muscle memory and rage.

Prep and First Run

Before the real course began, we had to prep the truck. Climbing in, I felt every warped step, every rusted hinge. Fuel gauges wobbled. Lights flickered. I checked mirrors, slammed doors, and adjusted levers that moved like they had a mind of their own. My breath formed clouds inside the cab. Fingers numb, I tested the brakes, shivered as the heater spat nothing but icy air.

"7-Alpha, brakes!"

I stomped the pedal. "It's not responding."

The instructor's voice cut through the air, sharp and impatient.

"Not responding? What do you mean, not responding? Try again — now!"

The truck lurched, reluctant, clanking. I yanked the wheel. The rear tires fishtailed on black ice. My stomach lurched. The cab pitched. Diesel smoke stung my eyes.

First Skid Drill

"Shift. Brake. Turn. Counter. Do it again!"

The words came rapid-fire over the radio as we entered the skid course. I spun the wheel sharply. Ice cracked like glass beneath tires. Gravel clinked under metal, scraping steel. The cab leaned, whining, resisting my command. My hands burned. Knuckles cracked. Teeth clenched. The instructor barked corrections constantly. "Don't fight it. Let it slide. . . . Control it, damn it."

A fallen branch appeared in my peripheral vision. I yanked left. The cab tipped sideways, scraping ice. Radio chatter exploded with warnings from instructors: "Eyes up. Eyes up, 7-Alpha. Control."

For one heartbeat, I let go of the pedals. The cab breathed with me. Snow tapped the roof like fingernails. Lungs clawed at thin, diesel-laced air. Then, chaos returned.

Hours on the Course

We drove from Saint John to Moncton to Stanley and back. Hours bled together. Every mile was a negotiation with steel, ice, and authority. Tires screamed. My engine roared. My jaw clenched. Pulse pounded. Every skid, every wheel slip, every overcorrected turn was a test. Fear pressed on all sides, hammering in rhythm with the engine. Obedience sharpened. Survival demanded everything.

Other drivers flinched. Cursed. Slid off the road. I saw them, heard them over the radio, "Medium Logistics Vehicle, Wheeled 4-Beta, ditch. 3-Delta, watch your tail." Every warning was a knife to my nerves, a lesson in vigilance.

Collision Close Call

A sudden black patch of ice sent the cab spinning. My stomach dropped. I counter-steered hard, feet stabbing pedals. Tires screamed. Gravel skidded sideways. Diesel smoke clawed my throat. The instructor's voice cut through: "Hold it. Hold it. You're overcompensating."

I gritted every tooth. Heart thundered. Vision narrowed. The cab, metal and diesel, became an extension of my body. Muscle memory took over. Every scrape, slammed door, and word I was never allowed to say drove my hands, my spine, my nerves. I bent, twisted, survived.

Moment of Breath

Hours into the day, my body burned, mind screaming. For a single heartbeat, I exhaled fully. The cab rocked gently. Snow hissed on the roof. Diesel fumes lingered thick in my throat. I felt hollow. Alive. Raw. Unbroken.

Then, we were back in chaos. Tires screamed. Engines roared. Instructor voices clipped through the radio: orders, corrections, warnings. I answered back with the only things I had. Focus, muscle, instinct, rage, survival.

Final Reflection

By the time the sun dipped low behind the frost-lined trees, I realized something. Skill mattered, yes, but survival was about absorbing fear, bending it into obedience, letting it sharpen every sinew, every nerve, every thought. The seeds of rage planted in childhood had found fertile soil behind the wheel of a clapped-out truck. I had driven through fear, through chaos, through winter itself and emerged sharper, harder, ready for the next battle.

CHAPTER 11

Life in the Field: Fall Training, 2 RCR

Inside the Hatch: Dawn Attack

Rain hammered the hull, drumming against steel like fists. Water streaked across the periscope, rivulets blurring the outside world into a grey smear. My hands burned on the wheel, knuckles raw under soaked gloves. Every pulse of the engine rattled through spine and chest, reverberating with the memory of my father's hand, the sting of old lessons.

My stomach knotted with each jolt, bile rising in my throat, twisting with old fear. Cold, wet mud pressed through my boots and up my legs, and my gut lurched at the thought of the bridge ahead. Every ton of steel, every ton of responsibility, every ton of my own fear pressed down through the hull and through my abdomen, a gnawing pit that never settled.

Blackout lights glowed faintly along the convoy, ghostly beacons in the fogged dawn. Engines hummed in uneven rhythm. The light armoured vehicle's thermals flickered, barely catching heat tracks. My stomach lurched again at a sudden shift in the treads, sending a wave of queasy adrenaline through my core.

I adjusted the throttle. The vehicle leaned, treads clawing at the mud. Branches scraped the side armour, snapping and whipping. Water sluiced through hatch gaps, dripping cold into my shirt. The smell of diesel and wet metal filled my nostrils, mingling with the faint tang of copper in my stomach. Muscle memory screamed. Gut twisted. Heart thrummed against armour. Lungs burned.

"Charlie One, move to checkpoint Bravo! Repeat, checkpoint Bravo!" Static crackled. A voice overlapped. Commands collided.

Ahead, the temporary bridge waited. *If it goes under, stay calm. Open the hatch only once submerged.* The words looped behind my eyes. I imagined cold water clawing steel, imagined it pulling me down. My stomach turned over, tight, roiling with fear. Memory and instinct tangled, each demanding obedience. Childhood lessons surged—wrong moves, silence, punishment. Now, mistakes could drown me.

I edged onto the bridge. Steel groaned beneath us. The LAV shivered, treads fighting the slick mud, yawing slightly with each shift. I drew a ragged breath, lungs burning, pulse hammering against chest plate, willing the steel to hold. Stomach knotted tighter. Adrenaline made bile rise.

For a fraction, I felt the bridge settle under us, and I dared to breathe.

Branches scraped. My chest tightened. Muscle tensed. I braced with my legs, jaw locked, feeling the harness dig into my ribs. Another light armoured vehicle groaned behind, mud spraying across our flank. Engine hums layered with muffled shouts and crackles over the radio. My gut churned, a twisting pit that seemed to echo the treeline ahead.

The forest swallowed us. Mud clung to treads, spraying grit against armour. Trees whipped past, branches rattling steel, testing control. The LAV jolted, treads fighting grip, and swerved, plowing through a shallow ditch that tried to throw us off balance. Branches snapped. Mud flew. I held on. My stomach rolled with every lurch, bile and fear mingling.

"7-3, report status. Over."

"Holding, all clear, 7-3. Over."

I adjusted the clutch. Teeth gritted. Shoulder pressed to seat. Every shift sent jolts through my forearms. Micro-muscles burned with each brace, each lean. Gut knotted, twisting, anxious, alive. Lungs clawed for air. Reflexes and memory tangled, demanding obedience.

"Delta Two, maintain spacing! Move! Move! Move!"

Static. A cough. Fractured syllables. *Move.*

Playgrounds and backyards surfaced in my mind. Small stakes. Big fears. Survive. Obey. Suppress. Pain and obedience—my body remembered. My stomach churned at the rush of each engine pulse, each jolt, each memory.

Another micro-lurch—steel pitched left, then right, catching the lip of a trench before swinging back. I felt it in every joint. A fleeting heartbeat of relief pulsed through me. I clung to the wheel, chest heaving, stomach twisting, and let a tiny measure of control slip through before the next surge.

Old lessons, sharp and automatic, coiled inside me. A body trained to survive. A child trained to obey. Gut and spine aligned in a tense rhythm, rolling steel through rain and mud, waiting for H-hour, waiting for the unknown to strike.

And all I could do was hold the wheel, brace every joint, breathe between engine pulses, and feel the symphony of gut-twisting fear, steel, mud, radio chatter, and fractured commands pulse through every fiber of my being.

The Infantry's Poison

The infantry taught me to be a man, but it came as venom, slithering into my bones, threading through my veins. My ribs press inward. My gut knots. My muscles twitch before my mind catches up.

Boots hammer gravel before sunrise. Cold mud clings to my feet, sucking at them. Rain stings my neck. *Find. Fix. Destroy.* Each syllable vibrates through me. My heartbeat skips, then doubles. My stomach coils. My hands tremble, ready to strike, obey, break.

Back in Meaford, fluorescent lights buzzed overhead. C7 rifles gleamed on tables, oil sharp in the air. Fingers fumbled pins and bolts. Every mistake sparked shocks through my nerves. Instructors snapped words like whips. *Pick it up. Know it. This is your lifeline.* My chest tightens. My stomach knots. My jaw clenches. My veins feel like braided steel. The order is simple. Obey. My body obeys before my brain can protest.

Mud drags at my boots. Rain pours down my neck and spine. Sleep deprivation bends my body into angles meant for pain. *Obey. Kill the fear. Remember the enemy.*

Every breath burns. Every muscle screams. My lungs fight for air. My heartbeat drums a war song that vibrates through my skull.

The concert again. Bass, sweat, shouting. The anger has its own life. My fists twitch. My chest hammers. My stomach heaves. Seventeen-year-old boy. Soldier. Body screaming. Nerves alive with anticipation.

Classroom drills, concert rage, mud, rain, rifles, fluorescent lights. They collapse into one pulse inside me. Memory and present fuse. My hands twitch, itch, convulse. My chest constricts. My stomach coils, bracing for orders that have not yet come.

Every nerve is a live wire. Every sweat bead a spark. My teeth grind against molten anger. Blood pulses hot, carrying the venom into every tendon, every marrow, every fiber of my being.

The poison has become me.

I am inside my body, and my body is a battlefield. Flashbacks hit like shrapnel. Orders crash over me like artillery. Rage twists my chest. Fear hammers my gut. Obedience presses along my spine like a weight I cannot lift, a chain I cannot break.

I am the poison. I am the anger. I am the obedience. Every heartbeat, every twitch, every shiver confirms it.

And I obey.

A Father in Waiting

Her fear filled the bathtub as she sat quietly, wondering how to tell her controlling mother. She was six weeks along, and the ultrasound to reveal the sex of our first child was scheduled for the same time I'd be deployed to Germany on exercise. Once, she had whispered about wanting an abortion—not because she didn't want the baby, but because she was terrified of her mother's judgment. The generational control ran deep, in her family and in mine.

When the hospital ultrasound came, they couldn't tell us the sex. We left with blurry images and more questions than answers. That fall, while the leaves turned, we paid for a private 3D ultrasound. I wasn't there to see the moment our child's features came into focus on the screen. Instead, I was in a Humvee convoy, bouncing across Bavaria, gripping the seat as the weight of fatherhood pressed down on me. Was our baby a boy or a girl? It didn't matter to me. I just prayed they had fingers and toes and everything they needed.

She sent me the pictures afterward. It was a girl. I remember holding the printouts in my hands, on another continent, realizing how much of life was already happening without me.

I wanted to be a good father—better than mine. We bought baby books. I started planning a better life. But underneath, I was haunted. Haunted by the knowledge that the military was sharpening something in me that had already been honed in childhood: rage.

I tried to silence it. But I knew the programming. I had seen the same rage circle our house in Debert when I was ten—my father screaming, the cycle spinning, generation to generation.

I wanted to be a better father than mine. I really did.

A Summer Without Celebration

We returned to Newfoundland for summer vacation, carrying the news of our baby like a spark. I hoped it might soften the hard edges of my parents. Maybe, for once, there would be joy.

But when I told them, there was no celebration. No widening of eyes. No smile. No reaching across the space between us. Only a pause. Then a flat, "Oh."

My chest sank. My hands went cold. My throat tightened. It was as if I had mentioned the weather, not the imminent arrival of new life.

I searched their faces for warmth. For some sign that they understood this child was part of them, part of our story.

Nothing.

The air pressed down, thick and still. My stomach knotted. My heartbeat stuttered. It was the same distance I had known all my life. Their detachment said more than words ever could. This baby would have no love. No celebration. It was not theirs at all.

In that moment, I understood. The truest inheritance they had to give was absence. Just like every birthday I had waited for, every report card I had hoped they would notice, every small hope left dangling.

Nothing had changed. And I wanted nothing more to do with them.

When I returned to Gagetown that August, the Army pressed in from every side. Long nights on the sniper demo. Exercises that swallowed weekends. Alone. Family absent. Every duty, every expectation pressing down, relentless and inescapable. My body carried it all: the fatigue, the tension in my shoulders, the ache in my gut. Every obligation pulled me taut, reminding me that there was no shelter from the weight of this life, neither at home nor in the unit lines.

The Ditch I Never Saw Coming

Before we left for Germany, I was driving the LAV III through the Gagetown training area, through dust so thick it scraped at my eyes and coated my tongue. The engine's diesel smell mixed with the heat of the sun, pressing down like a weight I couldn't shake. I was driving at roughly 50 kph and didn't see the ditch until the vehicle yanked violently beneath me. My chest slammed into the steering column. My neck snapped back. My back throbbed. Sweat pooled in my eyes and ran down my face. I tasted it, metallic and bitter, and gagged.

For a second, the world stopped. Only my heartbeat remained, hammering in my skull, echoing in my ears, loud enough to drown everything else.

I screamed into the intercom. Panic clawed through me, nerve endings alive with pain and shock. Static answered first. Then the crew commander's voice, sharp and unforgiving: "What the hell were you thinking?" Blame pressed against my skull like a fist. Shame sank into my gut.

We rolled into the base. The senior chain of command joined in. Words like hammers, striking me from all directions. No one asked if I was hurt. No one even noticed the tremor in my hands, the way my legs shook, how my body had been rattled loose. No medical. No report. Just expectation. Suck it up. Keep moving. Carry on.

Later, alone in the driver's hatch, I trembled. Cold metal pressed into my palms. Heartbeat racing. Brain spinning. I called home, searching for an anchor, for something, anything that would remind me I was still human. I cried. I wasn't angry. I wasn't violent. I was broken, raw. But on the other end, it was dismissed.

"Stop being dramatic. Stop acting like a child. You're angry again. You're abusive. Overreacting. Not calm enough." Her words cut deeper than the crash, deeper than the steel of the vehicle, deeper than any bruise. That pattern—the misreading and the dismissal—followed me after deployment, when the stakes were higher and when damage ran deeper.

No one understood that driving didn't just scare me. Driving haunted me. Every rumble of an engine, every shadow of a ditch, every subtle shift of the road tightened my chest. PTSD and hyper-vigilance rewired me and fractured me.

After the war, it wasn't just hard to drive. It became impossible.

CHAPTER 12

Home Soil and Haunted Skies

Germany: Cooperative Spirit

In the summer of 2008, I was called into the platoon office. The warrant officer looked up from his desk. "You're going to Germany. NATO exercise—Cooperative Spirit. Month-long deployment. Afghanistan training starts next week."

That fall, I returned to the land of my birth for the first time since my family moved away in 1987. I was born in Germany, but like so many children of military families, I had been uprooted and replanted far from my origins. My father spent eight years in Lahr but never once encouraged a connection to that place or to its culture.

My mother would phone and complain, saying, "He never wanted you to learn my language. He never wanted you to know where you came from." There was shame in it, a denial of heritage that had been stitched into my identity.

I ended up at Hohenfels, near the Bavarian border, on a base that still felt haunted by the ghosts of World War II. Cooperative Spirit brought together Americans, Brits, Aussies, Kiwis, and Canadians. Testosterone everywhere. Everyone proving they were hard enough for Afghanistan. The training was not just tactics. It was psychological conditioning. Forget fear. Forget hunger. Forget hesitation.

Autumn in Germany

The German fall was stunning. Wet leaves and trees on fire with orange and red gave me a strange sense of peace, like home in a place I had never truly known. I walked the base alone at night, letting cold rain strip my thoughts bare. It rained for almost three weeks straight. I did not mind. I needed the solitude.

Back in Canada, I had been our section's driver. That job followed me overseas. The first week in Germany, we were supposed to receive Humvee training while the rest of the section focused on prepping weapons, rations, and gear.

I sat in a stuffy classroom, jet-lagged and on edge, listening to an American sergeant brag about bombing down the Autobahn at 200 kilometers an hour. He laughed as if it were nothing. I sat there sweating.

Anyone who served with me knew one thing: I hated driving. The weight of responsibility, the lives in my hands put a pit in my stomach that never went away. Even now, years later, just driving an SUV can spiral my brain into panic.

I was the section driver. Old American Humvee. No license? Didn't matter. Instructors said, "Just drive." And I did, even though driving made my nervous system lock up. Hyper-vigilance behind the wheel was not a choice. It was a reflex.

One day, we were rolling up to meet our American trainers. My crew commander, a senior corporal, gave me a quick set of directions. "Park beside that Humvee. Tight. Close enough to talk."

I eased forward. Left a bit. Left again. The scrape of metal against metal. My heart jumped. Breath caught. Fist clenched. Five-inch scar.

An American sergeant exploded out of the vehicle, red-faced, spitting with rage. He made me get out and stand at attention. The stench of old cigarettes and coffee breath hit me in waves as he screamed. "What if there were people between us? What if someone was standing there?"

"I would have seen them," I said flatly. "I would have stopped."

His veins bulged. Fists clenched as if he wanted to swing. He barked a few more words I did not hear. It did not matter. I had already left the scene in my head.

When it was over, my crew commander lit into me. I told the truth. The brakes had stuck. They had been sticky all day. No one believed me.

The unit MPs opened an investigation. A female military police officer with something to prove made me get behind the wheel and prove my driving on a wide-open paved area. It felt like a trial, not a test.

It reminded me of Gagetown, where I nearly backed a LAV into the bay doors after a long day on the road. My nervous system had locked up back then, too. Hours of white-knuckle driving. Never knowing if a mistake would end in disaster or just another screaming sergeant.

The Kill House and Humiliation

In Germany, I stood in the dark with my section, night-vision goggles strapped to my face, waiting outside the kill house. A "kill house" is what soldiers call a live-fire training structure built to mimic urban combat—hallways, doorways, stairwells—the chaos of a city condensed into plywood and cinder block.

Weapons ready. Hearts pounding. The world glowed in sickly green through the lenses, depth and distance collapsing into flat shapes and shadows. For guys like me, with glasses wedged behind the goggles, everything was distorted. For a brain that wasn't firing the way it used to, it was a nightmare—every step uncertain, every corner a guess.

I had already suffered two TBIs by then. This would become my third.

We moved out. Something went wrong. My boot caught. Or maybe my brain misfired. I went down hard—somersaulting like a clumsy idiot—right in front of a general, of all people.

He looked down at me, confusion etched on his face, not anger. "You good?"

My face burned. Heat spread across my neck, my ears ringing. I nodded. Got up. Said nothing.

Inside the kill house, everything blurred. Strobe lights flashed. Smoke thickened the air, clinging to my throat. Blanks cracked like live rounds. Chaos swallowed me. My reaction time slowed. My coordination slipped. My hands hesitated over the weapon as my stomach flipped. But no one saw that. They only saw another soldier fumbling through the motions.

Then it was over. During the After-Action Review, there were nods, grunts, critiques. Then, back to prepping for the next round of chaos.

No one asked if I hit my head. No one checked. There was no space for weakness. Not there. Not ever.

I never made it to Lahr, my birthplace, during that trip. I had only twelve hours off during the whole month that I was stationed in Germany. Instead, I chose to visit Nuremberg.

There were other choices: Munich, Dachau. But something in me recoiled at the idea of standing in places so saturated with death. I was already sensitive to energy then, though I didn't fully understand it. I just knew that sometimes I felt feelings that weren't mine. Sometimes, the weight of history pressed into my bones, cold and unyielding, like it was trying to anchor me somewhere I didn't want to go. My chest tightened. My stomach knotted. I walked the streets, trying to shake it off, yet knowing I couldn't—not yet.

CHAPTER 13

Preparing for Deployment

Golf Company and Ghosts of War

It was December 2008, and we were in what we called *silly week*—a brief reprieve from the grind. Battalion sports days, ridiculous costumes, half-drunk competitions. All of it was an attempt to decompress after the chaos of training Golf Company. We were just starting the long road to readiness, slated to deploy in 2010 as part of the Provincial Reconstruction Team (PRT) in Afghanistan.

There were no slow days. Just C7 ranges, jungle lanes, section attacks, and platoon- and company-sized assaults. We ran mounted and dismounted fighting drills, trying to stay sharp, trying to forget the names of the guys we knew were already dying overseas.

One December night, I was eating supper, the TV flickering in the background like it always did. The weather outside was bitter, the kind that settles deep in your bones. Then the headline broke across the screen.

Three of our own from Golf Company had been killed by a massive IED hidden in a culvert.

It was all over the news during Christmas leave. Their faces were everywhere—on the screen, in the papers, seared into our thoughts. It was hard to enjoy the holidays with that kind of weight pressing down, a dark cloud hanging over everything.

When we returned to base, we held the memorial. Everyone stood at attention. Speeches, silence, rifles reversed.

But no one cried.

And it made sense to me then why my father never showed emotion except when his brain overheated and he exploded. The military had trained generations of men to harden up, shut it down, and carry on. Even when the grief was too big to name.

Fatherhood and Fractures

From the moment my oldest was born in February 2009, I was already preparing for deployment. I spent most of her first year in training—driver courses, live-fire ranges, grenade handling, comms, heavy weapons training, and close-quarter combat. Levels 1 through 5 light armoured vehicle ranges. I was learning how to kill a man with my bare hands while my baby girl learned to crawl without me.

The close-quarters combat training at 2 RCR pushed us past the limits of safety—headbutts, elbows, knees, strikes, helmets clashing. The instructors called it realism. What it really was: blunt force trauma, repeatedly. My head rang for days at a time, but back then, you didn't complain. You took the hit and you drove on.

My oldest daughter was still an infant, just learning to hold her head steady, babbling sounds that broke through the fog of exhaustion like sunlight. At work, I was a soldier, absorbing blows and drilling aggression into muscle memory. At home, I was a father, rocking her to sleep with my body aching, ears still ringing from the training pit. Two worlds colliding inside me, neither of them forgiving.

When I first held her, I felt everything at once. Joy and terror. Pride and doubt. A love so fierce it terrified me, paired with a weight heavier than any rucksack I had carried. I looked at her tiny fingers wrapped around mine and thought: *I will die for you without hesitation.* But in the nights that followed—when the crying stretched for hours, when her mother and I snapped at each other in sleep-deprived frustration—another thought haunted me: *Am I enough? Will I fail her the way I was failed?*

Training bled into fatherhood. I'd come home after twelve or fourteen hours of drills, my uniform still damp with sweat, and take her into my arms. I was still vibrating from adrenaline, and now I was supposed to soften, to nurture. Some nights I managed. Other nights I failed. I could feel myself fraying, lashing out at small things, then collapsing into silence.

My relationship with her mother strained under the pressure. We were young, unprepared, still learning how to survive ourselves while trying to raise a child. Sometimes, I felt shut out, like an outsider watching the bond between mother and baby from the cold edges. Sometimes, I felt completely alone.

No one told me that new fathers can spiral, too. That postpartum depression isn't just for mothers. For men, it comes in shadows of irritability, detachment, reckless choices, and shame that festers. We don't admit it. We bury it—until it buries us.

This was the year my identity began to splinter. Soldier, husband, father—none of it fit neatly together. My body was cracking under the blows of training, my mind under the strain of PTSD symptoms I didn't yet have words for, and my heart under the weight of fatherhood.

It was joy shot through with grief. A miracle laced with fear. A new beginning that forced me to confront every old wound from my own childhood, every unanswered question of what it meant to be a man, a partner, a protector.

This was the year I became both a father and a ghost of myself.

Roto 9, Provincial Reconstruction Team

We were just starting our training—us and all the sub-units. In September 2009, my section commander told me I'd be attached to the POMLT—the Police Operational Mentoring and Liaison Team. It was a mixed bag of trades: infantry, military police, artillery, all lumped together for one mission.

On paper, my role was simple: light armoured vehicle driver. But, like everything in Afghanistan, nothing stayed fixed. By the time we touched down, I'd become the RG-31 driver and the radio man. I volunteered for the radio because our vehicles rarely worked properly. Drivers usually just stayed behind, roasting in the steel coffin of the RG-31 while the rest of the section patrolled. Carrying the radio gave me an option—to step outside, to walk, to at least feel like I wasn't just trapped in a broken vehicle.

Close Quarters and Blackouts

Winter 2009. We were deep into close-quarters combat training for the deployment. Long nights in the LAV storage barn, breath steaming into the frozen air, everyone just wanting to get home.

We circled up again for sparring, like in battle school. Sweat slicked my skin, the concrete floor cold beneath my boots. Suddenly, the soldier behind me grabbed and pinned me. His weight drove into my spine. My throat closed. The world dimmed at the edges. Blackness crept in.

I went limp. For a moment, nothing.

Then I was back, fists flying, lost in a haze of adrenaline, instinct, and flashbacks colliding. My body had betrayed me by blacking out, then waking up fighting ghosts.

Those blackouts scared me more than the bruises. They reminded me that my mind carried its own shadows, heavier than any opponent in the circle.

Christmas and Shadows

By Christmas 2009, the year's weight pressed down on all of us. Tension hung over the barracks like smoke.

I felt it most in the quiet moments. The silence after a long day. The pause before lights out. It was as if every step of my life had been building toward this deployment, toward Afghanistan. As a kid, I ran through the woods pretending to be a soldier, playing hero like the generations before me.

But in 2009, those childhood fantasies started to twist. I began to see myself more clearly, not as the unbreakable hero I had once imagined, but as someone carrying fractures I didn't yet understand. Flaws that would scream back at me after deployment, when the blackouts, the blood, and the burning eyes would no longer be confined to training barns or barracks halls.

CHAPTER 14

Control Is an Illusion

Fort Irwin, California, 2010: Baptism by Storm

The rain hit hard. I knew immediately: I had no control. Not over the sky. Not over the wind tearing through the seams of our mod tents. Not over the cold crawling into my bones.

Fort Irwin. The Mojave Desert. "Dry, barren, predictable," they said. They were wrong.

Rain hammered the canvas. Each drop, a needle. My neck prickled. My stomach twisted. Chest tight. Teeth chattered. I tried to adjust my cot. Tried to lift my soaked gear. It was too late. Everything was mud, water, chaos.

The desert had its own rules. One thing I learned quickly: The desert does not care. Not about rank. Not about training. Not about pain.

We arrived expecting heat and sand. Instead, hypothermia. Mud sucking boots. Cots drowning under us. Trenches around our gear vanished in seconds. The Americans joked that we Canadians had brought the storm. I laughed once. The sound was hollow.

Final evaluations were underway. Soldiers were cut from the roster for mistakes too small to name. One slip. Two years of blood, sweat, and sacrifice, erased. Eyes scanned constantly. Hands shook. Breath hitched.

My brain replayed every failure, every punishment from childhood, every crack in my body and mind. This was not training. This was survival.

Inside the Tent

Two hundred men and women pressed together in white canvas. Mud, sweat, fear.

A generator tipped over. The thud made my heart leap. A dozen of us scrambled, fingers numb, muscles trembling, to right it. It was our only light in a dark, soaked world. Our only pulse of hope.

I lay awake. Wind screamed. Rain hammered the canvas. Every gust whipped my face, chest, and arms. My stomach lurched. Shoulders tensed before my brain even registered the motion. Air tasted sharp, metallic. I tried to breathe slowly. Tried to will calm into my bones. Failed.

My cot neighbour prayed. Softly. Steadily. I felt it seep into me. Some calm trickled down through my teeth, into my ribs, into my hands, into the tremor in my legs. For a moment, I was not alone. For a moment, the storm inside softened.

Then, flashes hit like sparks: Gagetown mud. Childhood fear. California dust. Muscles tensed at memory alone. Heart hammered. Mind jittered. The illusion of control cracked further.

G-Wagon Turret Duty

Fort Irwin featured mock villages so that troops could train in a realistic environment. For most of the exercise, I was in the G-Wagon turret. Rifle pressed to shoulder, scanning the soaked horizon. Fingers numb. Eyes burning. Every gust of wind, a threat. Every shadow, a story my imagination wrote too fast.

Memory flashes punctuated the scanning:
- My father's hard hand guiding, punishing.
- Childhood corners where fear lodged in my lungs.
- Diesel and sand from Gagetown.

Reflexes moved before thought. Muscles remembered drills. My mind screamed uncertainty. The military police unit we were folded into blurred lines. Who we were. Who we were supposed to be. In California, those lines would vanish entirely.

The horizon offered no mercy. The storm made every hill and every dip a threat. Every decision mattered. Every hesitation was a potential failure.

Patrol to the Mosque

We set out across wet desert terrain. Mud sucked boots down. Sand clung like glue. Silence pressed heavier than the storm. A mosque perched on a distant hill. Small. Vulnerable. Beautiful. Merciless.

A young soldier of Pakistani descent trained with us. He did not last long. During a failed landing zone capture, panic took him first. Hands shaking. Jaw tight. Breath short. Then, he was gone. Vanished. Fort Irwin tested nerves, training, identity. Friend and foe blurred. Even in simulation, it was impossible to separate self from machine, from fear, from failure.

Simulated Firefights

Night fell. Rain turned the mud slick and reflective. Torches flickered in the storm. Commands crackled over radios, punctuated by shouted corrections and shouted panic.

We moved in pairs. Eyes adjusted to black. Hands slick. Fingers fumbling with weapons and radio. Every movement, calculated. Every shadow, a threat.

California dust in my nose. Rifle jammed. Silence before simulated firefight. Heart hammering. Breath gone. Memories of Gagetown crashes. Childhood corners. Fear lodged in lungs. Reflexes tight. Body taut.

I fired my rifle in bursts, scanning the desert for enemies that were not real. Yet fear made them real. The machine depended on me. The men around me depended on me. The desert did not.

Exhaustion and Hypothermia

Sleep came in fragments. Fifteen minutes here. Twenty there, before a gust of wind or a scream jolted me awake. Mud cold against my spine. Soaked cots clinging to skin. Body shivering in futile rhythm.

Stomach roiled. Head pounded. Muscles trembled. I counted breaths, tried to slow my heartbeat, tried to make my body obey reason rather than panic. I was a puppet of the storm.

The desert had won again. Every soaked uniform. Every heavy boot. Every gust of wind. Every decision. Every hesitation. Every breath.

Night Turret Rotations

Darkness became a canvas for hallucination. Rain streaked like rivers across the windshield. Lights reflected on mud. Shadows twisted into figures. My rifle hand shook. Every microsecond demanded attention. Body. Rifle. Eyes. Nerves.

Sleep deprivation blurred time. My body wanted rest. My mind screamed caution. The illusion of control had been shattered.

Final Evaluations

Morning came. Mud crusted under nails. Boots heavy. Fingers stiff. Eyes dry from wind. Rain eased to drizzle.

Evaluators circled. Every mistake counted. Every hesitation logged. Some were cut. Some survived. I survived. By inches. By grit. By muscle memory and luck.

I walked across the muddy field, drenched, exhausted, heart hammering, mind raw. The desert stretched around me, indifferent. I looked down at my hands, shaking from cold and tension, and realized:

I had never been in control.

The desert had taught me, before Afghanistan ever began, that control is an illusion. Every plan, every drill, every decision can be stripped away in a single storm, a single gust of wind, a single lapse of judgment.

Mud clung to boots. Gloves stung. Heart hammering. Breath short. And still, somehow, I stood.

Escalation of Force

One scenario still clings to me. We were securing a meeting site, scanning the perimeter. I was up in the turret again, eyes locked on a man in traditional Afghan dress approaching the cordon. He ignored shouted warnings. I tried the few broken Pashto phrases I had picked up: "*Dreeshay! Pas naze!*" Stop! Do not come closer!

Still, he advanced.

I moved through the escalation of force, step by step, and finally fired a warning shot.

Seconds later, a Canadian MP sergeant stormed over, furious. The scenario ended, and we gathered under the tent for an after-action review.

"Who fired the warning shot from the G-Wagon?" the Canadian trainer asked.

I raised my hand.

He nodded. "Good call. That guy was a suicide bomber."

A wave of silence passed through the group. I allowed myself a small, quiet smile. But inside, the moment confirmed a suspicion already forming: that some of our military police were in way over their heads. Back in November, when I first joined the POMLT, I had heard the stories of incompetence in the leadership. Now, as we trained together as a full unit, it was obvious. My instincts and the years I had already put into the regular army told me the truth: we were being led by the blind.

The Mogadishu Mile

Then came the exercise no one wanted: the Mogadishu Mile, named after the infamous 1993 firefight from *Black Hawk Down*. It was a gauntlet, and most of the other units hadn't made it through unscathed.

My back was already wrecked. The mud clung to our boots like cement. Rain sliced sideways across our faces. We lined up, adrenaline masking exhaustion. I was soaked and miserable—the kind of misery only infantry truly understand.

I should have been home. My oldest was almost walking. Instead of holding her hand, I was strapping a C6 ammo belt across my chest, some half-broken parody of Rambo. While I trained in the California desert, my girlfriend had taken my daughter back to Newfoundland, visiting family the way she always did when I was gone for any amount of time. She was too overwhelmed to take care of a baby, the house, and the countless animals we had collected since we were together.

There, in Newfoundland, my daughter stumbled forward into her first steps. I wasn't there. I was shivering in a canvas tent, soaked to the bone, missing the moments that mattered. The military trains you to kill. But it never teaches you how to be a father.

On one training exercise, we held the objective, and then came the blinking lasers that simulated sniper fire. We broke for the landing zone.

That same soldier of Pakistani descent who had cracked days before was now sprinting beside me, silent and focused. I caught myself wondering what it felt like for him, preparing to fight in a land that carried his blood.

Mefloquine Madness

Mefloquine was an anti-malaria pill we were ordered to take under threat of court-martial. That pill changed me.

The changes began long before we boarded the plane for Afghanistan. In March, during pre-deployment training in California, I became rageful in a way that did not feel like me. I was screaming at senior leadership during convoy briefings, reckless in a way that could have ended my career. Something about that combination of mefloquine pumping through my system, the exhaustion of the desert, and the weight of soul pressure turned me into someone I barely recognized.

A week before leaving Canada for Afghanistan, I went to the base hospital and begged them to take me off that pill. I told them my moods were shifting, my head was spinning, and I felt like I was coming unhinged. They brushed me off. The orders stood: take the pill or face the consequences.

I begged the Forces not to deploy me. I told them something was wrong: I was changing, and I had not even been to war yet. But they did not listen. Just like they would not listen years later when I told them I was breaking.

The symptoms only escalated. I could not sleep. The ringing in my ears never stopped, and my head spun constantly, a 24/7 vertigo that left me feeling drunk in the middle of my home. My memory slipped like sand through my hands. I was dissociating so badly that sometimes I would watch myself from outside my own body, wondering if I was already dead.

And then there were the visions. Images I had never seen before, dark and demonic. Faces twisted in the shadows. Figures moving in my periphery. Some nights, it felt like the devil himself was whispering in my ear. The drug opened a door I could not close.

At the time, no one called it what it was. It was just another "heat-stroke." Just another "dehydration headache." Another hallucination dismissed as exhaustion. Another angry outburst, written off as stress.

CHAPTER 15

The Last Month Before War

In Case I Died

Pre-deployment training was nearly finished. A handful of us from POMLT stayed behind in New Brunswick while others slipped away on leave, disappearing into the arms of family and routine life. We remained behind, restless, sharpening edges. The final week was a blur of claymores detonating with Golf Company, live ranges at the Fredericton police headquarters, and zeroing rifles at dawn while mist clung to the pines. Everything smelled of cordite and wet earth. The air was thick with anticipation each day—another reminder that our number was coming soon.

And then my father reached out.

We hadn't spoken in years. Now, as if summoned by the shadow of Afghanistan, he decided it was time to "reconnect." My aunt told me it was the right moment, as he had just left his second wife. She pressured me like she always had, carrying the family's demand for reconciliation on her shoulders and trying to place it on mine. She wanted healing. I wanted silence.

His emails came like awkward small talk as he dipped his toe into waters he had poisoned long before. I wrote back, but only at the surface. I knew what this was. Not love. Not remorse. A transaction. His way of clearing his conscience before I stepped into a war zone. If I died, I knew he would show up draped in grief, play the grieving father for the cameras. Pretending he had always supported me. Pretending he had been there. But the people who really knew us knew better.

The Weight of Departure

At night, the anticipation turned to dread. I sat on the steps of our military house in Oromocto, rain pooling on my boots, staring across the base housing rows that all looked the same. In just weeks, I would leave my daughter behind in New Brunswick. She was barely two. I had already missed her first steps. Now, I would miss everything else—her first words, her first real laugh, the tiny milestones that stack into a childhood.

A soldier's duty often demands distance, but there was another reason I needed distance. I was suffering from mefloquine poisoning, though I didn't know the name for it yet. I only knew the feeling: a body locked down, shields raised. I couldn't let anyone get too close—not family, not friends. The armour was already up, and I was already halfway gone.

The war was pulling me forward, and I let it. *Better to be absent now than to shatter later.* That's what I told myself. That's how I justified the silence, the distance, the rainwater dripping down my boots while I rehearsed leaving the people who loved me most.

Packing for War

Only three days earlier, I had been in Gagetown, finishing my last rounds of packing. Now, it was April 26, 2010. I was bound for Petawawa, Ontario, for Departure, final administration, last-minute kit checks, chalks organized, movement coordinated. I was slated to be attached to a 3-Military Police unit for the tour.

Leaving Fredericton meant leaving my child behind in New Brunswick. That part cut deep. While other soldiers hugged their kids a little longer, I had to let go. I boarded the plane with that quiet ache sealed inside me.

When I landed in Ottawa close to 11:00 p.m., the terminal was empty. No duty driver, no welcome, just silence. I sat alone, disoriented and anxious, panic rising like it had years earlier when I slept on a bench in Calgary Airport in 2005—alone, invisible, carrying only shame and fear. My family had been no anchor back then: my father was a ghost wrapped in rage, my mother distant, my sisters silent. I still carried the impulse to reach out, but I never knew how.

In the absence of family, I had been lucky once. My girlfriend's parents had taken me in, fed me, made space for me, seen me. I didn't recognize it at the time, but they were a small pocket of grace in the middle of chaos.

Eventually, the duty driver strolled in, casual, as if nothing was wrong. "Hey, are you Private Wiseman?"

I was the only one there.

"Yeah, that's me."

We laughed, but it rang hollow.

The drive to Petawawa stretched an hour but felt like a lifetime. When we arrived, we couldn't even get a key to the shacks, as the commissioner's office had closed after midnight. By the time I stumbled into a dark, stuffy room, I was too tired to care. Before leaving, the driver paused at the door and said, "Good luck." It sounded like a throwaway line, but in my exhausted state, it felt loaded, almost prophetic.

The days that followed blurred together with paperwork, briefings, and endless waiting. I wandered Ottawa with a friend from basic training, overwhelmed by the size of the city and the chaos inside Bayshore Mall. At night, we drowned our nerves in beer and laughter, pretending we weren't about to walk into hell.

One evening, I found myself eating with some of my mother's cousins from Germany. For a moment, it felt like family again, with real food, real laughter, and a flicker of normalcy before the plunge.

Then, it was time. We boarded buses in Petawawa, bound for Trenton to catch our flight overseas. In a twist of irony, the flight stopped in Gagetown to pick up soldiers from my old unit. I had just left that place three days earlier, and now here I was, already on the road to war.

The highway stretched out like a long grey ribbon, carrying us toward the unknown. Our kit bags were packed tight in the back of the truck, the weight of them nothing compared to the heaviness in my chest. We spoke in half-sentences, nervous laughter filling the silence, each of us trying to mask what we already knew: this drive marked the end of one life and the beginning of another.

Somewhere in Ontario, the bus slowed as we rolled into a small town. We weren't expecting anything. But as we pulled into the main street, the entire community was there. Families lined the sidewalks, children on their parents' shoulders, Canadian flags waving in every hand. People cheered, clapped, and shouted blessings as we stopped. It felt surreal, this sea of strangers gathered just to honour us. For a moment, the war ahead disappeared. The noise, the red-and-white flags snapping in the wind, the warmth of their faces—it cut through the tension like sunlight through cloud. None of us said much, but the silence in the bus was heavy with emotion. Some soldiers pressed their faces to the glass; others bowed their heads. It was the kind of memory that etches itself deep, a reminder of what we were carrying with us.

Every turn of the wheels brought us closer to the airfield. Closer to the desert. Closer to the possibility that some of us might never return. The sun set slowly over the horizon, casting the landscape in a pale gold. It should have been beautiful, but all I could see was the shadow of what lay ahead.

I had spent those last days pacing the barracks, restless, trying to prepare myself for what was coming. But no amount of pacing or thinking could change the truth: never in my life had I imagined I would be going to war.

Would I be able to end a life? Would my life be ended? Would I return?

Everyone talked about IEDs, about instant death, but not about the invisible wounds. I thought if something happened to me, it would kill me outright. Quick. Clean. That was the bargain I believed I had signed.

But I had already seen the other side of war. I had seen soldiers from the rifle company hiding in dark offices, drinking their demons into the abyss.

And now it was my turn to find out what war would do to me.

Chain-Link Goodbyes

We boarded our flight in Trenton—a grey military transport plane packed tight with nervous energy. Some of the guys had never seen combat; others had been through two or three tours in Afghanistan and other places most people could not find on a map. The chief of defence staff and other high-ranking officials stood at the bottom of the flight stairs, shaking our hands one by one, wishing us luck with solemn eyes.

I choked down a lump in my throat as I climbed the steps to the plane, my home for the next eighteen hours as we crossed continents and time zones. Word had started as a rumour, but now it was confirmed—we would be landing in Fredericton shortly before suppertime, local time. I got word to my daughter's mom. We would not be allowed to leave the airport, but I did not care. Ninety minutes with my daughter was worth more than the next sixteen and a half hours cramped in a metal tube, headed into the unknown.

When I left a few days earlier, I had not expected I would get to see my daughter again before leaving the country. I had already locked away every shred of love and joy just to survive what I knew was coming. The summer fighting season was about to begin. The Taliban, rested from winter, would be coming out to engage and test us. It was what we had trained for and what we feared.

As the pilot announced our approach into Fredericton, my whole body buzzed with anticipation. The excitement was vibrating out of me. Others felt it, too. All around me were soldiers—many just like me, torn from their families, and now given this unexpected fleeting reunion. When the cabin crew, all Canadian Forces personnel, opened the door, a gust of wind rushed in, rattling through the fuselage. For a moment, I felt like I was home.

We left our gear on board and threw on our berets. Proper dress and deportment were second nature by now. The sun gleamed off our tan combats and polished boots. I felt like a superhero. I wore it with pride—pride for myself, and for the friends who never got the chance to deploy.

As we disembarked, I was taken aback by the crowd gathered behind a chain-link fence. Families waved signs as balloons danced in the wind. "Support Our Troops," written in marker and hope. I scanned the crowd, and there she was. My baby girl, waving from behind the fence with her mom. My heart cracked wide open.

I nearly ran down the runway just to get to them. The wind howled, and my hands were shaking as I reached through the metal grid to touch my daughter's tiny fingers. The two people I was willing to give everything for stood just feet away. Time stopped. We talked, not knowing how long we had. It could never have been enough.

As more soldiers began to gather near the plane, preparing for their leg of the journey, I knew it was time. My daughter and her mom left. And as they walked away, that familiar ache crept back in—the loneliness, the fear, the quiet surrender of being left behind before I ever left.

They were gone. Back to their lives. And I was left standing on the tarmac, gearing up for eight months of absence and missed firsts, baby smells, giggles, and milestones I would never see. I wondered if this was how my father felt when he disappeared into the night on his own deployments. I wondered if he locked away his love the same way I had.

But in that moment, I had to ruck up.

There was no room for sentiment in a war zone. No space for softness. That is how people die.

We lifted off from Fredericton and eight hours later touched down in Spain for our first fuel stop.

The war was waiting.

CHAPTER 16

Camp Mirage: The Gate Between Worlds

Stepping Into the Unknown

Our flight touched down at Camp Mirage in the UAE—a secret but not-so-secret Canadian staging ground for the war in Afghanistan. The sun was just setting as we approached. The pilot banked hard to the right. My body leaned with the plane, but my thoughts did not follow.

I stared out the window, breath held, heart quiet. I could not believe this was real. I was about to enter a war.

What would it be like?

Would my training kick in?

Would I freeze?

Would I die?

Those questions swirled with the desert air as we prepared for the final three-hour flight into Kandahar Airfield.

But first—Camp Mirage.

We landed under the cloak of night on April 29, 2010. The second the plane doors opened, the heat hit like a sledgehammer. I had never experienced anything like it. It was dry and humid at the same time—thick, suffocating heat. Sand blew through the open doors of the transport plane, riding the desert wind straight into the cabin. The air smelled like rust and sweat and jet fuel.

Over four hundred of us, soldiers from every province in Canada, sat in silence—tired, sunburned, nauseated, wired. The mission ahead was massive, but for me, even standing upright was a challenge. My head throbbed. My stomach was in flames. I could already feel the mefloquine we were ordered to take wreaking havoc on my brain, a storm behind my eyes. I stumbled off the plane and did my best to fall into formation.

The base staff shouted at us, ordering ranks. We were processed like cargo—one by one, issued plates, mags, weapons, ammo. Full fighting order. Gear on. No time to rest.

I asked to see a medic.

They took me to a small, aging medical building. A female medic met me there. I told her about my nausea, the dizziness, the fire in my gut and skull. I begged for a Gravol—anything to take the edge off.

She looked at me calmly and asked, "Do you know what a combat landing is?"

I stared at her, confused. "No," I said.

She explained that we would soon be flying into Afghan airspace. There would be no gentle descent, no smooth approach. We would go from high altitude—forty or sixty thousand feet—straight down to sea level in under a minute. Like a roller coaster, but one designed to dodge enemy fire.

I stared at her, mouth open.

"I can't give you anything," she said. "You will need your wits about you. Just in case something happens."

Something happens. Those two words hit harder than the heat.

This was real.

Not just stories anymore. Not just training videos, or gallows humour about "man love Thursdays" or the smell of burning shit. This was war.

As I left the clinic, I felt the world around me closing in—heat, fear, exhaustion, the ache in my chest from kissing my daughter goodbye just a day earlier. My stomach churned. My throat tightened. My legs were heavy, like my body already knew what my mind could not admit.

I was tired. Hungry. Lonely. Sick.

And scared.

What have I gotten myself into?

The question repeated as I stepped back into the dark.

The Delay at Camp Mirage

Word came down through the ranks: the Globemaster that was supposed to take us into Afghanistan had broken down. It had made it as far as Camp Mirage before something gave out. They had to order a replacement part—from Canada, of all places. We were grounded for a few hours, maybe more.

The air was restless. So were we.

We paced around Camp Mirage, jittery with nervous energy. No one talked about the fear directly, but it hung in the air like desert dust. Everyone was thinking the same thing: *What happens next? What is waiting for us?*

That is when we stumbled upon the kitchen. Not a mess hall—this was something else. A galley filled with foods I had never seen in my life. Dragon fruit, imported cheese, pastries stacked like little pieces of art. Häagen-Dazs ice cream by the freezerful.

It was like stepping through a portal.

The world was my oyster here. I could eat anything I wanted. No rations. No one judging me. No one shaming me for what I took or how much.

For the first time in a long time, I was not being policed—by the army or by my family.

There was something strangely healing about that moment. Amid all the fear, the nausea, the crushing unknown of what lay ahead . . . I let myself enjoy it. Just for a moment. I took what I wanted. And no one said a word.

It was a small thing. But for a kid who had been judged, controlled, and second-guessed his whole life, it felt like freedom.

Tarmac Dreams and the Flight into War

My brain was fried. Between the flight, the heat, the mefloquine, and the past three days of movement and stress, I was completely spent. I found a patch of open tarmac—true grunt behavior. A flat surface was as good as a bed. I dropped my kit beside me and let my body collapse into the soft warmth of the asphalt.

It was still April, still dark, and somewhere deep inside me, the animal part of my nervous system started to settle.

My brain kept spinning: *Will I remember everything? Will I let anybody down?* But those thoughts began to blur. My breathing slowed. My eyes got heavier. For a moment, I was at peace. Just me and the stars above, resting on the edge of war.

Word came down: The part had arrived. The Globemaster was fixed. It was time.

We were shaken gently from our shallow sleep. Backpacks tightened, weapons checked, helmets secured. The air was still cool and silent, but the energy shifted. The waiting was over.

We filed toward the plane, each of us locked in our own thoughts. It was still dark, but the interior of the Globemaster hit like a spotlight—harsh fluorescent lights washing out everything, stinging my eyes. We shuffled aboard, climbing up from either the front or the rear, depending on our chalk.

It was packed. Shoulder to shoulder. Nuts to butts, as they say in the infantry.

This was not a commercial flight. No flight attendants, no movies, no meals. Just steel benches, rattling gear, and a cargo bay full of young men pretending not to be afraid.

We all had our rituals, our little superstitions. iPods everywhere— guys listening to their favourite songs, trying to drown out the fear with something familiar. Some closed their eyes. Others joked quietly. A few just stared straight ahead.

I slid into a seat with my kit in my lap, everything stripped down to the present moment.

Across from me, I saw a friend. His foot was bouncing nervously, shaking uncontrollably. But he wore a smile on his face. That half-grin soldiers wear to keep themselves sane.

And I remember thinking: *How the fuck can you smile right now?*

But that was the only thing he had left. Years later, I realized that his smile was like mine—a mask.

CHAPTER 17

Kandahar

In Afghan Airspace

I was eager to prove my resolve alongside comrades who had already heeded the call to arms. Our platoon had conducted final training exercises as we made our last preparations. Now, I would face my first combat landing at Kandahar Airfield—an experience that cannot be understood until you've felt the weight of a Globemaster descending into a war zone.

May 1st, 2010

After eighteen sleepless hours since leaving Gagetown, the pilot's voice broke through the cabin at 3:00 a.m.

"We are now entering Afghan airspace."

Those words still echo in my mind.

A silence fell over the plane as we readied our weapons. It felt like a scene out of my favourite movie, and yet, this was real. It was the first time in my life that I had ever felt truly alone in the universe.

My mind drifted to my teenage years. Had all those war movies, books, and video games—from *Charlie Wilson's War* to *Saving Private Ryan*—been training me for this? Was this the moment I had been unconsciously preparing for since childhood? I thought of how I used to scribble war stories in my school notebooks, how I once saw soldiering as a calling.

That night, as the stars blinked above our flight, I took a moment to really see where I was, and who I had become. In just a few short years, my entire world had changed.

The pilot's voice returned on the intercom, confirming it: "We are now officially in Afghan airspace."

As we began our descent, I saw the first traces of morning light stretching across the orange sky. The horizon glowed like a burning ember, the kind of light that promises both beauty and danger. The reality hit me: we were about to do our first combat landing.

The plane banked hard, metal groaning under the strain. My stomach lurched as gravity seemed to shift sideways. The engines screamed, the vibrations running through the floor into my boots. Loose gear rattled in the cargo hold. The air smelled of hydraulic fluid and sweat, the kind of scent that sticks to your tongue.

Some of the guys laughed nervously—high, sharp bursts that barely covered the fear beneath. I gripped the edge of my seat, knuckles pale under my gloves. My heart pounded in rhythm with the engine's roar. We had trained for war, yes but we first-timers hadn't understood what it *felt* like until now.

A sudden drop—my insides shot up into my throat. The Globemaster jolted violently, slamming us into our harnesses. My ears popped. Someone cursed. Another made the sign of the cross. A few hours before, I had only heard about combat landings in theory. Now, here I was—living it. The ground rushed up, the Afghan desert swallowing the dawn.

At 0600 hours, the wheels touched down at Kandahar Airfield—the threshold between the world I knew and the one I was about to enter. I stepped off the Globemaster, heart pounding. Hazy morning light hung over the tarmac, blurring the horizon into shades of beige and smoke. The heat hit next—thick, dry, and sour with the smell of burning trash and human waste. Dust curled around my boots as they met Afghan soil for the first time. In that moment, I knew—nothing would ever be the same.

My first few weeks in Afghanistan were mostly quiet—at least on the surface. We were learning the terrain, the rhythms of the land, and the dangers that waited beneath them.

The six months ahead would bring patrols that pushed us to the edge, ambushes that tested every nerve, and operations that blurred into one another. At the same time, paradoxically, we were tasked with "winning hearts and minds." It always struck me as counterintuitive—to fight a war and build trust in the same breath. But I was just a small cog in a machine already in motion.

Our mission was to mentor the Afghan police. They were fighters—raw, undisciplined, but fearless. The war had shifted by then; the locals were tired. Some opened their doors to us, grateful for the promise of security and aid. Others saw us as occupiers. Either way, every encounter carried the weight of uncertainty.

First Day Outside the Wire

We were issued our kit and told we would be leaving for the police substation by Chinook helicopter. I had never flown in a Chinook before—not even in training. Back then, we just drove around Kandahar Airfield in a little pickup truck, trying to orient ourselves to the heat, the dust, and the ever-present noise of war.

Departure was scheduled for mid-afternoon. We were to be picked up at the shacks in Kandahar Airfield and driven out to the landing zone, where the Chinooks would pick us up to fly us to Masum Ghar, a Canadian forward operating base. Then, we would drive to our police substation. Everything felt surreal—the sun, the sand, the weight of exhaustion pressing down on me as I packed and repacked my gear, waiting for the call to move.

When the Chinooks finally came into view, flanked by Griffons for escort, the mood shifted. This was now. Business time. I remember staring across the tarmac, watching heat waves shimmer off the engines like rising spirits. The rotors thundered in the distance, drowning out even the constant backdrop of jets and small-arms fire echoing from the far side of the airfield.

The loadmaster approached, shouting over the chaos to brief us. His voice cut through the roar—sharp, authoritative, no-nonsense.

"You approach from the rear, not the side!" he yelled. "Straight into the door! Keep moving! Watch the rotors; they flex!"

We were carrying everything: rucksacks, day bags, full fighting order, and a kit bag each. The weight was crushing.

As I stepped closer to the plane, the heat hit me first—a searing wave from the twin engines. It felt like walking into the mouth of hell. Then came the rotor wash, like a hurricane made of dust and grit. It reminded me of the brutal windstorms back home in Newfoundland and Labrador, when the gusts hit 110 kilometres an hour and you had to lean into them just to stay standing.

So, I leaned in. Buried beneath my gear, I braced myself so I would not be thrown backward. My heart was hammering—part awe, part fear, part something I still cannot name.

This was it. My first step outside the wire.

I shuffled inside, dropped my kit in the centre, and threw myself into the cargo seat. My body slumped down. I adjusted my helmet and ballistic eyewear, muzzle-downing my weapon in my lap. *Holy shit*, I thought. *This is real.*

As the last few soldiers loaded in, the door gunner glanced back. He wore a skull mask under his helmet, crouched behind his machine gun like death itself. He did a final check, then gave a subtle nod.

We were about to leave.

The engines roared louder. I looked out the tiny side window and saw the Griffons already in the air. The Chinook bounced for a moment, then lifted, hovered about a hundred meters off the ground, and lurched forward.

The noise was deafening and silent all at once—a strange void of sound and vibration. I looked out through the slightly lowered rear ramp. And then, in an instant, we were at full throttle.

Below us: forward operating base mud huts, roads barely carved into the land. The war lay beneath us like a scar. Years of destruction and desperation stretched out across the landscape.

We stayed low, nap-of-the-earth flying, zigzagging like a roller coaster. My stomach rose into my throat as the Chinook banked hard left, then right.

Thirty minutes passed in a blur.

We arrived at Masum Ghar.

As the Chinook touched down, it blasted sand and dust in every direction. The crew screamed for us to grab our kits. I had held onto mine by the strap with my foot; I did not want to lose it in the madness.

We staggered down the rear ramp, stepping into the dust that swallowed us, like being birthed into another world. The air was thick. I ran toward the nearest concrete barriers, trying to get clear. Dust circled and stung. I looked around for a familiar face. A sign. Something.

Then, I saw them—the other soldiers from my home unit who had been in the country a few weeks already. Just standing there, calm. Like ghosts waiting for the new ones to arrive.

I approached them as the Chinook behind us roared back to life, kicking up another storm of sand. Moments later, it lifted into forward flight, vanishing into the haze.

Shells and Small Talk

May 2010

The Echo and Foxtrot POMLT teams were eating at TGI Friday's on the boardwalk—laughter, burgers, small talk. It felt almost normal. The surreal calm before the storm.

The restaurant was packed with service members doing their best to forget where we were. For a few minutes, it worked. Jokes flew. Shoulders loosened. Even I laughed. But when we stepped outside, reality reminded us we were in Kandahar.

A whistle cut the air.

Then silence—just for a second.

I froze. Everyone else hit the dirt.

But I just stood there. Staring.

Twenty feet in front of me, embedded in the gravel near the hockey arena and volleyball courts, sat an unexploded mortar shell—freshly fired by the Taliban. My stomach dropped. I could not move. My eyes locked onto it like it might disappear if I blinked.

The world around me detonated into chaos—alarms shrieked, soldiers yelled, jets screamed overhead as they launched into night ops. My hip throbbed from the weight I had been carrying all week, but adrenaline buried the pain. An American sergeant dove to the ground beside me. Our eyes met. He did not say a word, but his face said enough: *Move. Now.*

I dropped. Late, but alive.

As I finally bolted toward a concrete bunker, a different kind of fear gripped me—the kind that whispers, "You do not know who you are around." That bunker was full of Afghan locals, and in that moment of panic, uncertainty flared. Who was friend? Who was not?

I did not wait to find out.

I kept running—sweat blurring my vision, lungs burning, the base erupting behind me in bursts of dirt and fire. The green tent—our temporary quarters—came into view, and I dove inside as rockets kept falling. The ground shook. Shouts came from every direction. Word spread fast: Taliban might be inside the wire.

That night, we made a choice—stay in the tent, fully kitted out, and ride it out together. No one slept. We just lay there, armourer and armed, as the night dragged on with sirens, explosions, and the smell of burning earth.

By morning, Kandahar Airfield was still smouldering.

It had taken less than two weeks in Afghanistan for the war to get personal. Rockets had landed within thirty feet of me. One did not explode but it could have. It should have.

That night carved something into me.

I ran to find the other members of the POMLT, heart pounding, mission clear. I made a promise to myself: *If it comes to that, I will die beside them. I will fight to the last bullet— not alone. Not like this.*

It was no longer about the mission. Not really.

It was about each other now. About survival. Brotherhood. And something deeper—something that words could not reach yet, but I could feel it settling into my bones.

The war had come home inside my body.

CHAPTER 18

What the Desert Took

The War Beneath the Skin

For the first few months of the tour, we cooked our own meals. We followed in the footsteps of the last team—holding the line, scavenging rations, doing what we could. Then word came down from the higher-ups at Kandahar Airfield: the battle group was moving deeper into Panjwaii to prep for the elections. Our food budget would be "transferred" to the district center.

Translation: We starved.

We went from monthly rations to freezer-burnt mystery meat. I stood at the freezer one night, looking at grey sausages left by the last rotation, and muttered something dark: "I've got scurvy, boys." Gallows humour. It was all we had.

We were patrolling daily—sometimes for hours—trying to keep a presence in the green space so locals could feel safe. My body was breaking down. Mefloquine was chewing through my nervous system like a parasite. The combination of rage, malnutrition, and hyper-vigilance was making me someone I did not recognize.

One night, I stood behind our makeshift field kitchen, shirt off, scratching my back with a rusty cavalry officer's sword that someone had scrounged from God knows where. It was absurd. Medieval. I stared into the moonlit sand and whispered my mantra: "We are not in Kansas anymore."

That sword felt more honest than the C8 I carried. At least it did not lie about the world we were in.

No Chance to Say Goodbye

May 2010, Kandahar Airfield. Word came down that Colonel Parker had been killed by an IED in Kabul—750 kilograms, they said. A massive device. God. He was a good man. Solid leader. The kind who gave a shit about the troops, especially on those long, soul-wearing days back in Battalion. They said there would be a ramp ceremony here at KAF.

I waited for the military police to let me know the details. I wanted to be there. I needed to be there. They never told me.

Two days later, we were rocketed. The earth shook again. My chest tight. My anger deeper now—grief turned sour because I was not given the chance to say goodbye.

I was learning to drive the RG-31 at the time, doing laps around Kandahar Airfield. The instructor barked at me for not crossing through an American convoy. He had not been outside the wire. Not once. I could tell. His tone, his body language—he was textbook.

I snapped. "You don't drive through the middle of a convoy."

He checked himself. Fell quiet. We continued.

But inside, I was already somewhere else. My soul had packed up days before. I was hollowing out, piece by piece. The weight of this place—of the war, of the losses, of the bullshit bureaucracy—was grinding me down.

The Goat and the Gun

It had been only a few days since we got back to the district center from Kandahar Airfield. I had spent two hours on the thermal, eyes burning, ears ringing with silence. At three in the morning, through the thermal,

I watched a man fucking a goat. I blinked hard. For a moment, I even wondered what it would be like. That's how fried my mind was. No Pepsi. No sex. No sleep. Just the black imprint of the optics burned into my face. This place fucking sucked.

I called my daughter's mother on the satellite phone. Hearing her voice made me regret every lie I had sold her and myself about this war.

I told her 150 people had already died here. I never told her what it smelled like when flesh burned, or how the Kiowas—little birds, call sign *Shamus*—screamed overhead, launching out of Kandahar Airfield to lay down fire for the boys who just got IED'd at the bazaar. We cheered when the sky lit up, until the radio crackled, "Danger close." The high burned off fast. The Taliban still fought hard, even when the West rained hell.

One night, I asked a guy from the last roto if there was a fighting position on the mountain behind us. He laughed. "The Taliban don't climb mountains," he said. Later, word came down—figures had been spotted up there after all. Now, POMLT had to climb it. Me? I was just the dumb chicken-fucker who couldn't find a proper fighting position. Brain-damaged from mefloquine. That's what they thought.

My shift was over. The new guy was asleep in the air-conditioned sea container. I hated that door, awkward and loud in the dark. Still, I slipped inside, headlamp casting a dim red glow, trying not to wake the sergeant major.

I whispered his name. Reached for his foot, then his arm.

In a flash, his pistol was in my face.

Even in the dark, you know when a pistol is pointed precisely. Instinct took over—I slapped the weapon away and nearly tackled him. When he lowered the pistol, we both froze—two ghosts in the red light. I laughed it off in the morning, said it was nothing. But something in me cracked that night. A small, silent split I wouldn't recognize until years later, when the war finally followed me home.

Panjwaii's Children and the Burden of Seeing

As we walked through the alleys and compounds of Panjwaii, my weapon was always at the ready. Then, I heard it—a baby crying.

For a moment, I wanted to drop my rifle and run back to my own child. I missed my baby. I missed being a father. I missed being human.

In the bazaar, boys with bellies swollen from hunger sprinted toward us, waving the same little Canadian flags we had given them days earlier. One minute, they were asking for pens or bottled water. The next, they mimed an explosion with their hands—boom—as if to remind us of what waited around the corner. They knew what was coming before we did.

At first, I thought it was a game. Later, I wondered if those pens we handed out were being turned into triggers for IEDs. By mid-June, brothers were already dead from blasts. The Taliban had perfected using children as shields, couriers, and even bait. My heart broke every time I saw those poor children caught between two worlds. Still, I laughed it off. Because I had to. It became a survival mechanism in this place where death was around every corner.

We were losing guys almost every day. The Taliban's summer fighting season was in full swing. They had rested all winter and returned emboldened. Meanwhile, the Afghan government we were propping up was rotten to the core. The Afghan Uniformed Police smiled at us during the day, then sold our patrol routes to the Taliban at night. I was furious. Furious at the lies, the losses, the futility.

International Security Assistance Force, the United Nations–mandated mission, kept pushing the "hearts and minds" campaign—an old counterinsurgency doctrine meant to win civilian trust by handing out aid, flags, and candy so that locals might turn away from the Taliban. But in Panjwaii, it felt hollow. The people were trapped between us and the insurgents. To side with us by day meant risking Taliban retribution by night. And any trust we built could vanish the moment a firefight erupted, a compound was searched, or a child was caught in the crossfire.

The bazaar was crawling with Taliban. They moved freely through the grape rows and green spaces, using children as cover, knowing our rules of war bound us even when theirs did not.

Our patrols became parades of force. We blew up suspicious obstacles, held the roads with armoured convoys, and tried to control what little ground we could. A company of British soldiers was thrown onto the roof of the district center to provide constant security, but it barely made a dent.

The truth pressed down on all of us: in Panjwaii, hearts and minds were already lost.

The children watched us like they already knew how the story ended. Their games mirrored our war—tiny hands miming explosions, laughter dissolving into silence. Every time I saw them, my chest tightened. I saw my daughter's eyes in theirs—bright, hungry, innocent.

But out here, innocence was a luxury. These children had already learned what I was only beginning to understand: in Panjwaii, childhood ended the moment the war began.

A Graveyard in the Bazaar

I walked through the Panjwaii bazaar one day and found a graveyard—colorful banners fluttering above crumbling stones. It reminded me of *The Kite Runner*: the way the dead watched the living, the way memory clung like dust that never washed off.

I slowed, counting the silence between radio bursts and the bazaar's chatter, hunting for the sound that didn't belong.

And I wondered: *Will this be my last walk down this road?*

CHAPTER 19

Between Gunfire and God

Stood Up—RG-31 Jolt

The night we got stood up for the high-value target stop, we were driving the RG-31 toward the T-intersection between Route Hyena and Route Moncton—roads that bled out into the red desert and toward combat outpost Nakhonay, where India Company was starting to move in. We had been rocketed earlier that evening. The call came down from the camp sergeant major—my old boss from India Coy—that something was going down.

The British had been living with us for weeks, covering nights while the days blurred into a loop of patrols, workouts, chow, and restless sleep. Days of sandstorms had grounded air support—no choppers, no drones, no fast air. The Taliban were getting bold again. They had rigged an old mortar with a delayed fuse and detonated it nearby. Intel rumours said more than two hundred Taliban fighters were massing in our area of operation. The chaos was building to match NATO's surge. You could feel it pressing in.

That evening, a rocket slammed just outside the district center. Controlled chaos erupted. I scrambled out of our cramped room, half-dressed in frag vest and helmet, C8 in hand. The remote weapon system gunner was climbing up to mount the C6 machine gun when the belt-fed gunner sprinted past me, bipod extended, and *bam*—the damn thing nailed me in the chest. I flew back a few feet like I'd been sucker-punched by a freight train. Caught my footing, shook off the stars, and kept moving.

The field phone rang. In our kitchen, the major's voice crackled through: "We've got the target."

"Yes, sir," I stammered. "He's on his way, and so are we."

I bolted out of the kitchen, yelling for the C6 gunner. "Let's go! He's coming!"

By now it was full dark. We loaded into the RG-31. I slid into the driver's seat, idling the engine up to 2,500 RPMs. Tried jamming my monocular night vision goggle into my eye socket, praying for visibility through the ballistic windshield but all I got was glare.

"I can't see shit," I yelled to the RWS gunner as he armed his screen.

The route was claustrophobic—crumbled walls, scattered debris, and those damned concrete barriers staggered to stop suicide bombers. I tried predicting where they sat, squinting through the green haze, waiting for a ground guide who never came.

Then—*slam*.

The RG-31 smashed into a concrete barrier at ten, maybe fifteen clicks an hour. My head and torso slammed forward into the armoured glass, night vision goggles crunching into my eye socket. Pain detonated behind my eye, my neck snapping back against the seat. White flash. Ringing ears. Disorientation.

And then—we laughed. That stunned, awkward, half-delirious laughter soldiers use when rage or grief has nowhere to go. We limped forward, trying to shake it off, pretending the op was still ours to salvage. But it wasn't. The rest of the POMLT was already pulling back through the wire. The target had slipped away.

By the time we returned, we were just another RG-31 limping home in the dark. No one saw it. No one asked. No incident report. No check-in. Just another invisible hit buried beneath the tempo.

In the days after, my neck stiffened, grinding every time I turned my head. A deep ache pulsed behind my right eye, vision flickering at the edges. I started dissociating behind the wheel—present, but not. Another layer of damage, stacking up inside me, hidden under the lie I kept telling myself: *I'm fine.*

Blast Day

One day in Afghanistan stands out like a concussion wrapped in heat and smoke. I was running a range, teaching our POMLT mentors and our support assets how to effectively use the 84mm Carl Gustaf. We fired round after round—twelve in total from my shoulder alone—HEAT and anti-structure munitions. The kind of firepower that caves in walls and buckles steel.

It was not just the Carl G. There were other anti-tank systems being demoed that day, the air thick with overpressure and dust. Each blast slammed through my body like a shockwave of static. By the end, I could barely hear. My ears were ringing loud enough to drown out thought. I felt nauseated, dazed—my brain foggy, like someone had turned the dimmer switch down on the world.

And still—we cheered. Every direct hit on the mock targets brought a roar of approval from the line. It was loud, violent, triumphant. In the moment, it felt like victory. We celebrated precision and power, the clean break of a well-placed round tearing through its mark. No one mentioned the way our heads swam or how the horizon tilted when we stood still.

At the time, I did not think much of it. We laughed it off, same as always. But something was different after that day. The clarity never quite came back. That was the moment—though I would not realize it for years—when the cracks started forming deep in my cognitive foundations. The injury did not come from a bullet or an IED. It came from doing my job too well, too many times, with too little thought for the cost.

What We Carried Into the Fire: Panjwaii, Afghanistan, 2010

The heat was already pressing down like a weight we had not packed. My vest was soaked before we even stepped off. Seven mags loaded tight across my chest, one in the well, bolt forward, safety on. C8 in hand—my lifeline. Frag grenades in my side pouch. Medical kit stowed in my chest rig, right side—muscle memory: chest seal, tourniquet, trauma dressing.

What I could not pack was the growing sense in my gut that something was off.

We knew what was coming. That morning, our patrol commander gave us the frag order: we would be patrolling the green space in front of the district centre. The Taliban had been using it to move freely behind the bazaar. Our officer made it clear—we were looking for a fight. Every unit that crossed that invisible line had drawn contact.

My stomach sank as he briefed us from the rooftop.

Standard spacing. Eyes up. Heads on a swivel.

We stepped off from the relative safety of our little police station. My boots kicked up dust with every step—dust that clung to my rifle, my gloves, my soul. I adjusted my chinstrap, more out of habit than need. I turned to the RCMP officer behind me, trying to cut the tension with dark humour.

"Hey, you know how to make a tourniquet nice and tight, right?"

He laughed nervously. Local dogs trotted at our feet. The patrol commander ordered us into an extended line as we advanced toward a suspected Taliban lookout. I spotted an ISAF panel marker on the roof of one of the compounds. It raised red flags at once—something felt off.

We took a short halt along a mud wall in front of the compound while our officer formulated a plan. We crept along that wall, crossing to the other side of the road, expecting contact. The patrol came to a hole in the wall. The first half moved through into a farmer's field, taking cover behind a mud wall to provide the rest of the patrol covering fire while we crossed the farmer's field.

Just as our signaller and patrol commander moved into the centre of the field, the quiet of the humid morning shattered.

Ambush!

A burst of machine gun fire cracked through the air. My body reacted before my mind could catch up—instinct turning me toward the sound of the PKM machine gun, a reliable belt-fed 7.62×54mmR general-purpose machine gun developed in the former Soviet Union. The rounds snapped overhead. I hit the dirt and started crawling, trying to burrow into the warm sand, heart hammering. My nervous system started to shut down. Everything became muffled. All I could hear was the violent snap and crack of incoming rounds. I shook my head to clear it. We were under fire.

Then—

Everything collapsed into noise and light.

Rounds cracked from the front. I dove left, shoulder slamming into the earth, gear biting into my ribs. Someone screamed behind me—cut off mid-word. I rolled, fired, shouted, "Contact front."

My voice did not sound like mine.

Time folded in on itself. My chest was tight, but I could not tell if it was fear or the plate carrier pressing down like judgment. My hands moved on instinct—tap, rack, go. Muzzle flash. Dust. Shouting. And then—silence.

Not outside.

Inside.

I left my body.

I floated.

My kit stayed behind, strapped to a husk of muscle and bone, firing back, staying low, doing the job. But I—the real me—hovered above. I saw the arc of it all. The madness. The fragility. The futility. And during it, something else: light.

Enemy fire cracked the stillness of that Afghan morning. Rounds kicked up dust inches from my face. Moments earlier, we'd had our backs to the enemy, ignorant of the trap waiting for us.

The farmers we had passed were gone.

Spotters, I realized too late.

Will I die here? I wondered. *Will I ever see my daughter again? Feel her tiny hand wrap around my thumb?*

Revelation in the Ambush with the Holy Ghost and Gunpowder

The world went black with heat and dust as the first crack of gunfire echoed through the grape rows. I hit the dirt. Everything slowed, the way it does when death walks close. Rounds snapped past my head, the earth kicking up beside my face as I lay in that Afghan sand.

Someone was shouting for fire positions, for return fire, for anything. But I was gone. No, not gone—lifted.

My vision blurred, but not from sweat or sand. There was light. Not the sun through the haze, but something brighter, cleaner. Then, it happened. He pulled me from my body like smoke rising from a fire, and suddenly, I was above it all.

We watched from above me—the Savior, the Holy Ghost, Jesus. Not in form, but in presence. A warmth. A stillness in the eye of chaos. Below, my body lay in the dirt, weapon half-raised, teammates returning fire, the battlefield erupting in sound and sand. The acrid smell of gunpowder cut through dust and sweat like a warning.

Christ spoke, not in words, but in knowing:

This is not your day to die.

I wanted to stay. It was peaceful here. Safe. But the voice was firm and loving:

You still have work to do.

For what felt like eternity, I hovered in the split, half above, half below, watching myself fight as if I were just another piece of kit left in the dust. The firefight raged on, voices calling sectors over the radio like a foreign language.

Then came the pull.

A weight. A slow, gravitational draw, first in my chest, then my throat, then all at once through my spine like a cracked whip of light. My spirit slammed back into my body like a resurrection too sudden to be holy. I gasped. My body shuddered. Every nerve screamed awake, anchoring me to the dust and blood and sun-bleached ruin of that moment.

I clenched the rifle tighter. My hands still shook, but they were mine again.

A single tear cut a track through the grime on my face. Something in me had changed.

I was no longer just a soldier.

I was a ghost that had come home to his body.

Not whole, not healed . . .

but alive.

I shook my head and cleared my vision and realized I was back in my body, the enemy fire still pouring above me.

I flipped my C8 to full auto and started counting—thirty, twenty-nine, twenty-eight . . . Each burst a tether, keeping me present.

Orders crackled over the radio. Move to cover, one by one.

I covered the patrol commander, then the radio operator. When it was my turn, I hesitated. The Taliban machine gun still had us pinned. I looked over my shoulder—both men had made it to the wall.

Now, it was me. Alone in the field.

I summoned every ounce of intestinal fortitude the Royal Canadian Regiment had drilled into me, and all the strength of generations who stepped up before me. I knew I was not alone—there or ever.

I glanced back just in time to catch the signal: Get behind the wall.

It was my turn.

I placed my C8 into the cradle of my hands, muscle memory kicking in from all those practice ranges. The drills, the shouting instructors, the controlled environments—they were gone. Out here, it was real. No one was yelling commands. It was just me, the enemy, and whatever willpower I could claw from the depths of my soul.

But I trusted the people in front of me. I trusted the ones beside me. I trusted that under the cover of this crumbling wall, they would protect me—just as I would do for them.

And then I saw her—my daughter's mother. And I saw our little baby, waiting for a father to come home whole. That was what pulled me up. That was what forced breath back into my chest.

Cradling my rifle like an infant in my hand, I rose. Rounds snapped and cracked—some so close I could feel the air shift as they passed. I started to move. I did not even think. I just moved.

Tears streamed down my face. My voice ripped open in a scream I do not remember forming. But I remembered what Jesus told me.

This is not your day to die.

So, I ran, not from death, but toward life.

I zigzagged at first, then sprinted, weapon up, legs burning. I leapt over the mud wall and collapsed behind it, lungs heaving, heart thundering.

We survived. Barely.

But that was only half the mission. We still had to get the rest of the team, who were stuck behind the broken wall and under fire. As I orientated behind cover, the RCMP officer arrived, followed by two Afghan police, high on opium, giggling in the midday sun. A herd of goats drifted into view at our one o'clock—children with them.

A classic Taliban tactic: fire from behind civilian movement.

I barked at the RCMP to ensure those kids were not mistaken for hostiles. At the same time, our medic's voice crackled through the radio, panicked and pleading—desperate for the C9 machine gun to lay down suppressive fire. From behind a mud wall, the weapon kept jamming in the dry dust.

Five of our guys had set up a firing position and were calling out for life in the open.

The medic's voice broke into horror. I can still hear it.

A military police reservist from Ontario started kicking her—"motivating" the medic to move. She wanted to walk to the cover of the machine guns we had set up as covering fire, but they needed to run. But she was dead inside—in shock, frozen. Rounds were still flying as the far section started to push forward. I crouched behind the wall, rounds cracking overhead, shattering dry mud into a thousand fragments. I looked across to the patrol commander—he mirrored my position. We both reloaded.

I popped my head up, levelled my rifle across the wall as a brace, took a breath, and leaned in. Clicked my safety off.

And waited.

Through my scope, I saw him—a Taliban commander stepping out to give fire orders. He moved into a break in the wall, maybe a few hundred meters away.

This was it.

One to the head, one to the chest, I thought to myself as I controlled my breathing.

I squeezed the trigger.

He dropped. Instantly.

I watched the life leave his body, and something heavy latched onto my soul. It would take fifteen years to understand what that moment had taken from me.

As the firefight waned and the last of our patrol made it back, orders came that we were withdrawing. Forty-five minutes of contact but it felt like a lifetime. And it would feel like more than a lifetime in the years to come.

Something in me had changed.

I wanted more. More ammo. More targets.

I had killed. And I was ready to kill again.

Not for country.

Not for honour.

For blood.

As we regrouped and pushed through the grape rows behind us, my body ran on animal instinct. Hyperventilating. Adrenaline coursing. Eyes burning with sweat. We entered a mud hut, and I looked up.

Cannabis plants. Hanging upside down.

I thought, *What a wonderful world,* and wished I could take the edge off with a hit.

We kept pushing, linking up with the Quick Reaction Force. A lieutenant from the Royal Canadian Dragoons met us. As we passed, he asked me, "How was it?"

I grinned. "Fucking awesome. I want to do it again."

He told me to check myself for wounds. I had forgotten I had just been in the kill zone.

I ran my hands over my body. No holes.

The shock faded.

The weight settled in.

Two ranks formed. We started back toward the district centre. The radio operator ahead of me turned, face pale.

"Dave, I almost shot you in the back."

My gut dropped. It was the second time he had nearly killed me. I did not need to hear that. Not now. We were not safe—not even from our own.

Back at the police station, another soldier greeted us. "What the fuck just happened out there?" he asked. He had stayed back, doing laundry. From his position, it sounded like the world had ended.

Was it loud? I did not even know.

We debriefed. Minimal maintenance. No more patrols that day. Just a lot of *What the fuck just happened?*

I sent a short, frag-order-style message to my dad. He knew instantly what it meant.

I had killed a man.

He asked how I was.

I never answered. It was the job. That was the last time I spoke to him until 2017.

The ambush haunted me. The commander's fire orders still echo in my dreams.

No battlefield damage assessment was needed. You know what you did. You carry it in your soul. Forever.

The Taliban commander was dead. But something in me died, too. After that, I stopped expecting to live through the rest of the tour. Time shrank down—minutes, maybe hours. Days and weeks no longer existed.

If we killed ten of them that day, more came. Always more. They studied us. Watched our patterns. Counted our missteps.

And they used them against us.

CHAPTER 20

The Distance Between Worlds

Our daughter is crawling. Climbing. Tiny fists scrabble at the baby gate. Thirty steps from disaster. I feel it from halfway across the world. My chest tightens. My stomach knots.

Her mother sits at the computer, fingers hovering above the keys, coffee steaming beside her. Something shifts. Instinct. She bolts. The carpet swallows her footsteps as the gate trembles in the stairwell.

Our daughter clings to the rickety frame just as it gives way. A gasp. A crash. Her mother catches her mid-fall. The gate slams into her mother's foot.

Word reaches me: My girlfriend's foot is broken. And she wants me home.

Impossible. Impossible. Impossible.

My throat closes. My mind frays. Sleep gone. Thought gone. Only panic. Only helplessness. Only the thirty steps repeating, a loop with no end.

* * *

Explosions flash in my skull. Kandahar. Rocket attack. Dust swirls. Screams. The ground shakes. Blood tastes copper in my mouth. My stomach coils. Tiny hands.

Falling. Falling. Falling. I am helpless.

* * *

Leave

By mid-June 2010, my body is done. Mefloquine twists through my veins. Tremors. Hallucinations. Thoughts like shards of glass. PTSD is installed. Pulse hammering. Nerves screaming. Every cell alive with terror. Every breath, a battle.

I go to the hospital on Kandahar Airfield. Heat on my skin. Dust in my throat. Thoughts snapping. Light burning behind closed eyelids. Private Andrew Miller sees the frayed edges of me. Switches me from mefloquine. Relief. Brief. Suspicious. Malarone carries its own poison. Betrayal threads through my veins. Rage rises. Cellular. Unstoppable.

I am cleared to leave. Journey home begins. PEI. For Canada Day. Tiny hands. Screams. Gate. Dust. Rockets. Pulse racing. Stomach coiled. Every nerve taut. Every step weighted. I am split between worlds.

I want a hero's welcome from my father. The kind he never received. The kind we both hoped for. That will wait. For now . . . I am falling. Falling. Falling.

Half a World Away

Missing my baby hurt more than the hollow grind of war. Every day apart felt like punishment for sins that weren't mine. She was the only light in a world that had gone dark long before I boarded that flight. From the moment she was born, I had already been missing her, always missing her. Those two fleeting weeks of parental leave were the only time we truly had together, and even that came with a cost.

Had I followed the common path and skipped leave, like so many others, I would have had nothing. No first smiles. No skin-to-skin. Just static-filled calls and blurred photos from half a world away.

Still, I carried something to prove. Not to the uniform. Not even to myself.

To my father.

The man who starved us of food, of safety, of love. The man whose approval was a weapon. Somewhere deep inside, I believed that if I endured this war—if I came back hardened, bloodied, "a man"—he would finally see me. Maybe even say he was proud.

That was the lie that carried me. The truth was sharper. I had traded my daughter's first years for the ghost of a father who never really existed.

So, I lingered at Kandahar Airfield, caught in that strange purgatory—no longer on mission, not yet home. I slept late. Ate cheese fries at the boardwalk. My stomach twisted with each imagined laugh of hers. I spent hours in Canada House. Wandered the market. The base felt less like a war zone and more like a dust-choked city. But the war never really left. It hung in the air, close enough to taste.

When the call came, we boarded a Dutch Hercules. I spotted the flag painted on the tail and muttered half-joking, half-true:

"I hope they know where they're going."

Once, in Panjwaii bazaar, a Dutch plane had almost dropped its bombs on half our POMLT, along with Oscar Company. The irony wasn't lost on me, heading home and still not feeling found.

We filed across the tarmac, boots striking in rhythm. Fresh troops unloaded nearby, faces bright with curiosity, unaware of what waited for them. We exchanged silent nods, a warrior's passing acknowledgment. Inside, though, my soul whispered words I couldn't speak aloud: *Abandon all hope, ye who enter here.*

The flight carried us to the UAE, that desert crossroads of war and escape. Everything felt surreal. I hid in my room, watching movies and spooning ice cream, chasing small comforts that felt thin and false. At night, music from a live band drifted across the base, soft against the warm air.

I told myself, *I am safe.* My body believed it. My soul wasn't convinced.

Black Mark on the Road

Down the road, our engineers had scraped a makeshift road into the moon-like surface, carving through dust and rock to keep the supply routes open. Not long after, the Taliban placed stones deliberately in front of a newly installed culvert—an all-too-common sign that something had been disturbed underground.

It was the same stretch of road where the nomad village had sprung up earlier that summer. And it was where Private Andrew Miller and Master Corporal Kristal Giesebrecht were blown up in late June. They were on patrol toward Mackinac when the IED took them.

I was home on leave at the time. Safe. Quiet. Distant. Sitting in safety while our guys watched smoke rising from the district centre. I heard later how the blast echoed like thunder, how the armoured vehicle burned for hours after. Nothing could be done.

I can't even recall where I was when I first heard Miller was gone. Details blurred. The impact cut sharp. My soul cried out, knowing it was bad but the full weight didn't hit me until I came back to the district centre at the end of July.

We stood on the rooftop under the scorching sun. Heat and dust settled into my bones like it had never left. One of the POMLT guys pointed into the distance, about three kilometres out. "That black mark on the road," he said quietly. "That's where they died."

From where we stood, it was only a smear of darkness on pale earth. Heat rose off it in ghostly waves. The faint tang of burnt metal lingered in the air. A whisper of cordite clung stubbornly to the wind. What really happened out there—the aftermath, the remains—was too much to put into words. Still, it stayed with me. Haunting.

I was home. Safe. And they weren't. God, I hoped they died instantly. Or at least fast. Anything but burning alive in that steel tomb. And yet . . . I felt the shame of being alive while they weren't.

We patrolled past that blackened scar for months. Repeatedly. Until eventually . . . we forgot. Not because we wanted to. But because more names were added to the list. More scars marked the road. The grief stacks. The soul numbs. You learn this is the rhythm of it. The road keeps taking. You keep walking.

And still, when we passed that black mark . . . you wondered if the road would ever let you forget.

CHAPTER 21

The Cost of Staying Alive

Checkpoint One—Panjwaii, Afghanistan

I hadn't shit in a week. The pressure was unbearable. Morning light cut through the command post like a knife, dust swirling in golden spirals like ash in a funeral pyre. On the wall, two pictures froze me in place: the last rotation's officer and the Taliban fighter who had killed him. Their eyes met mine across time and war, silent witnesses to every misstep, every fear I carried.

I asked the sergeant if anything was happening today. I was thinking about taking the ExLax—desperate times. He shrugged. "Dust storms. The Taliban owns the ground; we own the sky." None of us believed it mattered.

Back in our cramped room, six of us packed like cordwood behind flimsy blankets killed time with *Company of Heroes* on beat-up laptops. War simulating war. Pixel explosions standing in for the real thing. My buddy tossed me the ExLax. I swallowed it with warm water, praying for mercy.

Hours later, the plan flipped. Typical army. We were heading out to Checkpoint One, an Afghan Uniformed Police outpost outside Masum Ghar, to teach vehicle search procedures. I wondered: would it be the laxative or fear that got me first? In hindsight, both.

We kitted up and moved out, threading behind Panjwaii proper with five-meter spacing. Our medic, still not fully recovered from the ambush, struggled from the start—boots dragging, body folding in the heat. She was never supposed to be here. A last-minute replacement after 1-RCR stole both our medics. Unprepared. Unfit. At the time, I told myself my anger was about the mission.

The patrol started like most: pre-patrol jitters, rations packed, weapons ready. I stood with my section at the edge of the district center, waiting for orders. Our mission was to patrol the outskirts of the Panjwaii bazaar, a zone we knew well but could never fully trust.

The landing zone we stepped off from had only recently been built. Months earlier, we had helped Oscar Company secure the area while bulldozers carved it into the Afghan earth. Now, higher-ups from NATO rotated through regularly. British troops would stay with us for the rest of the tour. ISAF wanted to swell troop numbers ahead of the September elections.

As we stepped through the gates, weapons were checked with a cold click. Each sound cut through the stale afternoon air. My stomach churned violently. A low, urgent rumble warned me that the Ex Lax had begun its slow, inexorable work.

Walking past the landing zone, rifle in hand, body trembling with cramps and nerves, I knew the mission was not about enemy contact. It was about surviving the next few hours without collapsing into myself. Every heartbeat reminded me of mortality, every step a test of endurance.

The street smelled of dust, diesel, and sweat. Soldiers' glances flicked between fatigue and calculation. Every detail carried weight. We were not boys playing war games anymore. We were men playing for keeps.

We halted often to let the medic catch up. My stomach twisted as my head pounded under the Afghan sun. I watched her shuffle, melting into herself, and I seethed. My mind ran loops: anger, fear, disbelief. I should have been focused. But the human body has its own agenda. Mine was reminding me, painfully, that it was alive. And uncomfortable.

A hand signal rippled down the line: halt, then move. We skirted the bazaar. A woman frantically swept dust. Dust sweeping dust. *Whatever floats your boat*, I thought. *Keep moving.*

Near the checkpoint, something shifted. Gravity thickened. The air seemed heavier.

Click. Click. Click.

Machine gun fire.

I looked up. The Chinook thundered low, barely a hundred feet off the ground. A twenty-foot trail of fire slashed the sky. Orange. Red. Unnatural. Beautiful in a way that twisted my gut. The bird was hit.

Instinct took over. We sprinted. Training and terror dragging us toward chaos. The medic stumbled. I stuck near her, half-pulling, half-pushing her into the checkpoint. Inside, the patrol sergeant was waiting.

"You're staying here," he said. "You, the medic, and one other."

Just like that, they were gone.

The three of us were left behind. No radios. No backup. Just us and Afghan police—some of whom we knew had Taliban loyalties. Shadows elongated in the bazaar, each one a potential rifle.

My gut gave out. I broke away, found a crumbled wall, and squatted. The shit burned down my legs. No toilet paper. I stripped the field dressing from my forehead and wiped. Dignity doesn't survive in places like that. Only the bare minimum to keep moving.

I returned to my post, shame tucked deep where fear already lived.

AK-47 fire cracked from the far side of the bazaar. Rounds snapped overhead. Griffon helicopters circled, laying down suppressive fire, but they didn't know we were pinned. I tried to wave them on to targets across the bazaar. Tried to scream. Nothing carried.

Time fractured. Seconds stretched like taffy. My hands shook. My boots felt glued to the dust. I counted—breath, heartbeat, step, breath, heartbeat, step—anything to survive the mental unraveling.

Then, the wind itself turned. A sandstorm rolled in, blinding, choking, like divine interference. Particles sandpapered against skin and eyes. Grit clogged every orifice. Breathing became a labour. Out of the howl, the rest of the patrol returned. They pulled us out, and we rejoined the push toward the wreckage.

The smell hit first: burning electronics, plastic, oil, flesh. Smoke churned in black columns, rising like a funeral procession. I didn't know how many were dead. None of us did. No time to process. No time to grieve. Only the next step.

We lingered at the corner of the crash site for some time, our interpreter resting against the wall as the three of us took position. We got orders: the Quick Reaction Force was coming, and we had to prepare to move.

Villagers gathered as we moved through the bazaar. Tension crackled in the air. A motorcycle engine revved in the distance. One of our guys fired a warning shot. The engine cut out instantly. As expected, a secondary attack from the Taliban.

The soldier behind me leaned in.

"You shit your pants, man."

I said nothing.

Back at the district centre, we climbed to the rooftop. The fire still burned—an orange glow against the Afghan night. Smoke drifted skyward, slow and relentless. Fingers sticky with soot, throat tasting of dust and fire. I didn't know whether to pray or scream. Instead, I stood. Waiting. Alive.

For a moment, time seemed to pause. The smoke carved ribbons into the sky. Shadows of soldiers moved like ghosts. My body screamed with exhaustion, fear, and shame. My mind—warped by heat, adrenaline, and excrement—searched for something familiar, some human thread to cling to.

Then, I remembered the officer's picture on the wall, and the Taliban fighter who killed him. Their eyes met mine in my memory again. Silent witnesses. Not judging, only watching. I swallowed, as much pride as bile, as much courage as fear. I took a breath.

We were still alive. That was a victory.

The Village of the Damned

The convoy slowed to a crawl. Dust swirled through the slats of the turret like smoke through a grate. The engine's growl softened to a low, anxious hum.

My body knew before my mind did. That coiled feeling in the gut—the static before a storm. I scanned the ditches, the rooftops, the shimmering horizon. Nothing moved. Too still. Even the wind seemed to hold its breath.

"Five and twenties," came over the radio, the tone flat, procedural.

Doors opened with a metallic thud. Boots hit gravel. The smell of diesel and sand mixed with the iron tang of anticipation. I watched the dismounts fan out—rifles low, eyes cutting through the heat haze.

Each second stretched thin, drawn tight between training and terror. My hand rested on the grip, safety off. Eyes flicked to the culvert again—those rocks, too neat, too deliberate.

A single crow lifted from the far treeline. The sound of its wings cracked through the silence.

And in that instant, I knew.

The earth was wired.

Clouds choked the morning sky. Only three of our vehicles pushed forward, flanked by a scattering of Afghan AUP pickups, their drivers bouncing like frightened children over the jagged dirt. Dust slipped into my mouth. My chest tightened. My stomach coiled. I could taste it—the metallic tang of tension, the familiar burn of fear that comes only when you've been here before.

We arrived at Combat Outpost Najet. I Coy had requested the Afghan police and POMLT for a village clearance just outside the wire. Same rinse-and-repeat loop we'd been grinding through for months. Clear. Sweep. Reset. And repeat. While a section of I Coy sat perched on their little mountain like gods behind glass, we trudged through the dust, carrying the weight of another day. Sunburned. Eyes sunken. Jokes thin. Hollow. Hollow joy, clinging to our bones like grit.

Orders came down from the commander: Search the village. Known for manufacturing and supplying IED components.

I exhaled. Of course they were. Everything in this valley was either broken or deadly or both.

The AUP were high. H-hour hit stupid early. That's the military term for the moment everything shifts from planning to survival. Before it is the waiting: the whispered radio checks, the dry mouths, the silence before ignition. After it comes the noise—the kind that rattles the soul and leaves your heartbeat somewhere behind you.

The night's fires still smoldered as the village began to stir. Smoke curled through alleys. Shadows turned into people. Silence turned into suspicion.

I kept my helmet on, orange lenses in the dark. I would swap them when the sun came up. Being back with my home unit felt real. Familiar. But I reminded myself: *Don't make an ass of yourself.*

We moved into position. I ended up near the commander. He stepped onto a berm, looked over the village, then turned to me.

"Listen," he said.

"To what?" I said.

"Wait for it," he said.

Seconds later, a fighter jet screamed overhead at 500 feet. Low. Fast. The ground vibrated. Air cracked. My chest shook. The roar hit me like a fist. Something inside me rattled loose. I laughed. Could not help it. Absurd. Overkill. And yet somehow—my first hard-on since the ambush. War has a sick sense of timing.

We pushed forward. Compound after compound. The AUP led. Followed by us. POMLT boots crossing thresholds, rifles raised, hearts half-numb.

First compound, smooth. The officer questioned the men inside through the interpreter. I held security at the doorway. Eyes scanning rooftops. Alleyways. Windows. Anywhere death could peek through a crack.

"Take a break," I told the AUP. "Drink."

They lit cigarettes like it was just another morning. I sat next to them, rifle across my lap, helmet on. Swapped out my orange lenses for black while I had a second. The sun was creeping up fast. Who knew when we'd get another pause.

For a moment, stillness. Suspended calm. No gunfire. No yelling. Just the village waking under the weight of foreign boots and burned-out hearts.

We moved deeper, winding through the maze of alleys. Then a group of boys gathered around an old man, slouched on a low wall. His hands were shaking. Eyes glassed over. Vacant.

They had found wire near his compound. Half-buried. Suspicious.

The commander questioned him through the interpreter, pointing to the wire. Where did it come from? What was it for? The old man mumbled, gesturing vaguely. Voice cracked like old leather. Confused. High. Mentally gone.

I stood a few feet back, rifle in hand. Scanning rooftops. Alleyways. Windows. How do you trust anyone here? Everything is an IED. A wire could kill. A battery could blind. Even an old man could have buried death for a child to find.

The boys pressed. The interpreter translated. The old man stared past us. Didn't see soldiers. Only ghosts.

We moved on. Deeper into the village. The alleyways twisted like the veins of some dying animal. The air smelled of cooking smoke, goat dung, and dust. Each footstep, a countdown.

Suddenly—a clatter. Metal scraping stone. My heart jumped. Rifle raised. No one. Only a tin can rolling down the alley.

I exhaled. Guts still coiled. Eyes scanning. Rooflines. Windows. Every shadow a threat.

We cleared the next compound. Wire, batteries, nothing deadly yet. The old man's village. Worn mud walls, sun-cracked. Children peered from rooftops. Curiosity and fear mirrored in their eyes.

We pressed on. Every compound, identical. Every alleyway, a maze. But the tension never let up. Every shadow could be the trigger. Every whisper, a countdown. My chest tight. Hands trembling. Heart thrumming.

By mid-morning, sweat pooling under my vest, I realized: war here is never clean. Never quick. No victory to savor. Only the temporary illusion of control. The Taliban slipped through, regrouped, returned. Like water through hands. And we? We walked on, carrying the weight, carrying the dust, carrying the ghosts.

The village of the damned. That's what it felt like. And tomorrow? Tomorrow, we'd wake up and do it again.

CHAPTER 22

Moments of Stillness Amid the Noise

A Pause in the Dust

It is mail day.

Chaos hums around the substation—dust swirling in shafts of weak light, the constant drone of helicopters, distant gunfire, and the thump of explosions like a slow heartbeat. But today, for a few minutes, there is a pause. I dig through the box from home, from those who still love me.

A stack of *Reader's Digest* magazines from my aunt. She always sends those. A few other books, too. God knows when she thinks I'll find time to read out here, but I smile anyway.

The moment I lift the flaps, a scent hits me—Canada. Hard to describe. Crisp, familiar, comforting. A ghost of another life. I dig deeper.

Cans of Chef Boyardee, boxes of Kraft Dinner. My favourites. The smell of pasta, tomato, and cheese. Memories cling to the smell—kitchen floors, Sunday afternoons, my mother's laughter echoing through the house. For a few stolen seconds, I am a kid again.

Outside, war continues—sporadic gunfire, a mortar's low boom, helicopters buzzing overhead like mechanical wasps. Inside the substation, it is quiet enough to pretend. Just for a moment.

I miss my family. Back home, their lives carry on without me—Thanksgiving dinners, school runs, birthdays. They laugh and cry while

I count sand and sweat and dust. And here we are, hollowed out, pushing through, barely holding on.

It is October. Summer's heat has finally eased into winter's first cold snap. The shower has been broken for months. We wash like animals now—camping showers, boiled water, wiping dirt and sweat from skin like it is a ritual of survival. Each motion, a reminder that we are still alive.

And still, I am looking for the cat.

One has been living under the kitchen for weeks. Silent. Elusive. A shadow slipping between crates and trash cans. I kneel, holding my breath, listening. The scuffle of claws on concrete. A faint meow. The twitch of a tail disappearing under the stove.

Finding it has become a mission. Holding it. Feeling something soft against my skin, a small, warm proof that gentleness still exists.

It is stupid. I know that. And yet I reach, fingers trembling slightly, ready to scoop it up if it lets me.

For one moment, I am not at war. I am not counting days or bullets. I am just here, and it is quiet. And something soft rests in my hands.

Panjwaii Nights

Some nights in Panjwaii, when the generator sputtered and the stars flickered through the haze, I'd lean back into a wall of sandbags and pretend I was somewhere else.

The memory of home drifted through my skull like a lullaby from a life I wasn't sure I'd ever see again.

Out here, the fireflies were tracer rounds. Every flicker of light came with a question: friend or foe?

There was no sleep, only waiting. Sand fleas bit through the fabric, tricking the brain into thinking each sting was something more sinister.

You slap your thigh—it's a flea.

You hesitate—it might be an IED wire.

When the Afghan police finally quieted and the interpreter stopped whispering, I let my mind drift somewhere quieter, just for a moment.

Except out here, you had to stay awake.

Sleep was when the dead came back.

And the only thing more dangerous than what lay outside the wire was what lived inside your head.

Years Later

She was five, maybe six. We lie on a blanket in the backyard, a jar between us, catching real fireflies this time. Not flares. Not tracers. Not illusions. Just glowing bugs drifting through the warm summer air.

She giggled every time she caught one. Her little fingers moved quickly, carefully, unafraid. The smell of cut grass, the heat of the sun on our shoulders, the soft hum of crickets—it all anchored me in this moment.

"Daddy, look!" she whispered, eyes wide with wonder, as if the world was still good.

I just watched her. The way the light danced off her cheeks. The way she believed.

For the first time in years, something in me softened. The same light that once meant danger now shimmered harmlessly in her hands.

And for a moment, just a moment, I believed in the light.

Waiting

Our immediate chain of command made conscious choices—small but significant ones—to make the back area of our compound feel like a sanctuary, as much as it could in a place like that.

We tossed a ball, crushed a workout, blasted tunes from a beaten-down speaker, sipped burnt coffee, and spit from too much chewing tobacco into empty water bottles. For a minute, we could pretend the world outside didn't exist.

But more than anything, we had to lay down the noise—the mental chaos, the static from the last patrol, and try to remember who we were outside the wire.

Just for a moment.

Just enough to keep from going numb.

Combat Mustache

By month four, most of us had adopted what the Americans called the "combat mustache." It was not just facial hair—it was defiance. Regulation-pushing, dust-covered, sweat-soaked defiance. The mustache was a middle finger to command and to the mirror, a signal to us and each other that we were no longer the same men who had boarded the plane in Trenton. We were becoming something else. Feral. Hardened. Half-shadow, half-joke, we wore our disconnection like armour. A tradition born of too many patrols and not enough hot showers.

I looked at mine in the cracked mirror above the plywood sink—the edges uneven, dirt clinging like a memory I couldn't shake. It made me look older. Meaner. Or just more tired. Either way, it stayed.

States of Being

By mid-tour, combat fatigue, mefloquine poisoning, and complex PTSD weren't just medical terms—they were states of being. Fractured. Furious. Barely holding on. Midway through, my best friend—a soft-hearted military police reservist from Ontario—was medevaced out. The pressure broke him. He needed rest. None of us blamed him. I envied him. Hated myself for envying him. He got to leave. I had to stay.

Back at the police substation, everything was falling apart. The Champion generator had been choking and coughing smoke since we arrived, thick black plumes clawing at the sky, a signal flare no one would answer. It burned oil like a cursed engine. We inhaled it anyway, day after day, lungs scraping against the carbon taste just to keep the lights flickering.

One evening, as the sun bled behind the mountains, it died for good. Silence fell. A hard, solid silence, like the air itself had been ripped away. We were in the dark. No lights. No radio. No thermal scope. No link to the outside world. It felt like the moon. Cold, desolate, endless.

The Afghan Uniformed Police, in a theater of false security, lined up their battered 4x4s facing our front doors, engines idling, like they thought that would matter. I couldn't move my eyes from the darkened perimeter. I was terrified. Comms was dead. Overwatch gone. Quick Reaction Force? Just a ghost.

I pressed my back to the wall. Heart hammering in my ears. Sweat slicked my neck, cold and greasy. Every shadow was alive. Every whisper of wind across the sandbags made me flinch. I felt the twitch of my hands. Fingers itching for a weapon that wasn't there.

I prayed. Quietly. Desperately. Sunrise couldn't come fast enough.

Someone—anyone—had to send a generator. No one did. The darkness lasted. The smoke hung.

My body coiled in tension I couldn't shake. My friend was gone, and the world had shrunk to black, to fear, to waiting. I counted breaths. One. Two. Three. Too slow. Too fast. I tried to remember who I was outside this wire, but the memory was faint, and the night was absolute.

The night pressed against us like a living thing, and I realized: Survival wasn't about bullets or guns. Not tonight. It was about holding on to what little resolve remained in a world that had forgotten us.

Invisible War

The C6 gunner and his number two dragged a day bag full of 7.62mm rounds spilled out like copper teeth. Every one of us knew it was coming. The Taliban moved behind the bazaar, ghosts in the green belt. Children at their sides. They knew the rules. We knew our limits.

So, we waited.

The radio dug into my back. Same weight my father once carried in the '90s. For me, it wasn't just comms. It was survival. Ever since the Chinook crash and the ambush, I swore I'd never be without a way to call in air support . No one came for us then. Not again.

Straps cut into my shoulders. But it wasn't just gear. It was months of tension. Trauma. Fear that lived in the body even when the mind went numb. My spine felt like it was folding in on itself. I wouldn't understand the vagus nerve damage until years later. All I knew then was a slow implosion.

I thumbed the handset and called Foxtrot, our sister platoon at Masum Ghar. A voice cracked back. Familiar. Concerned.

"You sound . . . distant," the officer said.

He didn't know. Didn't know I hadn't slept in weeks. That food slid through me like water. That the pill we joked about—Manic Mondays, Wacky Wednesdays—was poisoning me from the inside. Simple tasks now cost twenty times the energy. And no one noticed. Not in Afghanistan. Not at home. Maybe because we were all fighting the same invisible war.

CHAPTER 23

The Cost Arrives

Red Desert, Rusted Bunker

Orders came down for an operation near Sperwan Ghar. One RCR. Led by the only female officer commanding in the infantry I had ever known—tough, zero tolerance for bullshit. I respected her. I was nervous. Excited.

We packed our kit into the RG-31s. The POMLT would roll with the small unit, American special forces training the Afghan army, who were set to search compounds—the usual routine. We were the local face of ISAF, and everyone needed us, yet few seemed willing to support us. We were the redheaded stepchild of the task force.

Someone snapped a quick photo before we climbed into the RGs. Game face on. Go time.

The roads deteriorated fast as we passed MSG, thick with dust, choking like talc in the lungs. The American special forces opened their spacing and picked up speed. We lagged; our vehicles couldn't match the American RGs. White-knuckling the steering wheel just to keep up, I felt every rock and rut through my seat.

Out of the corner of my eye, I saw an old man with a child standing by the roadside. I reached for the radio, trying to get the Americans to slow down. No luck. Too fast.

A memory slammed into me—a light armoured vehicle in 2008, off-road, losing visibility, slamming my body into the steering column. The pain, the shock. It hit again, electric, visceral.

We flew over a narrow bridge. My ass clenched. I waited for the blast that did not come.

Still speeding, keeping spacing, we pushed beyond the bazaar chaos into the red desert. In the distance, a mountain jutted up, shaped like a nipple. My co-driver pointed. "That's it. We're close."

Then, the radio crackled.

The tankers were taking mortar rounds. Tiny combat outpost abandoned. Kits left behind. Just hearing it made my stomach drop. This was not something we had trained for. Numb disbelief filled me.

Where the fuck were we? Certainly not Kansas.

We crawled up the hill into Sperwan Ghar. My hope for this operation evaporated with every switchback.

Vehicles parked. Leadership tried to make sense of the chaos. We wandered the hillside while the orange Afghan sun bled behind us. The longer we waited, the more obvious it became: this operation was not happening. Not tonight.

Word came down: Stand down. Tanker situation took precedence.

We moved into an old Russian bunker dug into the mountain. Rusted metal groaned underfoot. Mildew and dust hung in the air, sweet and acrid. Shadows swallowed corners, turning them into pockets of threat. I stumbled through the maze until I found a worn-out mattress. Without ceremony, I collapsed. Gone in seconds.

That night at Sperwan Ghar is seared into memory—not because of what I did, but because of how I felt.

I was dead asleep when it hit. One second, out cold. The next, upright, heart pounding, every cell on fire. Artillery thunder cracked through the mountain and into my chest before my brain registered anything.

It wasn't enemy fire. It was our own guns. But my nervous system didn't know the difference.

I don't know if I reached for my kit or just froze. What I remember is the silence that followed—the eerie calm after the blast. Breath shallow. Mind racing. *Was that the last one? Will the next one land? Can I even react in time?*

Even when the noise stopped, I did not. Wide-eyed. Wired. Waiting.

Sleep in that place was not rest. It was a temporary escape. And some nights, even that got stolen—just like the roads to Sperwan Ghar had stolen my certainty, my sense of control, my calm.

News from Zangabad

We got word. The American special forces team we'd been running with since June had been hit out near Zangabad.

They had been training the Afghan National Army. Trying to carve out a foothold in Taliban country. Inch by inch, all summer, we'd been doing the same. I remembered standing on the roof a month earlier, watching the Americans parachute in. It felt cinematic back then, like something out of a war movie. But this . . . this was no movie.

Now, the cost had landed here. Our police substation.

Until today, we had been lucky. If luck even exists out here. No casualties in our corner of the war. But today , , , that changed.

My stomach sank. Cold. Hard. My knuckles dug into the edge of the table. The dust in the air pressed against my skin.

A few of the guys trickled back from the operation. Faces hollowed. Eyes that spoke everything without a single word. Broken. Tired. Shattered.

The Cost Arrives

The Americans had been our lifeline. When the military police turned their eyes away—gave our food budget to someone else—it was the Americans who stepped in. Energy drinks. Provolone cheese. Small miracles in a place that gave us nothing. I had never even tasted provolone before this deployment. Turns out, it is delicious.

Now the same men stood before us, staring into the dirt. Picking at their Rip-Its. Pushing their cheese around their plates with the flat edge of a knife. Something had shifted.

War had crept closer. It wasn't a distant danger beyond the wire anymore. It was here. Sitting with us. Eating our cheese. Drinking our Rip-Its. Watching us. The air tasted heavier, like the sky itself had gotten darker.

The room felt smaller. The dust, louder. And in every glance exchanged, I could see the truth we'd all been trying to avoid: this war could reach anyone, anytime.

Primal

The day I heard Corporal Pinksen had died, I was gutted. I didn't even know him—just another innocent-looking face in the rotation but it hit me like a blow.

Word came down: killed in action. Wounded. From I Company. My stomach sank. How? How the fuck was this still happening?

Another stupid IED. Another stupid patrol.

We were ordered into comms lockdown until the families were notified. That's when something inside me snapped.

I slammed the kitchen door. Stormed toward our room. Moving fast. Breathing fire. I passed our gear—neatly packed, ready to go out again, and felt that old gut twist of dread and fury.

When I opened the main door to our compound, two Afghan Uniformed Police sat on a bench just outside. High as fuck. Smiling like idiots. Eyes glazed. Hands twitching in rhythm with the heat.

I slammed the door behind me. Something primal broke loose.

"We're fucking dying for your country!" I roared in English. I yanked open our blue door, the metal shivering under my hand. "What the fuck!"

The echo bounced off the walls and into my chest. For a moment, I wondered if anyone could hear. Or care.

I slammed it shut. Collapsed. Face hot. Hands shaking. Chest heaving. I cried. Not just for Pinksen. Not just for them. For all of us. For the hope that had once clung to this place like dust and now slipped through our fingers.

It was all falling apart.

CHAPTER 24

Survivors of Panjwaii

Rest in Peace, Thor

We didn't plan on getting a dog in Panjwaii. One afternoon in 2010, the Afghan uniformed police traded him to us for a case of water. That's how Thor entered our lives, a lanky shepherd mix with sharp eyes and a wagging tail, trotting into the substation as if he had always belonged there.

In a place where trust was scarce and chaos reigned, Thor became steady ground. He patrolled the compound like he was on duty, padding along the mud walls, stopping to sit with whichever soldier looked the most frayed. At night, when gunfire cracked through the fields and mortars shook the air, his calm gaze pulled us back. He carried no rifle, no armour, and yet, somehow, he made us feel safer—a living reminder of loyalty, of home, of why we endured.

For his safety, we eventually brought him to a forward operating base. In war, humans can do unspeakable things to animals, and we couldn't risk Thor being caught in it. Dropping him off felt like betrayal. None of us knew if he would survive once we drove away.

Two years later, in the winter of 2012, I was home and in one of my darkest places. I flipped on the news and froze. There he was, Thor, alive in Canada. A Canadian soldier had brought him back. I reached out to his new owner, and she confirmed it in a heartbeat. I called the guys, and word spread quickly. Against all odds, he had made it home.

I didn't hear of him again until 2025. That day, news came that Thor had passed. Sixteen years after leaving Panjwaii. He had lived a good life in Canada, loved and safe with another veteran. I cried when I heard it, not just for the loss, but in gratitude that he had carried a piece of our war into peace and somehow survived it.

Thor wasn't just a dog. He was family. A brother-in-arms. A quiet shield when we needed it most.

Thor was a good boy. Always.

Glow-Sticks and Gunfire

The Afghans were something.

On the one hand, there was this strange, childlike playfulness living right alongside the tension and brutality of war. One evening, one of the POMLT guys decided to "fish for Afghans" off our rooftop—a bundle of glow-sticks duct-taped to the whip antenna, dangling on a length of paracord like bait.

Below, a cluster of kids—maybe schoolkids, maybe just a crowd of bored teenagers—leapt and swatted at the glowing lure like cats chasing a laser pointer. Their feet kicked up dust in tiny clouds, their laughter sharp and bright against the endless drone of generators and distant rotor blades. We stood above them, boots scuffing the sunbaked roof, sipping lukewarm coffee, spitting dip into empty Gatorade bottles. We laughed the kind of laugh you only learn in a war zone—one part relief, one part madness. Ridiculous. Hilarious. Completely fucked.

We were not mocking them. Not really. We were just coping with the heat, the boredom, the pressure of knowing any second might be the last. That night, there were no compounds to clear, no IEDs to find, no briefings to fake our way through. Just dust, glow-sticks, and a moment of levity dangling over a country we could barely understand.

War felt like that sometimes—like herding cats.

Trying to impose order on chaos.

Trying to guide a mission no one truly controlled.

Trying to lead people who did not trust us, did not want us, and never would.

But that was not the whole story.

Because what struck me most about the Afghans we met—the common folks—was their commitment to family.

A deep-rooted drive to provide for loved ones, to scratch out a living from whatever meager means were available. They were not driven by ideology. Most could not have cared less about who ruled them. Their priorities lived lower on Maslow's hierarchy: Food. Water. Shelter. And, if they were lucky, a chance to watch their kids grow.

The children, dusty and destitute, somehow wore smiles like armour. The parents, weathered and wary, carried a quiet dignity, the kind you earn when survival itself is a full-time job.

In our valley, the illiteracy rate hovered around ninety-eight percent. Few, if any, understood the world beyond their mountains. But they didn't need to. When your world is defined by whether there is enough to eat today, whether the well will hold water, whether your son will step over what's buried beneath the dirt, your priorities become razor-sharp. Simple, but never easy.

And yet, there was courage, too.

We saw Afghan soldiers stand tall when it counted. Fathers, brothers, sons, armed with rusted rifles and worn boots, ready to fight for a future they might never see. Their strength was not in tactics or training—it was in heart. In staying. In not quitting.

The same motivations that led us to wear our own country's uniform lived in them, too.

Soldiers are soldiers the world over.

Language is irrelevant. Culture is irrelevant. We all bled red. We all buried friends.

We all learned how to smile with tired eyes and keep moving forward. Sometimes, war was glowing sticks and laughter from a rooftop. Sometimes, it was blood in the dust and silence on the comms. And most of the time, it was both.

Crossing Back

Fluorescent lights buzzed overhead, flickering just enough to keep the shadows alive along the walls. Boots squeaked, zippers scraped, pens clicked against metal tables. Somewhere, a tray clattered. The room was alive with soldiers trading stories, joking, laughing about medals and bars as if tiny strips of metal could measure courage.

A few leaned back, eyes glinting with the thrill of imagined honour. Others whispered numbers, counted points, compared ribbons, already chasing invisible bragging rights. I watched all of it, a ghost among them, letting the noise slide past like wind over sand.

My fingers found the locket around my neck. The hinge stuck now. Months of nervous touch had left the once-smooth metal scratched and worn thin. I turned it over repeatedly, tracing the tiny engraved letters, feeling the weight of a promise I could not keep while here.

I did not care about a bar. I just wanted to go home. Sleep in a warm bed. Hold a woman's hand. Listen to the birds singing outside. Watch my daughter grow up.

The locket swung slightly as I pressed it to my chest, catching the faint light from the window. Inside, the photograph blurred under my fingertips—the soft curve of her cheek, the tilt of her head, her eyes bright and unshakable.

"I miss you, Daddy," the engraving whispered back. Fragile and impossible, a plea and a command. My chest tightened. My throat burned. Dust and iron filled my mouth. My vision blurred.

Around me, the world continued: boots clattered, pens clicked, men laughed. It all felt distant, like the echo of a dream I'd stepped halfway out of. Every laugh, every story, every medal chatter was a reminder of what I could not care about.

I closed my eyes. I imagined her small hand curling into mine. Morning light spilling across our bedroom floor. Coffee brewing on the counter, steam rising, birds singing outside. The steady rhythm of a life I'd been absent from for too long.

I breathed in. The locket pressed against my sternum, and for a moment, the weight of months, the dust, the noise, the waiting—it all lifted. Just a little.

I did not care about medals.

I did not care about ribbons.

I did not care about applause or recognition.

I cared about her.

Snapshots Against Death

Thirty days and a wake-up. That became my mantra.

Every night, I whispered the same word to myself: *Home. Hold on to that. Survive. Thirty days.* That was all I had to last.

We were burned out. Hollow eyes. Chain-smoking. Silence where jokes used to live. The air itself felt brittle, cracked at the edges like dry paint. Lips split. Skin rough. Tempers one spark away from fire. Eighteen months earlier, we had started this journey. In thirty days, it would be over for me. I just needed to last that long.

On Remembrance Day, we held a short ceremony at the district center before mounting up again. Orders came down: set up a new checkpoint near Folad. We'd been patrolling the area for weeks, always tense, always alert. One patrol stands out, though the details blur.

We were walking. Easier than relying on the busted RG-31s. The sand crunched beneath our boots. The sun pressed down until sweat stung our eyes. Out in the open desert, me, some attachments, and a cluster of AUP.

I was walking behind an Afghan officer when he suddenly dropped his pants mid-patrol. Squatted. Took a shit in the sand, as casually as if it were part of the routine.

I froze. Suggested we pause for security. Leave no one alone out here, even for a minute. No one cared. He balanced the PKM on his shoulder while relieving himself, flies buzzing in lazy circles, stench slicing through the dry, sunbaked air.

War had its rituals. Some of them were absurd. This was one of them. And somehow, in that moment, I laughed. And almost cried. And remembered that life here was fragile, and ridiculous, and entirely out of your control.

We had just left an old UN checkpoint, its walls pocked with bullet holes, concrete darkened by long-dried blood. The dust still smelled faintly of iron. You didn't need a report to know what had happened there. The walls themselves spoke—silent witnesses to executions, to finality, to the kind of violence that leaves nothing behind but echoes.

I walked away, thinking this will be the last patrol I ever move through here.

And then a little Afghan girl ran up. I crouched down for a photograph with her. For a heartbeat, the war vanished. Her smile was a tiny rebellion against the dust, the blood, the endless march. Innocence pressed against a backdrop of death. I let the moment stretch, fragile, fleeting.

And then, like always, we kept walking.

The sand still crunched beneath our boots. The sun still pressed down. Sweat still stung. But for that one fleeting second, home didn't feel so far away.

CHAPTER 25

Where War Ended and Fatherhood Began

Her Arms, My Salvation

I left Kandahar at the end of November 2010. Dust in my boots. Rucksack heavy. Stunned I had survived. I wasn't sure how. Only that I had.

We lifted off at oh-dark-thirty. Camp Mirage first. Then Cyprus. Stories followed us—decompression antics, drunken shenanigans, mandatory briefings. I did not care. I just wanted out. Home. Normal. To see the two people who mattered most.

Camp Mirage passed in a blur—packing kit, returning plates and weapons, clearing customs. Cyprus hit me like a wave. Sunlight. Warm, salty air. A few hours to Pafos. To pretend the horror behind us was already behind us.

The hotel lobby swarmed with three hundred combat-hardened troops. Like misplaced children at a birthday party, ghosts in flip-flops, lounging on luxury couches under chandeliers meant for tourists. Palm fronds brushing against the edge of reality. A former commanding officer smiled at the chaos, herding us with veteran patience. I registered for classes. Collected my room key. I was going through the motions. Just waiting to go home.

One night, at a Greek restaurant, the server asked where we had come from. Muscle memory tensed me. We chewed grape leaves. The world outside buzzed like it always did. No one knew we had just walked out of war. Why would they? They were alive. We were ghosts.

The next day, a cook raised his hand in a decompression class.

"I wasn't in combat like the infantry," he said. "But I made sure there was a hot meal ready every time. I never knew if it would be your last."

His words hit like a fist. I had been walking the edge between death and home. Hope had left me behind. Pieces of myself lay in the dust. And now, I was trying to remember how to be human again.

The Distance Between Steps

The air inside the aircraft was thick with fatigue and silence. Boots untied. No one spoke above a whisper. The roar of the engines filled every empty space between us—the kind of sound making thought impossible and memory too loud.

As we lifted off from Cyprus, I watched the tarmac and coastline shrink beneath us—the same staging ground where we'd spent our first nights out of Afghanistan, trying to remember how to breathe again. My chest tightened. I wanted to cheer, to cry, to feel something clean. But numbness had settled in where relief should've been.

Someone cracked a joke. It fell flat. Another soldier closed his eyes, mouth twitching like he was still hearing incoming rockets. A few of us pretended to sleep, heads bobbing with every pocket of turbulence. The smell of sweat and gun oil lingered—a scent that clung to us no matter how far we flew.

When the wheels touched down in Germany for refuel, the air felt too soft, too clean. Civilization. Coffee in real mugs. Soap that didn't smell like bleach. But even there, I couldn't shake the feeling that my body was still back in the sand, waiting for the next siren, the next shadow to move.

Crossing the Atlantic, I stared at the endless blue below—that vast, forgiving ocean between worlds. Somewhere under the hum of the engines, I felt the first tremor of what I'd later call grief. Not for the dead, not yet, but for the version of myself I was leaving behind—the one who'd believed he'd make it home the same man he was when he left.

Then the intercom crackled.

"Gentlemen, look out your windows."

Through the small round window, four CF-18 Hornets slid into view—silver ghosts cutting through the cloudbank, one on each wing. The maple leaf shimmered on their tails. For a moment, time stopped.

Another voice broke through the static, calm and unmistakably Canadian.

"Welcome home, boys. You're in Canadian airspace now. We've got you from here."

The words hit harder than I expected. A few of us looked up, blinking fast, shoulders trembling. We weren't just soldiers returning home—we were being escorted back, guarded, acknowledged. Some of the guys cheered. Others cried quietly, trying to hide it.

I pressed my forehead to the window, watching the sunlight flash across their canopies as they held formation beside us. Pride, sorrow, gratitude—they all bled together into something wordless, something holy.

Then, through a break in the clouds, I saw it—the first glimpse of Canadian soil.

Green. Vast. Alive. Rivers like silver threads winding through the land. After months of dust and desolation, the colour felt almost unreal—a living world we'd forgotten how to see.

The Hornets banked away, tipping their wings in salute before vanishing into the clouds. The cabin filled with quiet applause, low and reverent.

As the aircraft descended toward Gagetown, the engines softened, the vibration eased. The wheels struck the runway with a jolt that felt like both an ending and a beginning.

Rain streaked the windows—a cold Atlantic drizzle I hadn't felt in months. When the ramp lowered, it rushed in: clean, sharp, alive. We could smell home before we stepped into it.

The chain of command stood waiting at the bottom of the flight stairs, caps pulled low against the rain, rows straight, expressions unreadable. One by one, we made our way down, boots clanging on the metal steps.

When my turn came, I stepped off the last rung and onto the wet tarmac. The rain soaked through my sleeves. I knelt, pressed my lips to the ground, and kissed the cold, wet Canadian soil.

It tasted like earth. Like home. Like everything I'd lost, and somehow been given back.

The rain has stopped and the sun is beginning to set. Bus ride. Windows fogging with heat and breath. Fifty soldiers. Shoulder to shoulder. Half-broken. Half-horny. Laughing. Joking. Electric energy. Twenty minutes to base. To the Ortona Building. To 2 RCR. To home.

We rolled into the compound. Necks craned. There was a sea of cars. Our families were waiting. Somewhere out there—my daughter.

The buses stopped behind the LAV storage barn. One by one, we filed out. Shepherded into place. Fluorescent lights buzzed, burning holes into my skull. My breath quickened. Legs shook.

"Form up! Three ranks!"

Heart pounding. This was it.

Behind the Ortona doors—wrapped in paper for the kids' Christmas party—were our families. My family. My daughter. Half a year since I last held her.

"Right dress!"

"Right turn!"

"They're all here for you," the commander said, softer now. "Let it soak in."

Then: "Quick . . . march!"

Doors flung open. Bagpipes. Cheers.

Boots echoed. Pine. Gym mats. Baked goods. Life. Alive.

Step. Echo. Step. A flash of dust. Step. She waits. Step. Heart hammering. Step. Another memory flickers—Kandahar, sand in my mouth, gun smoke at the edge of vision. Step. She waits.

Then I saw her.

Not a baby anymore. Walking. Steady. Bold. Goosebumps crawling up my arms. Scalp tingling.

The commanding officer dismissed us. Chaos erupted. Shouts. Laughter. Arms wide. Tears flooding. Life pouring back into the room.

And there she was.

I walked through it like a dream. Scooped her up. Held her close. Face buried in her soft skin. Clean. Innocent. Safe.

I held her as if the war could not reach me. As if, here in this embrace, I could keep her safe from everything I had seen, and everything I feared.

Part 3

The Aftermath

CHAPTER 26

Mefloquine: The War That Followed Me Home

Symptoms of Mefloquine Toxicity

It would be years before my symptoms were acknowledged as mefloquine poisoning, but the effects of that drug wreaked havoc on my life. Intense and often uncontrollable episodes of anger, aggression, or emotional volatility can be triggered by mefloquine—an anti-malarial drug once commonly prescribed to military personnel, especially during deployments in areas like Afghanistan and Africa. Symptoms may include:

- Panic attacks
- Paranoia and hallucinations
- Violent dreams or night terrors
- Depression and suicidal ideation
- Explosive rage or uncontrollable anger (a.k.a. "mefloquine rage")

These symptoms may appear during use, or weeks, months, or even years after stopping the medication, especially in those with prolonged exposure or who were under extreme stress, such as combat veterans.

Characteristics of "Mefloquine Rage"

- Disproportionate reactions to minor stressors
- Loss of control, like being a passenger inside your own body
- Explosive outbursts, verbal or physical
- Shame and confusion afterward, especially if behaviour was out of character
- Often misdiagnosed as PTSD or a personality disorder

Many veterans describe it as a possessed state, where their actions felt hijacked, impulsive, and alien, sometimes leading to violence, self-harm, or severe relationship damage.

Why It is Important

Mefloquine toxicity is underdiagnosed and rarely acknowledged by military medical systems.

Veterans often endure decades of misdiagnosis, being labeled as "difficult," "non-compliant," or "unstable," when in fact they were harmed by a toxic pharmaceutical.

Documenting mefloquine rage is part of a larger fight to expose institutional betrayal, advocate for proper diagnoses (e.g., neurotoxicity, toxic encephalopathy), and receive appropriate care and justice.

Fury, Mefloquine, and a Failing System

There are days I feel like I am stuck in a rage I did not create.

A *mefloquine rage.*

A betrayal buried in my cells.

I fought for this country.

I served in good faith.

Now, I am stuck in fight-or-flight, trying desperately to hold on while waiting months, *years,* just to get a diagnosis that explains my brain, my pain, my crash.

I am angry at this body.

But I am even angrier at the system that left me here.

PTSD is not a weakness. It is a human response to inhuman circumstances, like sprinting through open ground while bullets tear through the air beside you while your nervous system decides between life and death, while your spirit calls out to something greater just to make it through. That is trauma. And trauma does not just live in memory; it imprints itself into the body, the breath, the heart.

Sanctuary Under Fire

I stepped onto that plane in 2010 as a sick and scared boy. Through this long, winding journey—through trauma, confusion, awakening, and return—I have fought my way back to the center of my authentic self. The part of me buried under layers of dismissed pain: mental, emotional, and physical.

The systems in New Brunswick, and across Canada, did not truly see me. Most professionals I met wanted to help. But many just wanted their piece of the pie: another case to study, another theory to apply, another box to tick in a framework memorized in a classroom.

I was never a chapter in their textbook.

I was a living, bleeding, breathing contradiction to their models.

And yet . . . here I am.

Alive.

Wiser.

Still healing.

Finally, finally being heard—by the world, and more importantly, by myself.

My military career was effectively over not long after I returned from Afghanistan—though it took me countless sleepless nights to admit that truth. I was not just injured. I was used up. Only wanted when I could perform. And now, my body no longer felt like mine.

The nosebleeds came regularly. My ears bled, too, especially after exertion. At first, I told myself I was just out of shape. But deep down, I knew something was broken.

A friend from another battalion emailed me a course list for an upcoming paratrooper course scheduled for March, after post-deployment leave. It should have lit a fire in me. I used to eat that kind of challenge for breakfast.

Instead, when I attempted the basic fitness test, the truth of Afghanistan hit like a freight train.

A standard run—something I had once done without thinking—left me breathless, disoriented, bleeding from the ears. My lungs burned. My vision blurred. My body was waving a white flag I did not want to see.

I laughed it off in front of others. Easier than saying what I feared:

My brain and lungs had been poisoned.

Burn pits.

Knee-deep in toxic sludge. Plastic. Batteries. Rotting food. Human waste. God knows what else.

My combat boots shuffled through the smoldering wreckage of the week's trash. I wiped sweat-slick eyes with a filthy sleeve. Ash mixed with tears. We wore bandanas over our faces—the only "protection" we had from clouds of toxic smoke. No respirators. No warning. Just orders.

And now . . . the ash is still inside me.

It wasn't just the war that damaged me. It was the silence after. The denial of what we endured. The healthcare system that said, "Prove it." The command chain that said, "Push through." Comrades who vanished. A body that betrayed me. Post-deployment, I was swollen—bloated from chronic stress, war, and the invisible damage of unacknowledged brain injuries. The government did not want to talk about the cost. Especially not the parts that made them look bad. And I? I was silenced in my own home, too.

The injuries began to externalize. I was not okay.

The man I had once been was slipping. Rage replaced grief. I smashed holes in walls. Broke computers. I was not the man I used to be. And I was never given the chance to be the man I could be.

My body was not mine anymore.

The mefloquine had stripped away everything that made me me, and left behind something primal. A ghost inside muscle.

Back home, my partner, a young woman with deep wounds, was fighting a different war. Her mother, abusive, fed shame and self-hatred wrapped in fake love and impossible beauty standards. My partner internalized it all. I watched her wrestle with the pain of her past but she raged at me for everything I could not fix in her, everything she could not face in herself. When I returned, her pain leaked sideways: control, anger, silence.

I was not immune. I shrank under it, starving to feel wanted. Even before deployment, we were in a cold war. Two wounded kids begging an emotionally volatile matriarch for scraps of love, and blaming each other when she did not give them.

She hated me for "taking her away" from her family. I hated that she could not see what I saw: her mother was just like my father. Different weapons. Same destruction.

Only difference? Her mother tried to buy love. Mine tried to beat it into me.

I sat back and watched it all play out. Even then, I knew: this was not going to end well.

My daughter's crying would trigger memories of Afghan children. Screams I could never unhear. Screams from behind mud walls in compounds we passed on evening patrols, just as the sun dipped beneath the horizon.

One night, I heard it too clearly: a child, no older than my baby daughter, screaming inside a nearby compound. I froze. Then the grunts of a man, some savage monster, taking advantage of her.

We kept walking.

And kept seeing the other children. Bloated bellies. Tiny arms reaching out. Screams piercing our armoured silence.

Everything became a trigger.

My house back in Canada was never safe—not even before deployment. Constant criticism. Attacks. As if survival itself were not enough. That home was not a refuge; it was just another front line.

Echoes in the Field

The field pulsed around me. Laughter ricocheted off helmets. Cleats tore into dry dirt. Jerseys whipped in the sun-baked wind. The whistle shrieked. The ball slapped boots in sharp bursts. I sat at the edge, chest pounding, hands tight in my lap, every nerve alight, unable to join, unable to escape.

A cold current rose inside me. Sharp. Familiar. Something old. Something I thought I had buried. The same abusive line that had run through the men in my family for generations.

Bang. Whistle. Shout. A teammate collided with another. Dust exploded into the air, tickling my throat. My body reacted before my mind could catch up. Heart thudding. Hands trembling. Stomach twisting. I froze.

Afghanistan had rewired me. Rockets. Blasts. Mefloquine poisoning. My nervous system screamed, jagged and erratic. Every sound, every motion, every vibration on the field mirrored the spikes in my chest. I felt it in my bones. Tremor. Tension. Flare of rage.

The ball bounced too close. I flinched. Breath caught. Time slowed. The field blurred at the edges. Behind me, a couple of soldiers laughed. "Faking it," they said. "Just trying to get money from Veterans Affairs." Hollow. Sharp. Cutting. They could not see the truth inside me.

Flash. My father's face. Pressed greens. Jaw tight. Silence that cleared rooms. Rage like fire. Ghosts of home and war intertwining. Pushing me to the edge of something I had sworn never to become.

Bang. Dust cloud. Ball rolls. Shout cuts sharp. Heart spikes. Breath held. Body twitches. Freeze. Hyper-aware. Hyper-vigilant. Hands clench. Eyes dart. Each collision, each cheer, each curse on the field maps directly onto the wiring of my nerves.

A flare of heat. Sun burning my neck. Sweat stings eyes. Dirt scratches my skin. The chaos pulses in perfect rhythm with my chest. I taste it in my mouth. Metallic. Dust. Salt.

Then—a micro-pause. The storm inside wavers. I see it. The shadow. The inherited rage. I name it.

I ache. Not for rank. Not for respect. Not for approval.

Just to love.

To be loved.

Without shame.

The game continues. Players move, ball spins, whistles cut through, dust rises. Waves of chaos rise and fall around me, around my body. My heartbeat slows in tremors, in small intervals of grounding. I am anchored in the eye of my own storm.

Breathe in. Breathe out. Tremor fades into awareness. Sun on my face. Dust in my hair. Noise surrounds me, but I am here. Present.

Alive.

My War Baby

Months before I came home, my girlfriend told me she wanted another baby and that she would not have sex with me unless I gave her a child. My ego took the hit. I had done the government's dirty work. I had watched friends die, held body parts, lived through ambushes and helicopter crashes. I felt entitled to some control over my own life.

When I finally came back from Panjwaii, it happened fast. Within a month, my youngest was conceived in wild, primal moments. We broke our bed as she tracked her ovulation like a military operation, ordering me to abstain in the days leading up to her fertile window. I obeyed. I didn't care anymore. My head was still spinning with childhood ghosts, the ambush in the green fields of Panjwaii, the Chinook burning in August, the rockets over Kandahar that May.

Even in those final months in the sandbox, I slept with a photo of my first daughter tucked into a locket, crying into my cot at night. I came home raw, still on fire, using sex to keep the war alive, the only thing that made me feel.

When my youngest was born, my warrant officer showed up at the hospital. Sunlight poured over him as he held her. For a moment, I blinked. He looked like my father. Same shoulders. Same jaw. Same silence that could fill a room.

And it terrified me. I felt like a boy again, waiting for judgment.

Something in me latched onto him. I didn't just see a superior officer. I saw the father I never had. When he cradled my daughter, I believed, for a heartbeat, that maybe he could cradle me, too.

A year later, in the India Coy lines, his voice shattered that illusion. "Because you're sick, lame, and lazy."

The man who had once held my newborn now discarded me with the same contempt I had grown up under. Just like with my father, the ground was pulled out from under me. The same wound replayed itself, sharp and final, like a rifle crack.

When I held my daughter, I knew I was not a killer. My soul told me I had to get better. I looked into her eyes and realized I knew nothing. This was my fresh start. Just like her, I had to begin again, seriously this time, determined to become a better version of myself.

I secretly called her my war baby. She arrived after the blood, fire, and heartbreak. She slowed me down. She pulled me back.

That first Christmas, I held her in my arms while the smell of dust and burnt metal still clung to me. Rockets echoed in the night. Gunfire cracked in my ears. My heart raced and I held her tighter, terrified I'd disappear back over there. Then, her tiny fingers wrapped around mine, anchoring me here, reminding me I had made it home.

I didn't feel like I deserved her. I was jagged, half a ghost. The war still hummed in me. But she didn't know that. She only knew my heartbeat.

My first daughter made me a father.

My second daughter gave me a reason to stay.

CHAPTER 27

Hurry Up and Wait

Kingston, Jamaica, July 2012

The Jamaican Defence Force arrived in Gagetown that fall. I watched them stumble through the snow. Pale faces, wide eyes, bodies stiff. They shivered. Foreign. Out of place. Like me.

By July, it was our turn. The Fredericton tarmac baked under the sun. Combat boots stuck to asphalt. Fighting order dug into my shoulders. Sweat pooled along my spine. We waited for hours. The Air Force moved slowly. Hurry up. Wait. My chest was tight, lungs shallow. Muscles screaming. Even before we lifted, my body felt spent.

Landing in Kingston, the cabin door opened. Heat hit like a fist. Diesel, burning trash, sweat. My stomach flipped. Skull pulsed. Ears rang with a high, whining pitch. Heart hammered. Hands shook. Vision blurred. Afghanistan. All over again.

By the time we wound into the mountains, I was outside the barracks, retching into gravel. Limbs heavy, trembling. Veins throbbing. Balance off. Fogged thoughts wrapped tight around my mind. A friend rested a hand on my shoulder. I lied. "Fine." Deny. Suppress. Continue. That was the rule.

The month blurred. Rice. Beans. Jungle sweat. Sleepless nights. My back ached from the American radio slung across my shoulder. Antennas hung under the canopy. Fog clogged my thoughts, scrambled words, slowed comprehension. Even breakfast was a battle. Wasps swarmed plates. Slap. Heart racing. Brain overloading. Every buzz, too loud. Every movement, exaggerated.

I forced myself to breathe. Counted to three. Felt the gravel under my boot. Reminded myself I was in Jamaica, not Kandahar. Brief pause, but only a few seconds. The panic never fully loosened.

One afternoon, I followed my battle buddy into Ocho Rios. Step. Step. Step. Muscles coiled. Heart stuttered. Breath caught. Market chaos pressed in. Hanging meat swung. Machetes flashed. Dogs lunged. Rot stung the nose. Lights too bright. Shadows too deep. Panjwaii, all over again. Hands shook. Fingers tingled. Two men stepped too close. Head throbbed. Vision doubled. Brain circuits shorted. Not Jamaica. Kandahar alleys. Waiting. Grenade. Death.

We ran. Feet pounding. Lungs burning. Vendors shouting, "Donations!" Panic and laughter tangled in my chest. Ghosts only I could see. PTSD: Ripped from the present. Dragged into the past. Body first. Mind second. Brain struggling to catch up.

Back at camp, the days stretched. I barely ate. Barely slept. Head buzzing. Nerves thrummed like overloaded wires. Thoughts scrambled. Shadows slithered. Strangers leapt into threats. Not hate. Survival wiring.

Some nights, I forced myself to sit. Close my eyes. Feel the warmth of a cot. Hear the distant cricket song. Just a few breaths. Tiny grounding. Tiny reminder that the world had not ended.

Meanwhile, my personal life fractured. At home, my kids' mother disappeared into silence. Denial. I did not love her anymore, maybe never had. But I clung to the illusion of family. Afraid. Desperate. After Jamaica, we flew to Newfoundland and Labrador. We married. Rash. Desperate.

What I did not know was that the system had already flagged me. A few post-deployment questions had tipped someone off. Two months later: PTSD.

And yet, the war had already arrived. Seeping into muscles, tangling nerves, fracturing thoughts. Skull pulsing. Brain fogged. Long before any paper said so, it followed me home.

From Patriot to Protester

I had just filed a claim for PTSD with Veterans Affairs. My hands trembled as I hit send; my chest felt hollow.

It would sit there, untouched, for two years before anyone even acknowledged it. Two years of silence. Two years of waiting, wondering, hoping this wasn't permanent.

At the time, I thought I was getting better. I thought I had support. I didn't.

And when I couldn't even get hard anymore, the questions started to creep in:

What am I good for? Who am I if I can't show up as a man, as a partner, as a father, as someone who still feels alive in his body?

They don't tell you that war kills more than people.

It kills trust. It kills feeling.

It kills the ability to look in the mirror and say,

I am still here. I still matter.

Everything felt orchestrated. Planned. My stomach knotted. My shoulders tightened, carrying the weight of a betrayal I couldn't shift. Like the people who were supposed to have my back had already decided I was disposable.

My career manager.

My former platoon warrant officer.

Men I once trusted. Men I bled beside.

They hung me out to dry.

I was six months short of everything that mattered: pension, medical, dental.

They called me a coward. Lazy. A piece of shit. Said I was faking it. That I just wanted the money.

These were the same men who came back from their fourth or fifth deployment, still chasing the high of war, unable to sit still in civilian life. They didn't know how to stop. And because I did, because I couldn't keep pretending, I became their scapegoat.

I didn't know then that my oldest daughter was living through the same nervous system dysregulation I was. She couldn't trust anyone. I saw it in her eyes, and it shattered me—like watching a mirror crack, reflecting all the trauma I thought I had buried. I had passed it on, the same hypervigilance, the same grief.

She deserved better.

I called the CAF assistance line, desperate, shaking, angry. My stomach churned. My chest tightened. I had been medically released just six months shy of everything that would have made survival a little easier. Not just for me. For my kids.

This wasn't just PTSD. It was betrayal.

It was about my children losing access to medical and dental care because their father dared to break under the weight of everything he carried.

I was pissed. My jaw clenched. My gut burned. I still am.

That anger lingered in every thought, every move, until one night I was watching a documentary about abortion rights in the U.S., and George W. Bush's face flashed on screen. My stomach twisted anew—not just at politics, but at all the ways I had been used.

I once drank the Kool-Aid. I once believed in the mission. But I started to see through it. Started to feel used.

Because the country I served with loyalty and blood had no use for me once the uniform came off.

And my children were the ones who paid the price.

The Day I Snapped: Christmas 2012

The day I went to the mental health hospital was supposed to be a day of celebration. Our unit's annual Christmas party. I was only a few years back from Afghanistan, already diagnosed with PTSD, and with Ativan running through my bloodstream like a leash barely holding back the panic.

We filed into the mess hall. The moment I stepped inside, it hit me: a wall of triggers in motion. Noise ricocheted off the walls—laughs, shouting, the clatter of trays. Lights stabbed my eyes. Alcohol flowed unchecked. The smell of sweat, fried food, and cigarettes hung thick, and something about it all made my stomach lurch. My chest tightened. My vision tunneled. My body felt like it belonged to someone else.

We took our seats. The commanding officer gave a few speeches. My boss received the Commander's Coin for pulling a family from a car crash. The room erupted. Beer bottles clinked like gunfire. Underneath tables, hands slid bottles of liquor into jackets and backpacks. Senior NCOs moved through the crowd serving the junior ranks—a ritual, a tradition, a system I barely tolerated anymore.

The turkeys were carved and passed hand to hand. We ate like animals, teeth tearing, swallowing, shoving, shouting to be heard over the din. Every slap of silverware, every laugh, every shoulder bump pressed against my nerves. Chaos became primal. My body shrank into itself. I dissociated. *Just get home. Just get home. It'll be okay.* That mantra, repeated like a prayer, was all I had.

Flashbacks began to flicker at the edges of my vision. Dust choking my lungs. The thrum of mortars in Panjwaii. Afghan children darting across streets while I pressed the weight of my rifle into my shoulder. My hands clenched under the table, knuckles white. I could feel the war crawling under my skin, a current I could not switch off.

Eventually, we were dismissed. One last formality before Christmas leave. But something had shifted. Something inside me broke. They called it PTSD. I did not argue.

Early words from a social worker haunted me: "You're carrying a lot more than just your kit bag." I ran from her truth. But she was right. My anger was not about my past. It was about betrayal. About the person I feared, wearing the same uniform, claiming the same values, but never living them.

Chaos waited at home. My wife's sister had come up to visit. My kids' mom, desperate to escape her own mother's abuse, was crumbling. She could not function. Everyone around her had to pick up the pieces. She was scheduled to leave for Newfoundland and Labrador that day, or the next. I cannot remember. Everything blurred.

When I got to our house, my brain was still buzzing, my body still drunk from tension and medication. I was a monster. Sleep was impossible. Every sound startled me. I compulsively checked doors, windows, and locks. She sat on the edge of the bed. I paced like a caged animal, fire burning through my gut. She screamed. She was leaving. I grabbed the Ativan. "I'm going to end the pain. For everyone. Especially me." My voice was raw, jagged. I was not the man who had deployed. I was barely functioning. Reactive. Angry. Sad. A shell.

I stormed out and called my new therapist. I do not remember if she answered or if I left a voicemail. But I got a message: Go to the base hospital. Just go. Wait there.

I obeyed.

I drove through the snowstorm, wind slicing the windshield, snow piling up like white knives. Heart hammering. My mind replayed firefights and ambushes. Dust, gunpowder, shouting. I could feel my body shrinking against the cold, the panic, the memories.

A civilian nurse practitioner greeted me, placed me in a room with the door open, and tried to contact my chain of command. I vibrated. Trembled.

A master corporal I respected arrived. He sat beside me. "It's going to be okay. We will get this figured out." His voice was steady. A tether.

The decision came: I needed to be admitted to the civilian mental health hospital. My soul screamed. But I did not argue.

We drove through the blizzard. I kept apologizing. "I am sorry . . . I am so sorry." My body shook. My mind screamed failure. Weakness. Contamination. Every snowflake that hit the windshield felt like shards of shame on my skin.

At the ER, they were expecting me. They placed me in a room. The master corporal explained gently, "You need to stay here for a little while."

Then the doctor walked in. Middle Eastern. My gut reacted before my brain could catch up. *Enemy. Threat. Fire.* I wanted to strike. The war was still inside me. But I did not. I complied. They admitted me. They medicated me.

In the ward, I ran into another Afghanistan veteran—an engineer. He had already been medicated into a fog. We exchanged a nod, enough to recognize each other. Soldiers. Survivors. Ghosts in the same hall.

I thought of the trip to Newfoundland and Labrador. I could not ruin the illusion of a perfect family. I worried more about appearances than about healing. I did not want anyone to know.

Four days later, I was discharged. Medicated. Feeling better, or so I thought.

Back at the base hospital after Christmas leave, I saw him again—the engineer. Still there. Still drugged. A zombie. In him, I saw my deepest fear. My soul screamed, *Do not let them do that to you.*

I would not.

CHAPTER 28

The War at Home

War Without End

The people I was subconsciously programmed to love never really cared—unless they were gaining something. My kids' mom, my parents—each relationship was transactional. I was the one bleeding out on both ends.

My wife wanted to escape her mother's abuse, but she was so dysregulated, so co-dependent, she could not function without someone else carrying her weight. Her sister came to help, but by then, everything was already unraveling.

She turned to the same weapons her parents had used: Silence. Cold, calculated withdrawal. Emotional detachment. History repeating itself in real time. No compassion. No affection. Only punishment through absence.

It was expected that I would take it. Endure it quietly, like always. But something in me had changed. Her mask slipped, and I began to see myself cast into the same roles I had sworn I would never become. Her father. My stepmother. Even her mother tried to dictate my future, steering me into courses and choices I never asked for, treating me like a puppet.

After deployment, nothing felt safe. Vulnerability? Impossible. Sharing my inner world with my wife always boomeranged back at me. She did not hold space; she consumed it. So, we bought things instead, stuff to fill the silence—pretending love had not died years earlier.

Anytime I tried to speak about Afghanistan, she cut me down. "You chose to go," she would say. "You made that bed. Now lie in it." Her words became law. The more she dismissed my pain, the deeper I withdrew—into silence, into self-medication, into darkness.

I had heard the horror stories: veterans with PTSD who turned violent, who terrorized their families, who became the monsters they feared. I swore I would never be that man. So instead, I turned the violence inward. I broke my own body rather than risk breaking someone else's heart.

The truth is, my war did not start in Afghanistan. It started in my father's house. That tour lasted eighteen years. Now, I was in a war with my wife, pretending everything was fine while everything was falling apart.

The Quiet Violence of Survival (2016)

By 2016, I was still pretending I was okay. My release from the military was set for July, but my wife refused to accept it. Denial was her coping mechanism. Mine was work. I kept working. Even as my brain burned, I tried to be a good soldier. A good dad. A good man.

But the cycles never broke. The same fears circled back. Over and over. I tried to hold together a world already crumbling.

This was the quiet violence of survival.

And the most violent part?

No one saw it.

And I didn't know how to scream.

At some point, I stopped being a man and became something else. Something primal. I wasn't thinking; I was reacting. Snapping at noise. Flinching at kindness. Every sound, a threat. Every silence, a setup. My body moved before my mind could catch up, as if the war had rewired my instincts and left my soul behind.

I wasn't living. I was hunting for a way out of myself.

Growling through grief.

Gripping rage like a weapon.

Terrified of softness. Softness had no place on the battlefield I had become.

They say trauma pushes you into fight or flight. But I stayed there. Years later, crouched, scanning, waiting. Waiting for the next hit. Even if it came from inside my own home. Even if it came from me.

In those early post-deployment years, I followed every military prescription: SSRIs. Antipsychotics. Mood stabilizers. Their so-called "polypharmaceutical treatment plan." None of it healed me. It just numbed me into silence.

And when the silence got too loud, I turned on myself. I started hitting my own body. Not to die, exactly. Just to make the pain stop.

By then, we were just roommates. She made it clear I was in her way. And I felt the same.

The End

The end was not a ceremony. It was not a salute. It was a slow disintegration.

I spent the last month of my military career in therapy, showing up every day to try and fix what I did not fully understand. Then one day, I turned in my kit, walked off CFB Gagetown, and went home. No mission. No orders. Just waiting. For what, I did not know.

July 28, 2016 was the last time I stepped foot on base. The last time I wore the uniform. I call everything after that *my Chernobyl Days*. A friend of mine once used that phrase for PTSD; the meltdown has already happened, and now you are just living in the fallout. That was me. Radiation in my bones, invisible damage I could not explain. Damage I could not escape.

I turned to rage, because rage made sense. It was the only language I had left after everything else was stripped away: identity, mission, structure. I was not Cpl. Wiseman anymore. I was just a man with ghosts. And they showed up every night, uninvited. The Taliban commander's face burned into my sleep. Not a memory. A haunting. My brain locked in a loop, paying some kind of invisible debt I could not settle.

I did not sleep during this time; I survived. My mind bounced between past and future, never landing in the now. Twenty minutes of rest before my body panicked and woke me up swinging, or sobbing, or screaming. Every night, a battle with no endpoint.

That was the collapse. Ego death. Role disintegration. My identity—military, father, provider—was shattered. The system I gave everything to betrayed me. Released me without tools, without guidance, without a plan. It was like being kicked out of the only life I knew, with a pat on the back and a file folder full of nothing.

Later, I came to call it *initiation by loss*. The unmaking of the soldier. The unraveling of everything I thought I was. I used to think healing meant fighting to get it all back. Now I knew it meant letting it all go.

The Day of Release

It was a July morning in 2016. The sun was already hot on the parade square, but I felt cold inside. My release papers were in my hand, the ink barely dry, the signatures final. Years of service, of sacrifice, of blood and silence—all reduced to a file and a number.

I thought I would feel relief. I thought leaving the weight of the army behind would mean freedom. Instead, I felt stripped bare. The uniform that had once defined me now hung like a costume in the back of a closet. My purpose, my identity, my brothers, all cut away in a single morning.

I carried grief for the younger version of me, the boy who had signed up believing in service, in something larger than himself. He was gone. The man standing there was scarred, cynical, and exhausted.

There was anger, too. Anger at how easy it was for them to let me go. After everything, I was disposable, a line crossed off a roster.

But beneath the anger, there was fear. Who was I without the mission? Without the structure? Civilian life felt like foreign soil: Full of hidden dangers. No orders, no platoon, no one to cover my blind spots. Just me.

And still, somewhere under it all, there was the faintest flicker of hope. That maybe freedom could one day mean healing. That maybe, stripped of the uniform, I might learn who I was meant to become. That July morning was an ending but also, quietly, the beginning of something I had yet to understand.

The Dog, the Drugs, and the Disbelief

It was October 2016. I was sitting in class at the New Brunswick Community College in Saint John, an hour away from our house, when my phone buzzed. A text from my wife:

Casey's not acting right.

I asked what she meant.

She's just . . . weird. Out of it. I'm not taking her to the vet.

That was all I needed to hear. I gathered my books, walked out of the classroom, and drove home, my chest tightening with every kilometer.

Casey greeted me at the door, but she wasn't herself. Her eyes were glassy, her movements clumsy. She staggered when she tried to walk. My gut clenched. Something was wrong, something I couldn't brush off.

I scooped her into the car and sped to the Animal Hospital. The vet gave her a quick exam, then looked up at me with a face that carried no doubt.

"She's high. THC exposure."

The words landed like a punch. High? On cannabis? I didn't even have a prescription yet. My stomach twisted as I shook my head. "That's not possible. I don't even use."

The vet shrugged. "She got into something. Edibles, maybe."

I stood there, numb, unable to process what I was being told. It didn't make sense. Not then. I tucked the memory away, foggy and unconnected, where so many other memories went. It would be six years before the truth came together.

Later, the pieces clicked. My ex and her new boyfriend, another former infantry soldier, were using in the house. He was a man my co-workers had once called my "twin," like some cosmic joke. He'd shown up before my release, living in his truck. She told me she was helping him out. Looking back, I wondered how long it had really been going on and how much of my life had already been rewritten behind my back.

Collapse in the Basement, 2016

I sat like an animal in the basement—exiled, vibrating, soul splintered. Underdiagnosed. No help. No language for what was happening inside me. Only shame. Only judgment. Only her eyes, sharp with silent accusation.

Upstairs, my daughter played. Laughter trickled through the vents like sunlight into a cave, But it could not reach me. Not down here. Not in this place where I had been buried by pills, by war, by betrayal, by the slow unraveling of my mind.

My wife hovered upstairs like a sentinel. She did not scream—she did not have to. Her contempt was quieter than rage, but it cut deeper.

She watched me fall apart and folded it into her story: I was unstable. Dangerous. A threat.

In that warped silence, I realized something brutal: Most marriages would scream for help. Mine screamed for proof that I was the problem.

I was an expert in approach and retreat, trained by war, raised by rage. But this?

This was psychological warfare in domestic form.

And in those years, I had no choice but to go silently—

Cut off from my child,

Cut off from myself,

Cut off from the rifle I once cleaned with pride,
Now replaced by a system that watched me rot.

Family? It was falling all around me. And I was the only one inside, trying to hold it up—with a nervous system collapsing and a basement full of ghosts.

The Weekend That Never Was

I booked a trip to Toronto. One last try. A weekend in a charming hotel, near a concert she liked. She said it was her idea, and I let her believe it. I wanted to believe, too, that this plan might soften her, that the ghosts in our home might stay quiet for one night, that we might find each other again in silk sheets and city lights.

But we never arrived at healing. Because the truth had already arrived before us.

I had become little more than a domestic servant to a woman who wore charm like armour but wielded contempt like a blade. She had been cheating on me for some time—with a former co-worker of mine, no less. A man I had once served beside. A soldier whose incompetence in uniform had been outmatched only by his indecency as a man. And she let him in, into her body, into our life, while I was still patching holes in my soul from the desert.

I tried to reconnect with the woman I had once called my wife. Not out of love—I think deep down we both knew that had been dying for years but because of the children. I stayed for them. I could not bear the thought of breaking their world apart, of becoming another absence in their story. I thought if I could hold the pieces of our home together, even just barely, they might never have to feel the kind of abandonment I had known.

The Rage That Wasn't Mine

I did not know it had a name at the time. I just thought I was losing control—some twisted mutation of war trauma and failure as a man. But there is a term for it now: mefloquine rage. A poison disguised as prevention, handed to us like candy on deployment. No one told us the cost—just take the pill. Do not miss a dose, or you might get malaria. What they did not say was that this little white tablet could burn holes through the lining of your mind.

The rage did not come all at once. It snuck in like a ghost. Symptoms were subtle at first—a short temper, insomnia, a constant buzzing under my skin. But then it escalated. A fork placed incorrectly on the table could spark an argument. A partner crying on the couch became a threat, a trigger, something I needed to silence—not out of cruelty, but to survive. I felt like I was drowning in stimuli, my nervous system on fire. I could hear my own voice rising and felt powerless to stop it. I was not me. I was watching him—that version of me—from a cage somewhere behind my eyes.

They called it PTSD. They called it anger issues. They called me dangerous, unstable, non-compliant. But they never asked about the drug. They never reviewed the warnings the manufacturer had started to include in fine print—the ones about lasting neurological damage, permanent mood disorders, hallucinations, and, yes, violent outbursts.

The Operational Stress Injury Clinic did not ask, either. They wrapped me in layers of diagnoses, gave me antipsychotics, sedatives, and antidepressants. One pill to balance the damage done by another. They never got to the root. They saw the man on fire and tried to douse the symptoms, not the match that lit him.

I started to question everything. How many of my worst moments— the fights, the breakdowns, the nights I wanted to put my fist through a wall or worse—how many were mine, and how many were symptoms of a neurotoxic drug that was never meant to be used long-term? I carried the shame for years. It corroded my relationships, my sense of self, and my ability to trust even my own instincts. But now, I know. The rage was not all mine. It was chemically induced, pharmaceutically engineered. A byproduct of military negligence and institutional betrayal.

I am still responsible for my actions. But I am no longer taking sole ownership of the why.

Steward McFluffy David, 2016

I told myself I got the dog for the kids.

But the truth is, I got him to try and save the marriage.

I thought it would bring us back together. Something to focus on that was not pain or blame. Something innocent and new, with no baggage, no backstory, no accusations. Just something good.

He was awkward, lanky, a goofy-looking little mutt with eyes too big for his body and a heart bigger than he should have had. The girls loved him instantly—especially my youngest.

She crouched beside him the first day and held him like he was treasure.

"What's his name?" she asked.

"I haven't named him yet."

She paused, tilted her head, then lit up.

"His name is Steward McFluffy David," she said.

I chuckled. "That's a long name."

"He takes care of people," she explained, completely serious. "And he is fluffy. And David is you."

And just like that, he had a name. Somehow both ridiculous and sacred.

I hoped he would soften the edges. Maybe give the girls something to smile about. Maybe make her look at me differently—like I was still trying, still showing up, still human. I took him on walks, cooked more dinners, cleaned more messes, offered more silences. Waiting for the air to clear. Waiting for her to meet me halfway.

But she never did.

The marriage did not get better. The house did not get lighter. The fights just got quieter, colder. And eventually, I was the one packing up garbage bags, loading the car, and walking out the front door with a heart that had held on too long.

Steward came with me. Into the silence. Into the pain. Into the hollowed-out version of fatherhood that came after.

He never judged me for failing. Never left when things got dark. He just stayed, tail thumping, eyes watching, heart wide open.

I got him, hoping he would help me save the family. Turns out, he helped save me.

CHAPTER 29

From Sedation to Sovereignty

Operational Stress Injury Clinic, 2016

As I transitioned out of the Canadian Armed Forces, fully loaded on polypharmacy, I did the required Veterans Affairs Rehab Program. For eighteen months, I struggled to explain the actual physical injury—the one the military discarded, and now the civilian medical system pretended did not exist. Until all the doctors told me there was no help for me.

My body felt dead. My mind was not far behind. I was desperate for someone, anyone in the medical system to understand that we are more than just a diagnosis on paper. We are more than PTSD or depression. We are whole beings, and what broke in us is not just mental—it is everything.

During those eighteen months, I was shamed and labeled. Years later, while scrolling Facebook, I found other veterans struggling with the same thing I was: mefloquine poisoning. Instead of taking the time to know the real me, the authentic me, the Operational Stress Injury Clinic had simply mirrored the same system the Canadian Armed Forces used: shame masked as care, control disguised as support. Another institution that chose manipulation over understanding.

They acted as if I were uncooperative—as if my silence, my despair, my dissociation were choices. All the while, I was losing my human spirit one blister pack at a time, choking down pills meant to sedate, numb, and suppress.

Even the civilian health system stopped listening. I sat in my family doctor's office, trying to explain what the military had done to my body, to my brain. She had no reference point—no understanding of the institutional betrayal, of the invisible wounds. I pleaded with her: "Something is wrong. My body is wrecked. My brain is injured. I have chronic traumatic encephalopathy. I have been poisoned by mefloquine."

My family doctor glanced up and said, "There's no way to test for a traumatic brain injury."

And something in me broke with her dismissal. My soul cried out—not for a diagnosis, but for someone to see I was not just a chapter in a textbook, a case number, or a psychiatric profile. I was an organism unraveling.

In the end, it was not the system that saved me. It was ketamine therapy—a psychedelic lifeline—that cracked open the armour of shame and helped me start to remember who I had been before the silence.

I stayed in the hospital for two weeks in 2017—numb again, sedated on a cocktail of pills. The fog rolled in heavy, and with it came the old silence. No one asked what had happened to me. No one dared utter "mefloquine" or "brain injury." They just wanted me stable. Manageable. Quiet.

I was admitted to a mental health ward again. The rain was relentless. I escaped to my car just to find silence. I called my father, not for support, but because my brain injury was screaming.

I sobbed. Uncontrollably.

His response?

"Everyone has PTSD. They do not cry about it."

I hung up.

That was the last time we spoke for six years.

Eventually, I tried writing to him. Not to reconcile. Just to under-stand. But his reply was venom. Threats. A restraining order. Just like his father had done to anyone who questioned him.

Without realizing it, I had followed the same pattern.

After the military spat me out, I had stayed with someone who was slowly destroying me. I thought it was my duty to hold everything to-gether, for the kids. For the illusion of family.

Then she met another man and kicked me out. Changed the locks. Told the courts she needed protection from me.

But I was the one who needed saving.

Eventually, I got that chance, but it cost me everything. I lost my kids. She taught them how to trigger me.

Looking back, I was venting pain into a post-military career that had no purpose, grasping for something steady in a world that had gone sideways. The betrayal cut deeper than I could admit at the time. Not just hers but the pattern of it all. Every institution I had trusted. Every person I had loved. Every promise I had tried to keep.

But even then, I stayed—for them. For my children. They were the only light left in a world that felt like it was dimming by the day. I thought if I could just endure a little longer, I might spare them from the fire I had already walked through.

Kindness Is Dangerous

When I finally began to claw my way out of the pharmaceutical haze, I was scooped up by a weed clinic deep in the woods—marketed as a sanctuary for veterans. They promised help for my traumatic brain injury if I chose them as my provider.

I was desperate. They seemed kind.

And kindness is dangerous when you've been discarded. It feels like salvation.

The owner's wife, a self-proclaimed trauma expert, said she had "taken psychology classes" and would oversee my medication tapering. No doctor. No accountability. Just a woman wrapped in her own wounds, controlling the narrative while calling it care.

Her husband, a veteran battling his own demons, ruled the clinic through fear. Behind the curtain of "healing," he screamed, manipulated, and humiliated. Yet in that small world, power was measured in ounces of weed and loyalty bought with free product. Silence was the price of belonging.

As I detoxed under their supervision—more like surveillance—my body screamed for safety. But there was no support. Just control disguised as compassion.

When the panic got too loud, I called my Veterans Affairs Canada caseworker, voice shaking.

"I'm seeing the devil," I said through tears.

Silence.

Then the line went dead.

My caseworker was drowning in files. My cries went nowhere.

Weeks later, another call came:

"You're being put on permanent disability. Veterans Affairs services are no longer required."

Another system, gone. Another person, removed.

The military medical machine had chewed me up and spat me out. They labeled my PTSD *non-complex,* as if war hadn't rewired every part of me—body, mind, and spirit.

So, I trusted the clinic.

And they dragged me deeper into the dark.

One Saturday, I arrived to find the husband shouting at his wife, his voice sharp and full of control. She told me to leave, embarrassed. But I couldn't move.

My inner child froze—watching another woman protect another violent man for the sake of image and survival. My fists clenched. My chest burned. I was nine again, standing in a kitchen, watching my stepmother shrink under my father's voice. The same script, just different actors.

He raged around the clinic, mocking me in front of other veterans—my art, my posture, even how I crossed my legs. Shame was his weapon, wrapped in the word *brotherhood*. And because he handed out free weed, no one called it what it was: abuse.

His wife, pale with fear, caught my eye.

"Sneak out while he's gone," she whispered. "He'll take it out on you next."

A month earlier, he had kicked his teenage son out—a boy crushed by his father's rage. I knew then that I had overstayed my welcome.

A few weeks later, at a doctor's appointment, a new practitioner looked up from her notes.

"Are you in therapy?"

I told her no. The clinic had said therapy was a waste of time—that I should smoke ten grams a day until I forgot why I was upset.

Her mouth dropped open. "Even I go to therapy," she said softly. "There's nothing wrong with it."

That moment stayed with me.

After everything I'd seen—the yelling, the manipulation, the quiet despair—I began to pull away.

Slowly, cautiously, I started to find my way back to healing.

Cannabis as Medicine, Not Escape

When I left the military, I didn't know how to grieve. Not for the war. Not for the people I couldn't save. Not for the version of myself that had come home haunted.

So, they gave me pills.

And I took them because I didn't want to die.

But I wasn't living, either. I was surviving in slow motion—body wired to react to threat, mind collapsing under side effects and shame.

Polypharmacy had become its own war zone—every pill a negotiation with my soul.

One night, after another nightmare left me shaking, I reached for something different:

A plant.

A medicine the system never taught us to trust.

Cannabis.

Not to escape—

to listen.

* * *

The first time I took CBD mixed with THC and sat in silence, I didn't float away.

I dropped in.

Into the wreckage.

Into the scarred places the pills had numbed.

I felt the buzzing in my jaw, the tension in my hips, the weight in my gut.

I lit a candle, placed my hand on my chest, and wept—not from pain, but relief.

I was feeling again. That meant something in me had survived.

Cannabis didn't cure me.

But it gave me a bridge between chaos and clarity.

I began tapering the meds—one at a time, when I could. Alone, mostly.

Each reduction became a recon mission across the terrain of my own body—tracking triggers, insomnia, and inherited rage.

Cannabis helped me sleep when my body forgot how.

Helped me eat when my stomach turned at the thought of food.

Softened the tremors. Loosened the guilt.

It even let me move again—stretch, breathe, pray.

Not to the God of chaplains and war, but the one who lives in breath, silence, and soil.

Some nights, I'd take a puff and whisper to the parts of me still hiding: "It's safe now. You're allowed to rest."

I wasn't getting high. I was getting honest.

This wasn't addiction.

It was sovereignty—taking back agency from a system that called me broken, reclaiming my body from a chain of command that treated symptoms like insubordination.

Cannabis didn't dull my pain; it taught me to hold it differently.

And with each layer of letting go, I remembered who I had been before the uniform, before the rockets, before the shame.

I wasn't just healing.

I was coming back to life.

The Tattoo: Winter 2017

My body felt foreign—aching joints, panic jolts at 3:00 a.m., nerves fried like comms gear left in the rain.

The army had long since packed me out, but the war hadn't. It hummed in my fascia, behind my eyes, in the quiet after every slammed door.

There were nights I couldn't lie down, only sit upright with my back to the wall, counting breaths like rounds in a mag. Hoping to make it to morning.

Somewhere in that year, I got the tattoo:

Grunt.

A word for the filthy, footsore, tired son of a bitch who kept the wolf from the door.

A confession. A reminder. A curse.

When I looked in the mirror, I didn't recognize the man staring back but the ink told me he had once been willing to die for something.

And that somewhere, beneath the fog and the ghosts, the tired son of a bitch still lived.

The ink didn't heal me.

But it reminded me I was still here.

Still breathing.

Still coming home.

CHAPTER 30

When Survival Became Surrender

Fredericton, 2017

My marriage was over. A makeshift custody order called for 50/50 custody and a schedule of alternating weeks.

The Sundays when I was to drop them off at their mother's were the worst. My oldest refused food, snapping at everything. My youngest, worn down by her sister's moods, ended up in tears before the afternoon was over.

The contrast made it sting more. All week, we found rhythm: Saturdays at the park, the swing chains creaking as they soared higher, their laughter echoing across the field. Afternoons at the kitchen table, slime sticking to counters and fingers, food coloring staining their palms. Evenings curled up on the couch, popcorn spilling across blankets, movie light flickering against their sleepy faces. For a little while, life felt whole.

Then Sunday would come.

I tried to set boundaries. I tried to create stability. But the moment I did, my oldest reached for her phone. A few taps, and her mother swooped in, rescuing her from "mean dad."

That was the game. If I said no, if I asked for respect, if I expected effort, I became the villain.

It had been that way for years. My oldest walked into my home expecting everything for nothing. One morning before school, she wiped oatmeal-covered hands across the couch. When I asked why, she laughed. "Because I wanted to."

Like nothing mattered. Like consequences did not exist.

And I saw it spreading. My youngest, watching, learning.

Their mom never had to raise her voice. From another house, she directed the play, guiding their feelings, pulling the strings, never once stepping on stage.

In 2017, everything collapsed.

It was early April. I was single-parenting the kids in our small apartment in Fredericton. We had just gotten back from the YMCA and had picked up groceries, snacks, and a cheeseburger pizza—something easy for supper. I felt off. That was not new; I had not felt normal since 2010, when I took my first mefloquine pill. This night was different, though. Something was building. The stress, years of it—professional, personal, spiritual, moral. Add in the mefloquine poisoning, and my nervous system was primed to explode.

We made dinner, watched some YouTube. I sent the kids to bed in the master bedroom, to the bed I had taken from the old marital house but still couldn't sleep in. I tried to rest in the second bedroom, but my body would not let me. My thoughts slipped into nightmares instantly. Then, the seizures began.

I was wide awake. Heart pounding. Fitbit screaming. Vision starting to fade.

I knew this was not just a panic attack. I had been dealing with those for years. This was different. This felt like the early days of mefloquine, like poison boiling under my skin. I stumbled out of bed, trying to ground myself. I checked my vitals. My blood pressure was through the roof. My hands were trembling so badly I could barely unlock my phone.

I dialed 911.

"I'm losing my vision," I told them. "And I have two kids here. I am scared."

The fire department was ten minutes away. It felt like an hour. I lived on the third floor of a disreputable apartment building downtown, one known for drug activity. Just that winter, one of the other units had nearly burned down thanks to a meth lab explosion.

As I waited, pacing and convulsing, I kept the 911 dispatcher on the line. "They're at the bottom of the stairs," she said.

"I'll go let them in," I offered, desperate.

When the firefighters finally arrived, I opened the door, expecting compassion. Instead, I was met with suspicion. Contempt. The paramedics scanned the apartment like it was a crime scene. They found some old prescriptions on top of the fridge.

"What are these for?"

"I haven't slept since 2010," I said. "I have complex PTSD issues. My nurse is coming tomorrow to take those to the pharmacy."

They did not hear a word.

They called the police. And child services.

While my children slept in the next room, I sat vibrating at the dinner table, clutching a bottle of water. Trying to be polite while I was judged and labeled. They did not bring a stretcher. They hooked me up to wires and forced me to walk, shaking, down three flights of stairs into the ambulance. Like I was not having a medical emergency.

At the hospital, I was shuffled into triage. Extremely angry. Mouth too dry to speak.

The receptionist glared at me. "Name?" she snapped.

I tried to answer but couldn't.

She rolled her eyes.

I asked her for a glass of water to help answer her questions.

She snapped back, "No."

I waited in the ER for hours. No nurse. No doctor. Just me, convulsing, burping, farting, shaking violently in front of a packed waiting room. Someone muttered, "Must be on something." That hit harder than anything my kids' mom had ever said.

Eventually, they moved me into a back hall just to stop me from making everyone uncomfortable. I sat there, shaking, from midnight until sunrise. The rage passed. The seizures stopped. I was not violent, but I had the impulse to grab the police officer's gun. Not out of aggression. Just desperation. Like my brain needed someone to finally hear me. I did not act on it. I knew the cost would be too high.

I did not know then that I was having a mefloquine rage attack. I would not find out until 2018, when I saw a video from another veteran while scrolling on Facebook. He was saying what I had felt for years: This was not just PTSD. This was poisoning.

Since my release in 2016, my symptoms had been treated like a problem to sedate. More meds. More labels. Borderline. Obsessive-compulsive disorder. Eating disorder. They never got to the root. Never looked at the injury. Never questioned what mefloquine had done. Even though the military had known since 1988.

That morning, I left the hospital against medical advice. The vibrations had stopped, and I took a cab home. Hugged my animals. I needed to breathe. So, I booked a trip to see my youngest sister in Newfoundland and Labrador. I wanted to reconnect. She was raw, too. Wounded. I packed bags, arranged a cat sitter, loaded the dog, and we left.

I stayed a month.

At first, it was healing. Then, it was not. Her apartment, dusty and full of cats, was overwhelming. I tried to clean. She told me not to. But I could not live in that. My allergies flared. My nervous system crashed again.

During that time, child custody issues escalated. I had been trying to get my kids' mom to attend mediation. She dodged every attempt. I could see her plan: wear me down. Pretend I did not care, so she could tell the kids the same lie she told herself.

Remembrance Day came. I stood on Newfoundland soil as a civilian for the first time since my service, alone. I did not miss the parades, the snot-freezing forced rituals in small towns. The only Remembrance Day I ever truly connected with was in Kandahar. Among brothers. Under buzzing generators.

My father did not see me. He had not visited me in the hospital the previous year, either, when I was admitted for two weeks, vibrating after the divorce. Even years later, people would throw that stay in my face, as if going to the hospital had been something shameful.

It was during my time in Newfoundland and Labrador that my kids' mother began recording our calls. A child services investigation had started. She moved quickly, spinning lies—fast and relentless. I could barely process one before the next hit. My brain, already frayed by trauma, flashed back to years earlier—Now it was happening to me.

The same emotional warfare, the same twisting of truth. My father had done it to my mother. Now my ex was doing it to me. Different players, same pattern.

The investigation eventually cleared me. I was not a threat to my children. But that didn't stop the damage—the fear, the doubt, the ache of being seen through someone else's lies. I went to court to prove what was already true. In the end, I was granted visitation, and slowly, the children and I began to find our way back to each other.

She used the court system as a weapon. She knew I was vulnerable. She played the perfect victim in public. But behind closed doors, she was relentless.

And ten years later, she still plays those games.

A Letter I Wrote During Therapy

To My Future Self—A Reminder from the Fire

Hey you,

I hope everything is all right. I know how hard the last year has been—hell, how hard the last *many* years have been. But listen, **you are a survivor**. You have come through the storm bloodied but unbroken. You *can* do this.

Remember 2017?

We hit rock bottom and still found a way forward.

The future is wide open now. It is yours to claim.

So:

- **Keep walking**—three times a week, minimum. Move your body like it is sacred.
- **Eat right**—fuel the machine, feed the soul.
- **Live for yourself and your kids**—your love is a legacy.

You are not chasing perfection. You are in **pursuit of happiness**. That is a noble path.

Take time to breathe. To heal. To smile again. You deserve peace. You deserve joy. Even on the hard days, **choose to live with joy**.

If you fall, get up.

If you break, rebuild.

Never surrender.

You have this.

You always have.

You always will.

With love,
—Your Resilient Self

CHAPTER 31

A Second Chance That Wasn't

British Columbia, 2018

Throughout my adult life, I have faced challenges posed by people who claimed to love me. Often, their actions were unintentional, born of wounds and neglect they carried themselves. At the time, I did not realize that complex PTSD has a way of pulling us back toward the familiar—not because the familiar is safe, but because chaos feels like home.

One of the first people I dated after my marriage ended was a childhood friend from Nova Scotia. I wanted to believe it was a fresh start. While I was frequenting a cannabis clinic in 2018, the owner's wife encouraged me to pursue her. Instead, the relationship quickly became destructive.

She lived in British Columbia. The four-hour time difference meant late-night phone calls that too often echoed the arguments I had once endured with my ex-wife. Samantha was also living with severe diabetes, and most of her visits unfolded in medical crisis. Her blood sugar soared to terrifying levels, and I had no idea how to respond. My instinct to please others meant I neglected myself. I went hungry. I forgot to eat. My only focus was her sense of security.

It was my second time in BC. The first had felt like escape. This one felt like exile.

I had been there a week—starving, surviving on frozen black bean burgers and scraps from her fridge. After years of pharmaceuticals, I was detoxing, unsupervised, on the casual advice of a clinic owner's wife. My brain and stomach were in revolt. My soul scraped for air.

That cold spring night, I lay trembling on a borrowed bed in a small apartment, crashing at the home of a friend I hadn't seen since elementary school—twenty years gone in an instant. A few hours earlier, something inside me had snapped. I didn't know about the effects of mefloquine then. In that moment, it felt like my brain was short-circuiting—every wire crossed, every nerve sparking.

Her fear met mine in the air between us. The pain we both carried seeped into the walls until the whole place seemed to tremble with it.

Inside, I shook—my soul perched in the corner, watching, powerless. She screamed, her pain lashing out like knives against my unraveling nervous system. When she wasn't exploding, she folded into silence, collapsing on the couch, eyes vacant, unreachable.

As I lay there drenched in sweat, all I could think about was getting on a plane—getting home, and leaving this relationship behind. My body knew before my mind did: it was over. In our talks, I'd seen it coming—her fear of stepping beyond the safety of her mother's house, her comfort in staying small. I couldn't live inside that anymore.

When I came back to her place, she was still spiralling. I was too far gone to defend myself. She stripped the bed and left me on the floor. I vibrated through the night, whispering the only prayer I could form: *Just make it home. Just a few more days. Just survive this.*

We ended that night.

Her caring mask—the one she wore for her coworkers—was gone. With me, it slipped. What remained was another unhealed person in a position of power, unable to hold space for pain without defaulting to shame, ridicule, or blame. Her judgment pushed me deeper into the abyss of my own.

In the middle of that storm, I picked up the phone and called someone back in Newfoundland—a "friend" who had stolen fourteen thousand dollars from me. I don't remember the words, only the sharpness—the fury bleeding through like broken glass. It was ugly. It was necessary. The truth had to cut its way out.

The next morning, I spoke with her mother. I mentioned the patterns I had noticed—both then and in the past. Her mother admitted something had happened during university. But if I'm honest, even back in our childhood in Nova Scotia, she had always carried this chaos. She had just been better at hiding it.

Years of unmanaged diabetes were now eating away at her body. She was receiving injections in her eyes just to hold on to her vision. Her blood sugar climbed unchecked, yet she still fought to control others—to dominate.

The body keeps the score. And hers was showing it.

What haunted me most was the thought that I was only a few misunderstood words away from being locked in a psychiatric ward—far from home, far from help. A few days later, I boarded an early flight back to New Brunswick.

The Hook

The first time I fell for a narcissist, I didn't know it yet. I saw strength, poise, a woman who walked like she knew something the rest of us didn't.

What I needed was safety. Structure. Someone to tell me I was finally home.

I ignored the red flags. They felt like family.

By the time we met, I was already unraveling, quietly, like an old uniform coming apart at the seams. Mefloquine was still in my blood. My nervous system flipped between combat and collapse. The war hadn't ended when I stepped off the plane. My body was still in Kandahar. My mind hovered between rocket attacks and the psych ward.

Then came her voice. Soft. Confident. A nurse who claimed she understood trauma. I mistook her for safe. I mistook attention for affection. I mistook control for care.

She made me feel chosen. Until she didn't.

False Freedom

In November 2019, I thought I'd healed enough to try again. At first, she seemed different. We walked backwoods trails in New Brunswick. My kids' mom had been rigid; this woman, a white-haired cancer survivor, felt free. At that stage of my life, I needed her energy.

Cracks showed early. Money trouble. No drive. "It's ADHD," she said. Back then, I knew little about ADHD. I did know trauma. Looking back, I wonder if that's what it really was.

Most days, we stayed in her basement apartment. We smoked weed, took mushrooms, chased endorphins. I went along until the cannabis started to trigger me. When I told her, she brushed it off as "just your PTSD."

Her friends mirrored her habits: hard drinking, chasing chaos. When I set boundaries, she stepped over them.

It felt like a bad patrol—someone always tempting fate. Except there were no rifles, no radios, no sergeant to pull us back in line. Just me, alone, trying to hold order against her chaos.

Sanctuary Trauma

One night in 2022, it all came to a head.

She chased me up the stairs.

Ripped the cane from my hand.

Drove it into me.

I stumbled into the kitchen, cold rubber underfoot, fluorescent hum above. Her face twisted with rage. My voice shook. *Stop.*

She didn't.

She could never admit she was capable of harm.

In that moment, I saw her clearly: kind one breath, cruel the next. She had already convinced others I was the abuser. But the truth stood right there, framed by the kitchen light.

I had felt this before in Panjwaii, when Afghan police smiled by day and whispered to the Taliban at night. The same duplicity. The same mask.

By then, I was wrecked. Manipulated into choices that would shape the next four years. Cut off. Alone. Half alive, hoping death would come as relief.

It wasn't until 2023, in a peer support course, that I learned the term for what I had lived through: *sanctuary trauma*, when the place that is supposed to be safe becomes the source of danger.

Once I named it, everything clicked. Six years of chaos, numbness, and hypervigilance. The reason I never felt safe, even in my own bed.

Even the relationship I thought would be different, gentler, healing, turned against me.

One night, deep in a mefloquine episode, my body breaking down, I tried to escape the noise, the chaos, the pain.

The Spiral

When the pandemic hit, I thought I was ready for isolation. I'd just bought my second home outside Fredericton. It was quiet, with a yard by the creek. I invited her to move in. My kids stayed every other weekend. On the surface, it looked like a life.

By summer 2020, during a lull in restrictions, we went to Newfoundland to see my mom. I hadn't seen her since 2012.

The house looked like it had when I first saw it in 1997. Broken deck. Piles of trash. Stench of urine and mold. She'd been sleeping on the couch since 2015, after her alcoholic husband's stroke. Two broken people sharing a living room.

What my girlfriend saw wasn't only a broken house. It was the wreckage I was raised in. She used it against me.

She said she was "on my side." But her love came wrapped in adrenaline and shame, the same counterfeit I had accepted for years.

By 2021, still in the middle of COVID, I felt trapped. That's when I learned the term *reactive abuse*—when the victim explodes after being pushed too far, and the abuser flips the script. On the surface, she seemed caring. Beneath: manipulation, dependency, addiction. Her parents funded Christmas trips. Friends bailed her out. I was meant to do the same.

She unloaded her history—blackout drinking, one-night stands, abortions, rage at men. The more I listened, the clearer it became. It wasn't men holding her there. It was her choices.

Meanwhile, I was trying to heal. PTSD from war. The strain of co-parenting with a toxic ex. Body and brain breaking down. Instead of support, she projected her pain onto me. She stole my Veterans Affairs medication to feed her dependency.

Her routine was chaos. Cannabis from the night before. Double espressos. No food. Then off to work on a mental health floor. In the evenings, she would unload on me.

The cycle was brutal. Screaming like her father. Therapy twisted into blame. Even her sister said I couldn't handle her.

Whenever I said no, she pressed until I gave in. Her needs always came first. I was drained, guilty, confused. When I told her aunt about the cane, she said I was overreacting.

Gaslighting became daily fare. By 2022, I was isolating, sinking.

The Therapy Trap

Therapy broke me.

I brought her to a session, hoping someone would see. Instead, two voices came at me at once.

Her rage.

The psychologist's frustration.

Both shouting.

Chest tight. Head spinning. Room closing in.

I left shaking, wondering if maybe I really was the problem.

But I knew this cycle. I'd lived it before.

I had one simple boundary: no yelling or screaming at me. After war and abuse, I would not accept it. She agreed, but the pattern crept back anyway. Criticism. Contempt. Defensiveness. Addictions circling the drain.

She cut me off, blamed me, and turned every conversation into an attack. I begged her to stop. I asked her to follow a checklist, to give me space to calm down. She drained me until I trembled on the edge of a seizure.

She insisted she cared. But the words were hollow.

My family ran on this cycle, too—nervous systems addicted to chaos.

I had survived enough.

The Cycle of Denial

Her younger sister lived in a hoard with her boyfriend. One night, I drove him to St. John's and asked to use the washroom. He hesitated, and I soon realized why.

Inside, the stench hit hard. Garbage and rot. Beer cases stacked four feet high. Every surface, buried.

I knew this family. Show the surface. Deny the sickness underneath.

And the cycle rolled on.

CHAPTER 32

Mistaking Survival for Love

The End of Endurance

By the summer of 2023, we were both running on fumes. We stayed at her father's place in a small town, the air thick with judgment and unspoken tension. Rest never came.

My head spun from the mefloquine: ringing ears, vertigo, nausea, flashes of light behind my eyes. Every sound cut too deep. Every word landed like a blow. After being yelled at for the entirety of a two-hour drive, my nervous system finally gave out. Trembling, disoriented, barely able to speak, I felt my body collapse into a full-blown attack.

That night, after her father kicked me out, I went to a hotel to calm down and revisit the plan she and I had agreed on before coming to Newfoundland. My body vibrated, shaking off the static built up over days of travel, stress, and the shifting weather. At some point, exhaustion won. I passed out fully clothed, lights still on.

When I woke, my body was still buzzing, but I could breathe again. My phone lit up with messages from her: *Come over. Dad wants to talk.*

I already knew the pattern: conflict, then false calm, then control. Still, I packed my bag, grabbed the dog, and drove the few minutes back to the house.

She was outside when I arrived, eyes darting, energy off. I asked how her father was. No answer. The eagerness from her texts had vanished. I asked if it was safe to come in. She said yes.

Inside, her dad sat at the kitchen table, flipping through a magazine, pretending to be calm. My body started vibrating again, every muscle braced. Then, without warning, he looked up and said the words I had been waiting years to hear:

"It looks like this relationship is over."

I exhaled. "Finally, someone's hearing me," I said.

His voice rose instantly with accusations and blame, objects flying across the table. I didn't respond. I just gathered my things, loaded the dog, and drove.

Before sunset, clarity came. The questions I had been circling for years finally found their names: criticism, contempt, defensiveness, stonewalling. The four horsemen of a dying bond.

I drove through the night in a single twenty-four-hour push. Headlights streaked past like memories. My hands locked on the wheel, body begging to stop. I didn't.

The next day, she flooded social media with photos: smiling faces, family captions, declarations of love. As if nothing had happened. As if cruelty could be erased with filters and hashtags.

Not once did she ask if I was okay. Only: *I knew you'd make it.*

As if my worth was endurance.

That week, I told her I couldn't do it anymore. I asked her to move out. She didn't. She stayed for another year and a half, pretending my words, my needs, my boundaries didn't exist.

By then, I had already left a hundred times inside my mind.

My body just hadn't caught up yet.

September 22, 2024—The First Stage of Failure

I woke at 6:00 a.m. Ate watermelon. Drank water. Took my pills and cannabis. Watched a Canadian Forces documentary. Made oatmeal for both of us.

She shuffled upstairs, mumbling complaints, and collapsed on the couch while I brushed my teeth. Her energy crackled like static through the walls. I suggested somewhere closer to go. At the top of the stairs, I hugged her. Her eyes looked dead. I held her longer, trying to anchor her. Told her I'd made oatmeal. She slumped again.

The oatmeal cooled on the counter, untouched.

She checked work chat—despite promising not to, and raged about short staffing. She poured it onto me.

We left.

In the car, her anger grew. I tried to validate, but every pothole kicked my body into survival mode. Head down. Dissociation. She screamed at another driver. I asked her to stop.

At the drive-thru, she joked loudly that I was high. I asked her not to. She snapped. Directions turned to accusations about my tone. Lips tingling. Foam gathering. Panic overload.

I begged her to pull over. She refused. Said I was making it about myself.

I tried to help her find her headphones. She yelled that I wasn't meeting her needs. Words circled.

Finally, she announced we were going home. Parent voice. Child me.

She stopped under an overpass and jumped out.

I laughed—cracked and broken—then tried to breathe.

Later, at home, I asked if she could hold space for me. She said yes. Within minutes, we spiralled: blame, shame, gaslighting. I was the problem.

I asked again for help.

"What do you need?" she snapped.

The words died in my throat. My dog pressed against my leg.

After another PTSD surge, I tried to regulate. She sat in a hoodie with noise-canceling headphones. I was vibrating, not realizing she couldn't hear me. Dissociation tugged me out of my body.

The world rarely accepts that soldiers can have brain injuries. They just see anger.

By the time she drove me downtown, my shirt clung with sweat. Hands shook on my knees.

It was the first stage of failure—not the argument, but the symbols. My body knew the ending before my mind admitted it.

When It Broke: December 22, 2024

Everything imploded.

We fought. I had her removed from the house.

She mocked me with my own rank—weaponizing what I'd bled for.

She body-slammed me in the hallway.

Then put on headphones while I begged for help, mid-seizure.

The music in her ears was louder than my pain.

That was the moment I realized I could vanish, and she might not notice until it inconvenienced her.

Her job. Her trauma. Years of spillover.

I had taken it all—soldier, partner, healer.

But I was dying.

This wasn't a relationship.

It was war.

And I had no battlefield left in me.

Patterns Beneath the Pain

An hour after I woke, she came up to say goodbye. The coffee machine gurgled downstairs. Bitter smell. She hadn't eaten.

The rhythm I knew: push to the edge at work, collapse at home.

She dodged deeper conversations—especially about shared responsibility. When I was direct, she labeled it PTSD. I wasn't picking fights; I was offering solutions. My needs were reduced to symptoms.

In the consistency of her behavior, I sensed the root: she may have needed me to fix her from the beginning. Not consciously but the energy carried that whisper.

Like being handed a broken mirror and told to piece it together while the shards cut my hands.

December Collapse

As 2024 wound down, the winter pattern returned. She spiraled, blamed, turned cold—a mental-health nurse whose own trauma ran the house. Somewhere along the way, she convinced her circle that I was the problem. I was still begging Veterans Affairs to acknowledge my brain injury.

By then, she was months into ADHD treatment. Her once-measured voice had sharpened to glass. Work stress came home. We clung to couples counselling, but every session looped back to her mother's death. I'd been watching that cycle since 2023.

One night, after being screamed at through my night terrors, I wrote the counselor at 1:00 a.m. and tried to get the truth on the record. By daylight, my girlfriend denied it. In her story, I was always to blame.

In September, I received my Quilt of Valour. It should have been a sacred occasion. Instead, her ego hovered. A nurse friend, a former soldier, came by and started bashing men. I sat there—not confused, just done. She had discarded my essence years before.

I had cycled through roles: lover, friend, roommate, her toy, then—worst of all—her father figure. She raged at her childhood. "They gave me a dog instead of therapy," she said.

I answered softly, "I'm sorry they made you feel that way." I meant it. I always tried to hold space.

But the cracks widened. I asked her not to touch the cannabis Veterans Affairs prescribed to me. She ignored me. Add four to six coffees a day, and her system lived in fight-or-flight. Even my therapist began to see through her mask.

When I slipped into a mefloquine rage, she escalated: louder, closer, blocking my movement as I begged her to stop. She denied it. I knew it was over. I'd known for a long time.

A week before the final rupture, I asked her to sleep upstairs. I wasn't sleeping. Nightmares snatched me awake to her shouting. Comfort had left years before.

Even when I begged for space, she slid into my bed, weed-dulled, pressing against me while I slept. If she wanted pleasure, I was expected to provide it. If I wanted anything, I was shamed.

It was finished.

The Night It Ended: December 22, 2024

By nightfall, I knew there were only two exits: she'd leave, or one of us wouldn't survive. If it came to that, I feared it would be me—lost to a mefloquine surge.

She hadn't eaten all day. By afternoon, she was curled on the couch, hoodie up, Bose clamped over her ears, crying. Veterans Affairs had funded her therapy for years. Nothing changed. She wore pain like armour and swung it at me.

I stood in the kitchen, cooking lunch for us both. I asked her to eat. She refused. I asked her, gently, to cry in the bedroom so I could breathe without drowning in someone else's sorrow.

She snapped the pen from my PTSD workbook in two. I told her to stop breaking my things. She hurled the book across the room. I stared at her—her eyes were cold, like eyes I'd seen in war and in abuse.

That workbook had carried me through nights when I was overwhelmed by memories I'd told no one about. She knew that. She didn't care. Her crisis eclipsed my panic. My trauma became a footnote.

By evening, my body gave out: another seizure, a storm of PTSD, mefloquine toxicity, emotional warfare.

When the night softened, I asked her to dance in the sunroom. Loyalty is a reflex you learn in war. So is sacrificing yourself to keep the peace.

For a moment, it worked—until she swung a metal water bottle at me. I flinched. I asked what she needed. "A bath," she said. I cleaned the tub. She skimmed the water with a strainer, mocked my body hair, refused the bath, and stormed to the bedroom, screaming.

Sweat poured. Panic rose. She called me by my rank. The switch flipped. Combat circuits in my brain came online. We wrestled. She pinned me with her feet. I shouted, "She is raping me!" She screamed back, "No, you're raping me!" The bed—once a place for intimacy—was a battlefield.

She kicked me in the stomach.

"I'm not going to jail for you!" I yelled.

I broke free, ran for the door, and stopped only to cool my spine in the bathtub. She followed, screaming. I ripped the door from its hinges to get away.

Marks covered my body. The second time in a week.

"I'm calling 911!" I shouted as she scrambled through the basement, packing.

The RCMP came. It was two days before Christmas. The station was closing for the holidays.

After New Year's, I filed a twenty-page statement. The officer disappeared for a month. When she finally called, it was like she'd never met me. I reminded her I'd filed in person. She hung up. A week later, she said her sergeant wasn't going to do anything. "Gaslighting doesn't count."

They didn't have a place for an abused man.

I agreed to no contact. Not long after, the emails began again, pulling at the same threads. Trying to drag me back.

This time, I didn't answer.

Closing Reflection

Afghanistan taught me to live on the edge, waiting for the next rocket, the next IED, the next ambush. That kind of living rewires you. Survival becomes your only language.

I didn't expect to find the same battlefield inside my own home—the lies, the betrayals, the body keeping score long after the fighting stopped.

I'd survived war.

I'd survived abuse.

What I wanted now was life.

I stood at the window as snow fell. Cold glass pressed against my palm. Breath fogged the pane. Silence thickened in the room. The house was dark, finally empty, finally still.

I was done mistaking survival for love.

CHAPTER 33

A Door Reopened

Ketamine Therapy

In 2021, on the advice of another veteran, I started ketamine therapy. He made it sound like salvation. Later, I found out he got a cut for every referral. A few years after that, he was back again, this time pitching a "wellness retreat" in Ontario. By then, it felt like business, not healing.

It was the height of the pandemic. I was desperate. Years of pills had packed weight onto my body, wrecked relationships, and left my mind numb. A friend had killed himself the year before. I could feel myself sliding toward the same edge. So, I said fuck it and signed up.

But I was already drowning in an abusive relationship. She seemed supportive, spoke the language of healing. Then one night, after a flashback, I asked her for comfort. Instead, she mocked me, tore me down. That was the moment the mask came off.

From then on, control tightened—what I wore, how I raised my kids, how I lived. My brain injury was flaring, and my back needed care. Any request for compassion or space turned into a fight. To her, injuries didn't exist. Boundaries were "anxious attachment."

I started to see her father in her. The same man who later screamed in my face while I was having a stroke. The same family who branded me "dangerous." No one stopped to ask what I had survived.

Something shifted in me that year. For the first time in a long time, I chose myself. I wrote her a letter, told her I was choosing my health over her toxicity, and cut contact for a year.

But the truth is, I kept going back to people who treated me the worst. I accepted the bare minimum. I accepted disrespect. I accepted the lie that my needs didn't matter. That I didn't matter.

It was the part of me that had grown up trying to earn love by disappearing. The soldier in me that had been trained to endure no matter what. The child who still believed that if I could fix my parents, I would finally be safe.

But I see it now. I am not here to be used. I am not here to be broken in order to keep someone else comfortable. I can choose peace. I can walk away. I don't need permission to matter.

For days before my first ketamine session, I was nervous. On the day, I fasted for three hours. Later, I'd learn that fasting can make a mefloquine attack worse. I walked in, cautious but hopeful. My friend told me nothing I would see could hurt me, that I wouldn't be shown anything I wasn't ready for. But he was wrong. We are not all the same in this three-dimensional world. Ketamine would reveal that to me.

It opened a door that had been shut since my deployment—a world of love this physical realm could never replicate.

March 24, 2022—My Birthday

I sat in the treatment chair, finally in a place where I could begin to accept my painful childhood. I found myself longing for my dad to let go of his past and try to build something with me. I thought of every birthday that had passed without him ever admitting he might have been part of the problem.

I placed the little white lozenge under my tongue and let it dissolve. Within minutes, a rush surged through my brain as I slid into the world of the ego-less. Everything began to dissolve.

Stars.

Light.

Fire.

Flames danced off high cliffs, glowing with impossible beauty.

And then Jesus appeared. He came to me with open arms, cradling me, and spoke with a gentle voice:

"Stop suffering. I am your father. You do not have to suffer anymore."

I was in awe. As I rocked back and forth in the chair, repeating his words aloud, the nurse walked into the room to check my vitals. I heard her start crying as I echoed Christ's voice into the space. Then, the wave took me again. I slid back into the ketamine trance as He carried me forward.

In recovery, I still carried the weight of not wanting to let people down. It was a small moment, but it reminded me how deeply I had been conditioned to push through, no matter what. This time, though, I let the body lead.

For the first time, I believed it. I did not have to suffer anymore.

Session Five: The Gallows Walk

The fifth ketamine session felt like being led to the gallows—an old prisoner, resigned but still afraid. As my therapist and I walked down the narrow hallway of the clinic, an unnerving sensation coiled through my body. I could not name it—dread or reverence. A trembling awareness that something irreversible was about to begin.

We said little. The silence between us throbbed louder than words.

I settled into the recliner, its softness at odds with the storm inside me. My heart raced—part fear, part nervous anticipation. What would I see this time? What would be shown to me?

I slipped the pill into my mouth, began to swish it around. It was bitter and metallic, like the taste of fate.

And then, slowly, I began to drift—driving off into the unknown, no map, no promises. Just me and whatever was waiting on the other side.

But it was not all stars and salvation.

Somewhere in that fifth session, the medicine dragged me into the pit—no angels, no voices, no light. Just black. Just stillness. Just me.

I lay there—dead-eyed, unmoving—trapped between lifetimes, my body frozen in the recliner while my soul sank through layers of grief I had not even known existed. No visions this time. No cosmic downloads. Only the truth: I had lived most of my life dissociated, dismembered from myself, following orders, playing roles, surviving rooms from which love had long since fled.

This was the night I met the weight I had always carried but never named.

It was not the war or the abuse that broke me in that moment; it was the realization that I had adapted to it all. I had shaped myself around betrayal. I had normalized absence, made silence a spiritual practice. I was not crying because I was healing. I was crying because the truth was unbearable.

They call it the dark night of the soul, but no one tells you how long the night can last. Or how loud the silence can become when you are finally forced to listen.

I begged for the session to end. I wanted to tap out, scream for help, escape the vortex. But the medicine does not rescue you—it holds you there until you remember that you are the one who walked into this fire, and only you can walk out.

When I finally appeared, breath shallow, tears crusted to my face, the stars were still above me. Still watching. Still waiting.

Something died that night. But something else was quietly reborn.

The World I Know

They said it would want to fall through yourself. They did not tell me it would want to come home.

Ketamine was not a high—it was a burial. Not of my body, but of the world I knew.

The world I knew wore a uniform. It saluted the flag and swallowed the lies. It buried friends and called it peacemaking. It kissed babies goodbye and came back a ghost.

That world ended in Panjwaii—in blood, dust, and silence.

I died in Afghanistan. But they did not send my body home in a box.

They sent me home walking, breathing, ыtill able to tie my boots and scream in my sleep.

Years later, I found myself in a padded chair, тestled beneath a weighted blanket. The clinic was quiet, sterile but kind. The nurse handed me a small white pill фnd a glass of water.

I swallowed it like a prayer. The room dimmed. Lo-fi played low. My body sank into the heavy warmth. My soul prepared for liftoff.

I left again—тot with a rifle this time,иBut with surrender.

Ketamine cracked open the floor of my being. Time stopped. Ego scattered like bone dust.

And in the stillness, I met the part of me that never left Eden.

Christ did not come with a crown; pe came barefoot, ыmelling like the old cedar swing in my grandmother's yard.

He did not speak. He just looked at me.

And I remembered.

The world I know now is not their world. It does not kneel to command. It does not shame my wounds.

It breathes, weeps, sings in tongues. It makes room for the fireflies and the dead.

What the Oath Didn't Cover

I did not come back healed.

The pill brought me back true. Sleep did not come easily that night. My mind was still sorting through everything that had been stirred up. But eventually, it came. I let myself rest. No judgment.

Thoughts of the war crept in. I did not want them, but they came anyway, quiet at first, then all-consuming. I woke in a panic at 5:00 a.m., heart pounding, body on high alert.

I could not stay in bed. I got up and did yoga, trying to move the fear through my limbs. Then, I went outside. Nature felt steady, unchanged. The air was cool, the world still. I stood in it for a while.

The fog in my mind slowly began to lift.

That day, I tried to be easy on myself. Moved slowly. Let the energy settle. That is something Reiki had taught me—healing does not always look like progress. Sometimes it looks like stillness. Like letting go of the need to push.

Just showing up for myself felt like enough.

The Shadow I Did Not See

When I signed on that dotted line and swore the oath, I thought I was just becoming a soldier. I did not realize I was also enlisting a lifetime companion—one that would not show up in my kit bag or orders but would follow me like a shadow long after the war ended.

There is a meme I saw once—funny in that tragic, too-real kind of way. It shows a kid labeled "Me Enlisting in the Military," standing in front of a wall, casting a shadow shaped like Darth Vader. Inside that looming silhouette were all the things no recruiter ever mentions: PTSD, anxiety, divorce, hearing loss, disc jelly gone, depression, clicking shoulders, crunchy knees, memory loss, sleep disorders. A goddamn medical release horror movie.

That shadow of mine got longer every year. At first, it was just the knees and the back. Then came the anger I could not explain. The silence that followed me home. The nights I could not sleep without a bottle, a pill, or a weapon nearby. The distance it all put between me and the people I loved, and sometimes people whom I barely knew but who tried to help.

You do not see it coming when you are that young, when you are full of fire and wanting to prove something—to your country, to your father, to the voices that told you that you would never be enough. You think you are walking into the light, but you do not realize that your shadow is growing behind you. And no matter how far you run from it, it stretches.

They handed me my discharge papers like a diploma. My last paycheque was really a receipt—for the cost of everything I left behind, and everything I would carry going forward.

Welcome Home

I was lying on the trampoline, the night sky open above me, just after completing my twelfth round of ketamine treatment. The Big Dipper watched overhead, and stars streaked silently across the darkness. A single tear slipped down my cheek. I was in awe of the beauty, and I was in mourning—grieving the loss of my soul for almost thirty-six years.

The last time I'd truly felt at home was with God—before this life—when I was chosen to come to this planet to help create a world of love and peace. Now, under the vastness of the sky, I made a wish on a shooting star. I was crying, not just from grief but from the overwhelming realization that the ketamine worked. It really worked.

I am one of the lucky ones. So many of my brothers and sisters never got this chance. Some are still suffering. Some never made it home at all.

But I did.

There is a divine plan at play—one that somehow saved me from the horrors of war. This is my second resurrection. The first happened in the burning sands of Kandahar, when all hope was lost. But this one is different. Calmer. Grounded. Not born of hate, but of love.

The Door Fear Guarded

"Where your fear is, there is your task."

—CARL JUNG

That was the lesson I did not know I was being taught—until I found myself lying on the trampoline under the Big Dipper, tears slipping down my face, ketamine still softening the edges of my mind.

Fear had ruled so much of my life. Fear of war. Fear of peace. Fear of being known, and, even more, fear of being forgotten. I had buried it beneath armour, beneath addiction, beneath duty. But in that quiet, weightless space, ketamine opened inside me, and the veil lifted just enough for truth to land.

It was not the war that broke me—it was everything I refused to face afterward. The screams I swallowed. The children I could not save. The man I became to survive it all.

Ketamine did not erase the fear. It illuminated it. It whispered:

"This way. Right here. The place that terrifies you? That's where the healing is." I thought healing would feel like floating. But it wanted to fall—into grief, into memory, into God.

And in that descent, I found the task. The one thing I had avoided my whole life: feeling it all.

Letting it move through me.

Letting it change me.

Because the only way out of fear was through the door it guarded.

And that night, under a sky that had watched me both live and die a thousand times over, I finally walked through.

CHAPTER 34

When the World Fell, So Did I

Summer 2021

Afghanistan was falling. The headlines collapsed into me like shrapnel. The world I had given my body and soul to was crumbling on live TV, while I sat on a couples trip in Prince Edward Island. Blue skies. Quiet beaches. Salt in the air. How do you enjoy a vacation when your soul is breaking?

At Richard's, a seaside shack known for fish and chips, the gulls screamed overhead and the vinegar stung my hands. I tried to smile, but my phone lit up with Kabul: families clinging to aircraft, children starving on sidewalks. The food turned to ash in my mouth. The salt hurt my lips, the gulls shrieked overhead, and still, all I could taste was dust. My body stayed at that picnic table. My mind was still in Panjwaii.

The Taliban's final offensive began May 1, 2021, eleven years to the day after I first stepped into that war. I didn't need the news to tell me. Once you have killed, once the ghosts of children have found you, they never leave.

And they never left me. Their faces still surface. Dust-caked. Lips cracked. Eyes too wide for childhood. Some ran to us for candy. Some out of sheer hope. Many never made it home. Their eyes follow me, asking a question I cannot answer: Why you, and not us?

That is survivor's guilt. Not just surviving firefights. Surviving *them*—the children. Carrying their silence. Carrying their absence. Carrying the truth: I failed them.

Later that week, at the Dunes, rain battered the glass while tourists bought trinkets. I watched a country disappear. Afghanistan was gone. So was everything I had given: my body, my mind, my soul.

Around me, people numbed themselves with food, wine, and laughter. No one wanted to talk to me. That had always been the pattern. I could hold everyone else's pain. Mine made people turn away.

When her mask slipped on that trip, I finally saw it. She had never truly understood me. And in her eyes, I saw not just her but my father. The same cold refusal. The same hunger. It was not just a partner I lost that week. It was the illusion that I was finally free of the cycle.

Months later, I tried to outrun it. Six triathlons. Swim. Bike. Run. Again and again, as if I could outpace the screams in my sleep. They call it *moral injury*, but that phrase is too small. It was helplessness. Rage. The cries of children still rattling through my dreams.

As Afghanistan fell, so did I. Into the silence of children I could not save.

Court Papers and Broken Promises

We had an order.

Signed, stamped, filed.

Clear as day: I was to have time with my daughters—Tuesdays after school, every other weekend, half the holidays. It was not much, but it was something. A fragile lifeline in a sea of chaos.

She agreed to it in court.

Nodded to the judge like it meant something.

But the moment the ink dried, the games began.

Tuesday came—no kids.

No explanation.

I texted: "Are you on your way?"

No reply.

I called.

Straight to voicemail.

The next day, I asked what happened.

She said, "They didn't want to go. You should respect that."

I reminded her we had a court order.

She said, "You think a piece of paper means more than their feelings?"

That is when I realized: she never planned to follow it.

To her, the order was a performance. A box to check to avoid consequences she never believed she would face.

And she was right.

I filed police reports.

Documented every denial.

Tried to get enforcement.

They shrugged.

"It's a family matter."

"Try to work it out with her."

"The courts don't like punishing moms."

Each time she broke the agreement, it chipped away at my daughters' trust in me—not because I failed them, but because I was not allowed to show up.

She told them, "He didn't try hard enough."

Told the courts I was unstable, angry, unfit.

Weaponized my trauma like proof.

She would show up to court calm and composed.

I would be shaking with paperwork in my hand, sleep-deprived, emotionally gutted, begging someone to enforce the only thing that said I mattered.

But the system does not enforce parenting orders the way it enforces child support.

You can get jailed for owing money. But not for withholding children.

And that is the quiet violence no one talks about. No bruises. No blood. Just missed birthdays, unanswered calls, and the slow erasure of a father from his children's lives.

But I never stopped showing up.

Even when it broke me.

Even when the only thing I could do was keep my name—their name—on my heart and keep fighting to be part of their story.

Because no matter how many court orders she broke, I kept my promise.

I never left them.

Even when I was not allowed to be nearby.

2022: The Part That Still Bleeds

That summer, we planned a trip to Newfoundland and Labrador. I was excited and nervous, like a boy again. I hadn't seen my grandmother in twenty years, and my inner child was eager to reconnect with her.

But something inside still haunted me. A ghost. A father I would never be good enough for. I kept imagining what I would do if he showed up, if he tried to hug me.

Would I push him away? Or would I hold him tight, just once, and try to rewrite the past?

When we arrived, my grandmother greeted us at the door. She was smaller than I remembered, but her eyes lit up the same way they had when I was a boy. We sat around her table, crowded and warm, the smell of salt meat and boiled vegetables filling the air—a Newfoundland dinner, simple but rich, the kind that spoke more than words ever could.

My kids laughed with my sisters they had never met, their voices rising above the clatter of forks and plates.

Later, we took pictures, four generations pressed together in the frame, smiles wide, shoulders touching. For a moment, it felt like the past and present had stitched themselves into something whole.

But the deeper hours came in the basement apartment, just my grandmother and me. The laughter upstairs faded into silence while she spoke of old wounds. She told me how my grandfather had suffered in his final days, his body failing but his mind still clutching the ghosts of his own past.

Sitting there, I saw it clearly: the trauma that stretched back generations, passed down like an heirloom no one wanted but everyone carried.

At one point, she tried to give me all her photographs. She was afraid that when she died, my stepmother would take them and throw them away. I refused, not wanting to be pulled into the middle of the family drama. Still, her fear stayed with me, another weight layered onto the grief that already lived in that basement.

Later that week, we packed up the car. I hugged her tight at the door, holding on longer than usual. I knew, deep down, it would be the last time I saw her in this world—the kind of goodbye that lingers in your chest long after the moment has passed.

On the drive home, the kids slept in the back seat, their soft breathing like waves against the quiet hum of the highway. Outside, fog rolled in from the Atlantic, wrapping the cliffs and villages in a grey hush. I thought about how the nervous system cannot tell repair from repetition until it is taught otherwise—how it keeps circling back, confusing familiarity with love, chaos with intimacy, survival with connection.

For years, I had mistaken that pull toward the past for love, believing that if I just explained myself enough, forgave enough, endured enough, I might finally earn safety. But what I was really chasing was the child in me, the one who still waited by the emotional doorway, hoping someone might return with gentleness, recognition, or apology.

The truth is, safety is not found in returning to the wound.

It is found in tending to the part of you that still bleeds,

in becoming the adult who can finally offer that child what no one else could: tenderness, validation, calm.

As the road unwound through the fog, I let the ache stay where it was, inside my chest—not as something to fix, but as something to hold. For the first time, that felt like enough.

The Ones We Lose at Home

In late summer 2022, I lost a friend. Tyson killed himself. He wasn't just another soldier; he was a strong advocate for veterans, the kind of man no one believed would go that way. His death cracked something in me, and the shock tore through every layer of my life.

At his funeral, another veteran told me about a retreat called Dimensions, a cannabis-friendly psychedelic space for healing. I brushed it off. I had already tried ketamine therapy, also at his suggestion, and while it had opened me up, it had also left me scraping the bottom. My home was in pieces, my relationships lay in ruins, and my sense of self was barely intact.

I didn't see it at the time, but something had already been set in motion. The word *trauma*, and later the term *generational trauma*, did not fully land until the summer of 2023. By then, the cracks were too wide to ignore.

Some of us are born sensitive. We feel what others cannot. Even as children, we know when something is wrong, even if no one dares to name it. That sensitivity had always been my curse and my compass, and now it was dragging me deeper into truths I could no longer outrun.

The toll of PTSD showed up in ways that stripped me of control. There were mornings when I could barely stand before I was doubled over at the toilet, my body purging the weight of everything that had come undone. For months, it was how every day began.

Because We Already Bury Too Many

I walked into Princess Auto that day for something simple. Rope. Nothing more.

The place smelled of rubber and motor oil. Fluorescent lights hummed overhead. Ordinary. Too ordinary for the weight I carried. Just weeks earlier, I had buried a friend, a good man, a soldier who held the line overseas and cracked in silence back home. I was still numb, carrying that raw, metallic grief in my chest.

Near the back, I asked a group of employees where the rope section was. One of them, older, grey around the edges, turned to me with a smirk.

"You just need enough to hang yourself, or what?"

His words hit clean and fast. Like a sniper round through the soul.

I didn't answer. Just stood there.

He didn't know I had just buried a friend. He didn't know that, for some of us, a rope is never just a rope. It is a grave marker. A scream no one heard in time.

That kind of comment isn't edgy. It's ignorant. Dangerous.

What haunted me later wasn't only the words, but how easily he had spoken them. As if suicide was a punchline. As if we don't already bury too many. As if silence isn't already killing us.

I walked to aisle twelve and found the rope myself.

Because some battles aren't fought with fists or rifles. Some are fought in silence, with nothing but breath. One inhalation at a time. One more day without letting the rope win.

CHAPTER 35

Proof at Last

Winter 2023

An ear, nose, and throat specialist finally named what my body had carried for years: traumatic brain injury. Post-concussion syndrome. The assessment traced the shadows I knew too well—losing balance when the world tilted, shrinking from sounds that cut like knives, living in the fog that stole my focus and my time like pages torn out before I could read them.

To hear it named was a strange kind of justice. Proof, after years of dismissal. For so long, my symptoms were written off as exaggeration or weakness. Now, there was evidence. Relief washed through me, but so did grief. This was not just a phase I could "push through." It was an injury, a scar carved into my nervous system.

The diagnosis became more than a medical file. It was recognition. It was legitimacy. It gave me a place to begin again: with treatment, with recovery planning, with the hope that I could meet myself with compassion instead of doubt. The diagnosis did not end the struggle, but it ended the gaslighting. And that was enough to begin.

Traumatic Brain Injury (TBI) History—David Wiseman

Military Training and Service-Related Incidents (2007–2010)

1. Obstacle Course Fall—Quebec, 2007

While undergoing infantry qualification in Quebec, I fell during an obstacle course. The fall was significant but went unreported at the time.

2. Repeated Exposure to Blast Waves—84mm Carl Gustaf Rocket Launcher

During infantry training in 2007, I was exposed to repeated blast waves while firing approximately ten rounds from the 84mm rocket launcher. Later, while deployed in Afghanistan, I fired approximately twelve additional 84mm rounds, along with other anti-tank munitions, in a single day—a level of exposure far exceeding recommended safety limits for cumulative blast impact on brain function.

3. Close Quarters Combat (CQC) Training—Knockout and High-Impact Tosses

During "Hell Week" leading up to graduation from infantry training, I lost consciousness briefly after a blow sustained in CQC drills. These exercises involved being thrown over the heads of other trainees, resulting in multiple high-impact landings on my back and head.

4. Blindfolded and Masked Stress Drills

I took part in training that included sensory deprivation (blindfolds and masks), a form of stress inoculation training that can heighten disorientation and post-concussive symptoms, especially when layered onto earlier injuries.

5. Load-Bearing Fall—Final Defensive Exercise

During a fighting withdrawal scenario in my final defensive exercise before graduation, I tripped and flipped forward, landing in a gully filled with water. I was carrying a full rucksack, a C9 light machine gun, and a pickaxe. I did not report the injury due to fear of disciplinary action or being recycled on course.

6. LAV Crash—Gagetown Training Area

I crashed a light armoured vehicle in the training area while driving at approximately 50 kph. Visibility was severely reduced due to dust, and the vehicle ended up in a ditch. I experienced a violent jolt and potential whiplash, though it was not formally reported or treated.

7. Whiplash Incident—Fort Irwin, California (Pre-Deployment Training)

While in the turret of a G-wagon en route to a range, our vehicle crested a berm, and the driver braked hard. My head and torso were thrown forward, then snapped backward, striking the turret ring. I experienced dizziness, acute back pain, and limited mobility the next day. This incident was recorded via a CF98 injury report, but I returned to training prematurely, ignoring the severity of the symptoms.

8. RG-31 Jolt—Afghanistan

While responding to a high-value target, I was driving an RG-31 when I hit a wall or obstacle. My head struck the windshield on impact and then rebounded sharply against the seat's headrest. This incident contributed to cumulative concussive symptoms and neck strain.

9. MLVW Rollover—Sniper Course

While serving as staff on a sniper course, I was a rear passenger in an MLVW returning from the range. The corporal who was driving did not notice a hole in the road, and the vehicle flipped. I was asleep in the back, inhaling diesel fumes, when the vehicle went airborne. I was thrown inside the compartment as gear and unsecured equipment flew violently through the air. The incident was jarring but went unreported due to the prevailing "soldier on" mentality.

LAV 25mm gunner

Gunning the 25mm (M242/Bushmaster) from an LAV/LAV-25 exposes the gunner to several biomechanical risks that can cause concussion / subconcussive brain injury and longer-term neurological effects. The likely mechanisms are *blast/overpressure, repetitive low-level blast, military occupational blast/ acoustic pressure,* and *high impulse vibration/acceleration* from firing and vehicle movement—all of which are being investigated as causes of persistent cognitive, vestibular, and autonomic symptoms in veterans.

Cumulative Observations

These events reflect multiple exposures to blunt-force trauma, blast overpressure, whiplash, and physical concussions—many of which went untreated. Symptoms include, but are not limited to:

- Chronic headaches
- Neck and back pain
- Cognitive fog or memory lapses
- Sleep disturbances
- Emotional dysregulation
- Sensory hypersensitivities
- Vestibular issues (dizziness, disorientation)

This history sets up a clear pattern of mild to moderate traumatic brain injuries, compounded by repeated exposures in both training and combat environments.

ISSUES Ver 2.4 FEB 2018	MEF	PTSD	TBI
ANGER	X	X	X
DEPRESSION	X	X	X
ANXIETY	X	X	X
UNUSUAL BEHAVIOR	X	X	X
MOOD CHANGES	X	X	X
SLEEP PROBLEMS	X	X	X
CONCENTRATION	X	X	X
CONFUSION	X	X	X
IMPULSIVENESS	X	X	X
PERSONALITY CHANGE	X	X	
AGITATION	X	X	
NIGHTMARES	X	X	
FEAR OF CROWDS	X	X	
PARANOIA	X	X	
RESTLESSNESS	X	X	
SUICIDE IDEATION	X	X	
HYPER ALERTNESS	X	X	
BOWEL DISORDER	X		
FLASHBACKS		X	
UNABLE TO MULTI-TASK	X		X
MEMORY LOSS	X		X
LIGHT SENSITIVITY	X		X
DIZZINESS	X		X
NAUSEA	X		X
HEADACHES	X		X
VERTIGO/BALANCE	X		X
SPEECH (APHASIA)	X		X
RINGING IN EARS	X		X
VISUAL IMPAIRMENT	X		X
PERSISTENT COUGH	X		
TREMORS / JOLTS	X		
SKIN RASH	X		
TROUBLE SWALLOWING	X		
MUSCLE WEAKNESS	X		
IRREGULAR HEARTBEAT	X		
Count:	34	18	19

The symptom checklist prepared for me by the mefloquine toxicity specialist as part of my formal diagnosis of traumatic brain injury.

Part 4

Healing

CHAPTER 36

Trauma and Transformation

The Field Beyond the Fire

It was July 2023. I'd just driven twenty-four hours straight from Newfoundland, my car packed with what was left of a broken life. My girlfriend's father had kicked me out because he didn't understand the effects of TBI, and for the first time in years, I had nowhere to go but inward.

A veteran friend had told me about a wellness retreat in Ontario. Something in me said yes before my mind could argue. I even canceled my therapy appointment—something I never did. This felt different. Sacred. For once, I chose myself. Not duty. Not survival. Just honesty. Healing, at last, was becoming a priority.

The retreat sat nestled deep in the Algonquin Highlands. Pine-scented air drifted across the lake. Wooden cabins lined the forest path, smoke curling from their chimneys in the cool mornings. At night, crickets sang against the crackle of fire pits. It was a place designed for stillness. Yet, inside me, alarms still rang. My body, wired from years of vigilance, braced for impact with every sound.

Massages left my shoulders rigid. Somatic sessions dragged out memories I had thought were buried. Still, a shift began. For once, my body wasn't braced for the blast. Warm water held me. Clean food fortified me.

This is what calm felt like.

By day six, the tears came—not because I was broken, but because my nervous system, after years of war and survival, had finally come home.

The retreat unfolded into something I had not thought possible: three sacred ceremonies woven with drumming, firelight, and the scent of sage. Each ceremony peeled back another layer, leaving me raw—not exposed, but held, finally, in dignity instead of pushed through systems. Forty-two aftercare sessions waited on the other side, proof that this was not a quick fix but a path.

Then, a vision unfolded. Traumas of war rose, not as pain but as memories asking to be seen. My friends—so many who had not made it, or who had lost their battles with PTSD—surrounded me in glowing light.

We hovered together above a green field in Panjwaii. Below stood my younger self, battle-worn and fractured. With us were the 158 Canadian soldiers who paid the ultimate sacrifice. I could feel them, not just as memories, but as presence.

There was no fear. Only solemn knowing. A great honouring.

I wept, out of not sorrow but reverence. For them. For myself. For all we carried and all we lost.

A younger me crouched in the dust, sweat-soaked and wide-eyed. Dust rose. Bullets snapped overhead. He looked at me and screamed:

"Don't let them forget us!"

He turned his head once more, eyes pleading, then faced forward. Dust thickened, choking the air. The world slowed to a single breath. He pulled the trigger. The rifle kicked. A Taliban commander fell. My younger self vanished into smoke, leaving me with the dead and the living alike, knowing not all of me had come home.

Years after my release, I'd sat shaking in a crowded coffee shop with another veteran. He looked at me steadily and said, "That version of you died over there."

At the time, I wanted to argue. That soldier was all I had left to lean on. I clung to him, protector and survivor, for thirteen years.

255

But during the retreat in 2023, I finally understood. That version of me had died in Afghanistan. I had been dragging his ghost behind me ever since.

What I came to know was this: The protector I thought I lost had never left. He was not buried in a war zone. He was always within me— quiet, steady, waiting to be remembered.

The protector was never buried in Panjwaii. He had been here all along. Not in my rifle. Not in my uniform. But in the breath, the stillness, the strength to heal. In the choice to live, without apology.

The Familiar Flame of Cortisol Love

I was only just reading their texts when they started screaming over me.

Interrupting. Accusing.

Each time I opened my mouth, they cut me off: Stop. Stop. Stop.

I begged them for mercy, the same way I had begged as a child.

But my voice, soaked in decades of pain, came out sharp.

I sounded just like my parents. Rage. Indifference. The inability to see me.

The more I asked them to stop, the more they escalated. Louder, frantic, invasive.

They weren't hearing me. They were defending their egos, not their hearts.

And I was furious, my nervous system hijacked by mefloquine, trapped in a feedback loop of panic and poison.

The air was thick.

Electric.

Like war.

My chest buzzed, ears ringing as if mortars had landed inside me.

In that storm, I remembered something from the Dimensions aftercare program.

They had a name for this.

Cortisol love.

The kind of love that does not soothe but sears.

The only love I had ever known.

Dismissive. Reactive. Contemptuous.

Adults who never learned to regulate their pain, so they flung it at others and called it love.

And I kept returning, tormenting my soul.

Hoping someone would stay calm.

Hoping someone would listen.

But it always ended the same.

Gaslight.

Twist.

Collapse.

Rewrite.

Then the tears, not from remorse, but from adrenaline.

Then the manipulation. The soft voice, the collapse, the rewrite of the story.

And once again, I became the villain for crying out in pain,

for naming the pattern that had been killing me from the inside out.

This is what it feels like when narcissists win. Not because they are strong, but because I still care. Because I still try to soothe them even as I drown. Because some part of me still believes I am unworthy of love that does not hurt.

I had just turned forty.

A lifetime of cycles behind me.

And for the first time, I knew I could choose differently.

Why Do We Raise Our Voices?

A TBI Reflection on Love, Loss, and the Echoes of War

I sat still as the dust began to settle. Another relationship circling the drain. Just months before, we had been planning to travel to Europe in the fall of 2023.

Looking back, I realized I had known long before. The previous summer, something in me had registered it: We were no longer on the same frequency. What once felt like harmony now sounded like two radios tuned to different stations.

Her PTSD, sharpened by the pressures of hospital work, was flaring. I, meanwhile, had just come out of twenty-two sessions of ketamine therapy. Stripped bare. Layer after layer of trauma exposed. And beneath it all, a quieter, more stubborn wound: a brain that no longer worked the way it used to.

The TBI was yet undiagnosed. But undeniable.

Time had become slippery. Words tangled. Patience vanished before I knew it was needed. My nervous system lived in overdrive. And when I raised my voice, it was rarely out of anger. It was the absence of a brake pedal. No filter. No regulation. Just raw signal.

The grief of losing my kids the year before still hung in the air. I was dissociating, trying to function in a system with no map for men like me. And now my partner was spiraling into her own ghosts. Burnout. Rage. Trauma resurfacing.

One night, searching for answers, I stumbled on a video about why people raise their voices when love begins to die.

Clarity hit.

In couples counselling, we had been given material on John Gottman's "Four Horsemen of Relationships": criticism, contempt, defensiveness, and stonewalling. Watching the video, I saw our cycle clearly for the first time.

I also saw the truth. She had not loved me for a long time. For me, love had died in the winter of 2022, the day she labeled our fights "reactive abuse"—a phrase she had picked up from TikTok or the hospital.

At first, I resisted. Then, I realized I recognized Gottman's four horsemen. I had been living with them for years. I just hadn't known their names. And the recognition terrified me more than war ever had.

Because I knew that feeling.

It was the same as being a child again. Wanting comfort but fearing punishment. It was coming home from deployment, only to become the emotional punching bag of a partner who could not hold her own pain. It was guilt. Shame. The desperate scramble to fix everything before I was destroyed.

One memory stays vivid. Just after Afghanistan. Sitting on the couch while my kids' mom raged at me from the kitchen. Our military neighbour leaned through the window, cigarette in hand, chatting like nothing was wrong. I mouthed, *Not a good time.*

We laughed. But it was not funny. It was survival.

By the end of the day, the kids' mom and I were not speaking. I was cleaning, apologizing, trying to repair what I could not even name.

That is what TBI does. It scrambles memory. Erases filters. Makes boundaries impossible. Loving through TBI feels like staring through a cracked windshield. Everything distorted. Every emotion either too fast or too slow.

In this state, you do not raise your voice to dominate.

You raise it because you are drowning.

And when two people are drowning, one in PTSD, the other in a broken brain, every word can turn into a landmine.

Now, I look back not with hatred but with grief. Because the man I am today is still that boy. Still that soldier. Still that father. Searching for safety in a world that does not know what to do with tenderness, brain damage, or the quiet need for peace.

We raise our voices not out of cruelty, but out of desperation.

It is the last sound our soul makes when everything has become too much.

The Sound of Christ Consciousness

There are no words that can fully describe what happens when Christ breaks through—when the veil lifts, even for a breath, and you are held outside of time.

I have touched it, between bullets and breathwork, ketamine and collapse. Christ, not as dogma, not as the stained-glass Jesus they taught us to kneel before, but as Consciousness. Pure, unwavering Love. In those moments, language fails.

But sound remains.

One night, after another fight with my partner, her rage sharp as shrapnel, I felt like a ghost in my own home. My body shook, my nervous system fried, tears caught in my throat. Even grief was not allowed to move freely.

So, I waited until she slept.

Outside, the night air bit through my coat. Stars burned cold above me. I lay on the frozen ground and let the quiet wash over me.

And I wept.

Not only for war, or children I missed, or the friends I had buried. I wept for the part of me always blamed for breaking. For the man who carried so much and was still called weak. For the soul that had forgotten the feeling of safety.

The tears came in waves. I did not hold them back. The Divine held what no human could. Presence itself became Christ within me—not judging, not fixing, only seeing. Whispering:

You do not have to earn love by being strong.

You do not have to stay to prove your worth.

You can leave. You can heal.

That night, I began to believe. Not because life around me changed, but because something deeper remembered the truth: I was not created to suffer, to shrink, or to stay small for anyone's comfort.

The silence became a bridge between trauma and transcendence, between a battered body and a soul still willing to sing. A sacred echo of Christ Consciousness reminding me that even in captivity, even in grief, all is well.

And when the night finally stilled, the silence itself kept singing.

Revaluation 2023

"He who looks at himself, risks to meet himself. The mirror does not flatter, it shows accurately what is reflected in it—namely, that face we never show the world because we hide it with the persona, the mask of the actor. This is the first test of courage on the inner path, a test which is enough to frighten most people, because the encounter with oneself belongs to those unpleasant things one avoids as long as one can project the negative onto the environment."

—CARL JUNG

At the center of my soul, the mirror showed me how far I had drifted.

The little boy who once loved Legos, Teenage Mutant Ninja Turtles, swimming for hours, biking until dusk . . . He was gone.

What remained was a mask, crafted to appease, to endure, to survive in a world that taught me being myse lf was never safe.

Homecoming—Germany, 2023

"Ave Maria" rose in my mind like an echo I could not shake until I realized it was playing through my headphones.

The air was still, cool, clean, almost sacred. Germany did not feel foreign. It felt etched into me, as if my blood had been waiting to return. My boots struck the stone streets of the city's old quarter, each step reverberating against the quiet facades. Somewhere distant, a bell tolled.

The first notes of the hymn stopped me. Not for the song itself, but for what it stirred: grief, reverence, remembrance. My soul stood at attention.

I slowed. Let it in.

For years, I had been moving—through war, addiction, broken love, and the numbness of survival. But here, on this soil, something shifted. It was as if the land remembered me, even when I had forgotten myself.

Ave Maria, gratia plena . . .

An old church appeared ahead, doors shut, presence undeniable. I paused at the steps, closed my eyes, and let the weight rise: the children I missed, the brothers I'd buried, the pieces of myself left scattered across deserts and silence.

Tears came. Tears not of weakness, but of recognition.

I was no longer a soldier. No longer someone's broken project. Just a man on ancestral ground, letting the pain speak and grace rise.

The hymn carried me like absolution. No choir. No priest. Only a man, a memory, and a melody whispering through the air:

You are still here.
And that is enough.

The Caretaker's Curse

As we left the Moulin Rouge, my senses were fried: champagne corks popping, lights strobing, music clashing with clinking glasses. Even with earplugs, I could not protect myself here. Not in this city. Not in that place.

We stepped into the neon-lit Parisian night.

She screamed.

Louder.

Unrelenting.

"*You're crazy!*"

People stared as they passed. I begged her to stop. For anyone, the situation would have been hard. For me, with a brain injury, PTSD, and years of struggling to hold myself together, it was unbearable.

Sometimes she used to offer hugs afterward. Lately, she had not been. The woman I had met in that quiet basement apartment, the one who understood my breath patterns before I did, was gone.

She ran from me now.

When I tried to speak, all I got was correction. Instruction. Not support. Veterans Affairs pays her to be my caregiver.

A book I read at Dimensions, recommended by the counsellor there, named it: codependency. I cannot unsee that now.

I told her I needed a caregiver, not a caretaker. She looked at me like I was speaking German again, like the boy who lost his mother tongue to a father's shame.

My agency had vanished years ago. Every time I asked for help, she told me what I needed instead. Her job came home, and I became her patient.

"Take an Ativan," she screamed.

"*You're crazy—take the pill!*" Her voice split the room open.

I was on the floor, shaking, convulsing, clinging to a pillow like it was the last safe thing in the world. Freezing water hit me, shocking my chest, stealing my breath. It felt like punishment.

I waited. For the internal storm to pass. For her voice to fade. For the world to settle.

Back at the Airbnb, we fucked like animals. Pleasure masking pain.
Pleasure, avoiding truth.

She said it was just me, that I was the one addicted.

In my marriage, my kids' mom sought pleasure the same way.
Then shamed me for it. Told me the only way I knew how to love was
with my body.

I thought I had broken in Paris. Instead, I broke open.

Return to Innocence

The first layer was noise—rage, orders, radios—the war still echoing.

The second was memory: her face as I walked away, the crater in the
road that never left me.

The third was silence, the kind that hums.

Then came more—the betrayal in her scream, the birth of my daugh-
ters, the forgetting of who I was.
Time unspooled. Names vanished. Medals meant nothing.
And then I heard it —

a drum,
a chant,
a voice I had always known.

It spoke without words,
calling me back through the noise,
back to the beginning.

And in that place, I remembered: I was a boy once.
Before the walls.
Before the rifles.
Before I learned to kill what I loved.

264

That boy still lived.

In a field of fireflies.
In the wind on his face.
In the belly laugh of his daughter.

I did not rise from trauma.
I dropped beneath it.

And found
Not a warrior,
Not a veteran,
But a soul unarmoured.

A return.
To innocence,
To the boy who still waits.

CHAPTER 37

2024: Being Awake During Surgery

Veteran Peer Support Certification: A Full-Circle Moment

The certificate arrived in the mail on a cold morning. Frost clung to the window. The kettle whistled in the kitchen. I stood there with the envelope in my hands, holding it longer than I needed to, fingers running over the raised seal. It was only paper, but it carried years of weight.

I thought back to the nights when I could barely hold myself together. Survival back then meant white-knuckling through flashbacks, drinking too much coffee just to stay awake, or sitting in silence because words were impossible. The idea of helping anyone else felt out of reach. War, trauma, and moral injury had stripped me of more than I could name.

And yet here I was, a certified Veteran Peer Supporter through the Mood Disorders Society of Canada. The scars I had once tried to hide had become proof of experience—a kind of credential no classroom can provide.

The course gave me skills and language, but the heart of it was simpler: Presence. Learning to sit with another veteran in their storm without trying to fix them, without flinching from the chaos. Just being there. I realized compassion is its own kind of weapon—one that protects instead of harms.

When I slid the certificate back into its envelope, I noticed the circle in the design. It stopped me. Full circle. The boy who went to war. The man who almost didn't make it home. And now, someone who could stand with others in their darkest nights.

It did not feel like an ending. It felt like a beginning. Like the first ripple of a stone dropped into water, spreading outward long after the hand is gone.

A Hand Against the Glass

On Friday, January 19, 2024, I drove to the school to pick up the kids. No one came.

That afternoon, I sent the girls' mother an email: I would be by at ten the next morning.

Her reply came sharp and fast. If I showed up, she would call the RCMP. Do not knock, she wrote. Her fiancé would be the one to answer. The words carried no room for doubt: cold, aggressive, threatening.

Still, I went.

I parked in the driveway and stayed in the car. The steering wheel felt icy beneath my palms. My breath fogged the glass. I did not move. Did not touch the door handle. Just sat. Waiting. Hoping.

Through the window, I saw him. He raised his middle finger. I stayed calm. Did not react.

Then he came charging out of the house, boots slamming against gravel, fists tight. He lunged for the doors, yanking at the handles, pounding the side panel. My stomach knotted. My palms were slick against the phone. My heart hammered in the sealed silence of the car.

"Coward!" he screamed. "No one will believe you!"

I hit record, hands shaking, knowing he wanted a fight.

When he stepped back, he roared for me to get off the property. I left. A few blocks away, I called the RCMP. Filed the report.

By that evening, two more emails arrived from the girls' mother. They were putting up "No Trespassing" signs. If I came again, they would press charges. The subtext was clear: stay away or else.

But Sunday was my visitation day. I tried again.

This time, I parked on the public road, far from their house. His truck blocked the driveway like a barricade. I stayed put, doors locked, engine running. He came out again, phone in hand, snapping pictures of my license plate, shouting that I was trespassing, though I had not crossed the line.

I waited. Ten minutes. Fifteen.

Then, just before I pulled away, I saw our youngest. Standing at the bedroom window. She lifted her hand and waved.

That wave shattered me.

This time, no one came to the door. But she came to the window. And that was enough to break me.

Home Was Not Safe, Either

Although I was to heal on many levels, the effects of the mefloquine continued to rear its ugly head at times. It always began with something small: a drawer left open, a meal refused, a tone that cut sharper than it should have. To anyone else, it looked like an argument. To me, it was a battlefield. My pulse spiked. Vision tunneled. Fists clenched on their own. Something ancient and chemical surged through me like a trip wire snapping.

Then, the taste of copper. My cheek torn open again. A self-contained detonation. Rage turned inward until it leaked out. I swallowed hard against the metallic warning in my throat.

She called it emotional abuse. I called it survival. But the truth blurred. Her silence felt like a threat. Her defiance, an ambush. My body reacted as if I was still in Panjwaii, watching the tree lines for RPGs, scanning the ditches for bombs under trash bags. I tried to breathe, to regulate, but the drug was already in motion. Mefloquine rage was not a mood; it was possession. I could see myself from the outside: voice too loud, body too close, some part of me begging to stop, but the override switch was gone.

And then came the crash. The porch at night. Boards creaked beneath my boots as if they might splinter under the weight of me. Weed smoke hung heavy in the cold air. My hands shook, shame crawling up my spine. Inside, I could hear the click of the bathroom lock, the muffled sound of her crying on the other side of the door. I wanted to die. Wanted to be held. Wanted her to know it was not me, not really. That I had been poisoned by a country that needed bodies for its wars and did not care what happened after. But how could she believe me? She never saw the blister packs. Only the rage. The torn books. The holes in the drywall. The man she no longer recognized.

They told me I was dangerous. That I needed help. But they were the ones who had given me the pills. They put the rot in my brain and then punished me for the stench.

No one warned us the war would follow us home. Not just in nightmares or medals. But in the bloodstream itself.

The Small Margin

The morning starts heavy.

My head throbs. My hip aches. Even my teeth hurt. I take my meds with lukewarm water and sit for a while, waiting for the fog to lift. It doesn't. Later, I have a haircut, and I feel more anxious about it than I should. I've learned to stop judging that. Anxiety doesn't care how small the task is.

By afternoon, I'm driving toward Oromocto for my appointment with a new therapist. The air feels dense, like rain is thinking about falling. We're trying two treatments today: fear reconsolidation therapy and a vagus nerve stimulator. I got her card from an acquaintance I met in a Facebook group for veterans. I don't know what to expect, only that I'm tired of living like this. I want my nervous system to know what peace feels like again.

Lately, even the smallest things cut deep. The other day, I told a friend that I was hurt. His flakiness had been wearing me down. I don't like it when someone says one thing, then throws mental health labels at me when I speak my truth. They insist it isn't rejection, but my body says otherwise.

When I came home from that appointment, hoping for repair after the previous night's cycle of emotional abuse, the same patterns played out again. A month later, nothing had changed. The body remembers even what the mind tries to excuse.

I'm tired of being gaslit by people who think they're helping.

Recently, I began using a device called Vagustim. It clips gently against the skin and sends tiny pulses meant to activate the vagus nerve, the body's quiet invitation toward safety. The effects are subtle: a softening in my shoulders, breath that moves a little deeper, a faint sense of spaciousness returning to my chest.

It's not a cure. But it creates a margin, a breath between stimulus and reaction. For someone living with the aftermath of trauma and brain injury, that margin isn't small at all.

It's the beginning of peace.

CHAPTER 38

The Poison Is Named

April 15, 2025

I had my neuropsychology appointment this morning. It has become my mission to be the first veteran to force Veterans Affairs to officially recognize mefloquine poisoning.

They have started sending guys to Crux Psychology in Halifax for their assessments. I had mine today. What an incredible clinic.

After years of questions no one could answer, years of being told it was PTSD, depression, anxiety, childhood trauma, a neuropsychologist looked me in the eye and confirmed what I had always known in my bones:

Toxic brain injury.

From mefloquine. From other poisons I was fed in uniform.

Not imagined. Not exaggerated. Not weakness.

Injury. Inflicted.

All of it finally had a name: the memory lapses, the rages, the confusion, the crushing fatigue, the spinning compass inside my skull. The dissociation. The smell triggers. The unbearable sound sensitivity. The light that hurt. The panic in a grocery store. The blank stare in a conversation. The night terrors. The suicidal thoughts. The overreactions. The under-reactions. The shame.

Now they all had a source. A reason.

The moment the words left her mouth, my whole nervous system shifted, just slightly. Like an invisible weight lifting. Like a ghost that had haunted me for years finally stepping into the light.

This was not just psychological. This was chemical. Neurological. Medical. Military.

And in truth, I had known all along.

I knew when the pills made me feel strange.

I knew when the lights turned too bright.

I knew when I started forgetting names, when my soul began to fracture.

I knew when my reactions felt foreign, like they did not even belong to me anymore.

Now it is confirmed. The military gave me poison. And I have been living in its aftermath ever since.

There is grief in this moment.

Grief for the years lost chasing my tail in therapy.

Grief for the damage to my kids, my relationships, and my spirit.

Grief for every time I was blamed, for being "too much," "too angry," "too broken."

But alongside the grief, there is truth. And with truth comes freedom.

I finally have my answer.

Now I can write the next chapter with rage, with love, with fire in my bones.

The war did not end in Panjwaii. It followed me home. But now I know its name.

And knowing its name means it does not get to win.

The Day the Medal Came

The day the Sacrifice Medal arrived in the mail, I stared at the envelope for a long time before opening it. No ceremony. No phone call. No knock on the door. Just a quiet bureaucratic gesture slipped into the mailbox—an official acknowledgment that something had been taken from me, something I would never fully get back.

Inside was a letter stamped with my service number and name, saying in formal tones:

I am pleased to inform you, the enclosed Sacrifice Medal is awarded to you under the authority of Her Excellency the Governor General and Commander-in-Chief of Canada on behalf of His Majesty the King, in recognition of wounds you sustained during your deployment to Afghanistan in 2010.

I read it, but it felt distant—like reading a stranger's obituary. It was not just the neck pain, the tinnitus, or the cognitive fog that still hovered like smoke after a blast. It was something deeper. A spiritual rupture. The war had torn something loose in me. Left me raw and drifting, staring at my own reflection and not recognizing the man looking back.

That medal, etched with the silver maple leaf and forged in royal intent, was supposed to honour my wounds. But how do you pin a broken nervous system to your chest? How do you decorate a brain altered by blast waves and mefloquine? How do you translate moral injury—the soul-level ache of doing what was asked, even when it shattered your sense of self—into a piece of military metal?

I tucked it away in a drawer that day, unsure if it was a badge of honour or a quiet apology.

The letter tried to make it noble:

The Sacrifice Medal [...] may be awarded posthumously to those who die as a result of military service.

I thought of friends who never made it back. And others who did, only to die slowly—by silence, by bottle, by rope. I was still breathing, but some days that felt more like punishment than mercy.

I see the medal differently. Not as absolution. Not as closure. But as an echo—proof that what happened was real, even if the system never truly saw it. Even if most people around me still do not.

It is a symbol that says, "We see you." Even if that vision came too late.

Never Pass a Fault—The Way of the Cross

In war, "Never pass a fault" meant survival. A frayed strap, a loose bolt, an untied lace, anything ignored could cost a life—yours or someone else's. We were trained to correct, to notice, to act. That motto shaped me. It made me vigilant. It made me sharp.

But no one told me what to do when the faults were not in my kit but in my soul.

No one told me what to do when the cracks ran through my nervous system, when I could not sleep, when I flinched at kindness, when I mistook love for war. I passed those faults for years. Stepped over the grief. Avoided the memories. Silenced the screams inside. I wore stoicism like body armour long after I had stopped wearing the uniform.

Then came the dark night. Not a firefight, but the battlefield of healing. The medicine. The silence. The unbearable stillness of facing myself. That is when the motto came back to me—not as a command, but as an invitation.

Never pass a fault.

Jesus did not pass the fault, either. He did not avoid the pain; He endured it. Mocked, beaten, humiliated, crucified. He bore it all. A suffering so holy the sky itself went black. And through that agony came the resurrection. The miracle was not in avoiding the suffering. It was in passing through it.

And I realized: The pain I was carrying—the confusion, the heartbreak, the loneliness—it was not meaningless. It was the path. It was my cross. My own resurrection did not come through avoidance. It came when I stopped running. When I wept like a child on the floor. When I let the grief break me open.

Growth does not come without breaking.

Transformation does not come without surrender.

Resurrection does not come without the cross.

So, I grieved. I cried. I let it all out. Because sometimes, life is just sad. And that sadness is sacred. I had to feel it fully, or it would keep haunting the edges of my life. Unprocessed pain always finds a way back—through anger, through silence, through the way we hurt others without meaning to.

Now, I carry the motto in my heart.

But it no longer means control.

It means compassion.

Never pass a fault—in myself, in others, in the broken world.

Tend to it. Stay with it. Do not look away.

Because through the pain, something holy is rising.

What I Lost (A Story Rewritten)

There is a grief deeper than death. It is being erased from the heart of your own child while you are still alive.

My oldest is sixteen now. Grade ten in high school. I hear she is doing well, pulling 70s and 80s in her courses, walking the neighbourhood, gaming, and drawing characters from imagined worlds. She likes Blind Bag figurines and is considering becoming a historian, "depending on what it pays." That is my daughter—curious, cautious, capable.

She lives with her mom full-time now. She says it is better that way. That she is happy, cared for. That her needs are met. And I pray that is true.

But I have come to understand that there is a difference between being kept safe and being kept small.

Her mother was always good at shaping belief. She could cry in front of a judge and turn cruelty into concern with a few well-placed words. Withholding affection unless it served her. Love as a reward for obedience. I saw it when we were together, but it took years, and therapy—for me to name it: narcissistic, controlling, emotionally extracting.

When our oldest daughter was little, she clung to me like I was her anchor. We had weekends filled with cartoons, treasure hunts, and late-night talks about the universe. But as she got older, that bond weakened—first subtly, then all at once. It was not just the mental health collapses I went through, or the war I carried home in my body. It was the slow, quiet erosion. The poisoned well. Words whispered behind doors I was not invited through anymore.

She says now that I locked her in her room one night in 2022. That I denied her food and the bathroom. That I screamed and got angry. I did—at least some version of it. I was unwell then. Dysregulated. Fighting to survive my own mind. But in a house where truth is a tool, not a principle, even facts become weaponized.

She says I did not buy her hygiene products. That I shamed her. That I made her throw pads in the living room trash as a "walk of shame." It guts me to imagine that is how she remembers it. I failed her there. Or someone taught her to frame it that way.

She says she showed people videos of my episodes—her way of asking for help, she claims, when she didn't know what else to do. At the time, it felt like betrayal wearing the mask of concern. But now, looking back, I can see the desperation beneath it—the helplessness of someone who didn't understand what trauma looks like when it breaks the surface.

I know she called the Kids Help Phone once. I know she started panicking when I came to her school in grade nine, trying to reconnect. She said it felt fake.

These days, she says that my emails do not make sense. That I am "too far gone." That I look unhealthy now. That I drop therapists when they get too close. That I scream, cry, lock myself away. She is right.

But somewhere inside, I still believe the love between us is real, buried under layers of pain and projection. She says she might talk to me again "if you work on yourself." She says she worries about me.

And that is the cruelest part of this disease—this legacy of trauma. I tried to protect her from the broken man I was, and instead she was handed a version of me shaped by someone who needed me to stay broken.

I have been many things: a soldier, a patient, a father. But to my oldest now, I am a shadow. A cautionary tale told in quiet moments. A man she has been taught to fear or pity, but not love.

And still, I hold the door open.

Even if she never walks through it.

Echoes Through the Hallway

My youngest is thirteen now—the same age I was when I started hiding my heart to survive the emotional landmines of my own family. She lived in a house where peace had a price and love came with conditions. Middle school, dance class, track and field—those were her sanctuaries. Places where she could move freely, breathe, forget. But at home, freedom came second to loyalty.

My youngest daughter started visiting me in Fredericton in December 2024, some Wednesdays after school. We kept it simple. McDonald's, homework, conversation. No pressure. Just a safe space where she could be herself without performance. She told the social worker, "I enjoyed the visits. They went well." Then, they just stopped. No notice. No explanation to either me or her.

That was not the full story. But when you grow up under the influence of someone who needs to be the centre of gravity, someone who controls the narrative, you learn to doubt your own truth. You learn to assume silence means abandonment, not obstruction.

My youngest told me before: "Mom and my sister talk about you all the time." Not with tenderness. Not with nuance. With sharp tones and whispered accusations. And when they fought over me, over politics, over everything, my youngest turned up the volume on her TV. Trying to disappear. That is what children do when they live with someone who confuses control with care.

She said she still wanted to come back. Her older sister dissuaded her, saying if she went back, she (the eldest) would have to, too. She tried to convince her that Dad would do something to her, but she knew he would not. That line was drenched in guilt—not hers, but guilt planted, watered, and pruned by someone else.

My youngest was torn between loyalty to her sister and the truth in her heart. "Dad would do anything for us," she said, recalling the lake in our backyard, the trampoline, the days we spent at the beach. But the present was a trap. "I want to see my dad, and I don't want to upset my sister or anyone." Her eyes welled up. "I'm scared of hurting someone else."

That is the cost of growing up with a narcissistic mother. The child becomes the regulator of adult emotions. She tiptoes around someone else's fragility. She learns that her joy must not threaten the parent's narrative. That wanting love from both parents makes her selfish. Disloyal. Dangerous.

My youngest did not say those words, but they hung in the gaps between every sentence.

She had no contact with my side of the family. Did not know where her paternal grandparents lived. Did not know she could reach out. Her world had been carefully pruned, curated, and edited, half her story erased.

And yet, she still hoped.

She did not see me as broken. She did not fear me. She feared the fallout. She feared the pressure. She feared being made to choose again.

The line that stuck with me most: "Everyone has something wrong with them." That was her olive branch. Her truce with the dysfunction around her. A gentle permission to love a father whom others had made taboo.

She is a child not confused, but cornered. Not angry, but exhausted. Trying to belong to a mother who needs her to reject me, and to a sister caught in her own trauma, while still holding on to her memories of who I had been to her.

This is not about one home, one divorce, one parental conflict. This is about generational trauma, the kind passed down in silence and guilt, not genetics. The kind that dressed up as protection but taught you to hide your heart. I knew that wound. I carried it in my nervous system in the way I flinched at silence and worked too hard to prove my worth.

My father had disappeared when I was young, too—not just from our house, but from his own emotions. My mother, brittle and angry, shaped her identity around survival. I never got to be the boy who just loved and was loved. And now I watch as my daughter turns up the volume to avoid hearing her own heart break.

My youngest is trying to survive two histories colliding—hers and mine. And in a house where only one version of the past is allowed, she has learned to disappear gently.

That is the legacy I never wanted to leave her.

CHAPTER 39

The Loneliness of Healing

A Day in the Life

Each morning starts the same.

My brain, never truly at rest, jolts awake with a low-voltage panic. Before I even sit up, it is already calculating:

Will I have enough money?

Who will be angry at me today?

What conversations will leave me flushed, ashamed, or spiralling?

The same looping thoughts, the same mental arguments, repeat like a cruel algorithm I never consented to run.

My body feels it, too. Jaw clenched, ears humming, stomach knotted tight. A fire churning in my core.

This is how I greet the day.

Me and my brain injury.

Today marks another birthday I cannot be there for.

It's been three years since I last spoke to them.

This morning, I cried, grief swelling like a tide, unstoppable once it hit.

There is a terrible kind of loneliness that comes with healing.

When you start to feel again, you start to lose. Friends. Family. Lovers. All the people who once matched your dysfunction vanish when you stop playing the same game.

I have lost so much in these years.
The small ones I no longer tuck in.
Friends who ghosted when the mask cracked.
A partner I once imagined building a life with.
As I heal, I lose.
And as I lose, I see more clearly.
Every day begins in fire.
Every loss, another tariff.
And still, through the smoke, I see.

The World Is Burning Now

The world is burning now, or maybe it always was.

That country to the south flexes its fear like muscle—threats and tariffs, old Cold War posturing wrapped in modern cruelty.

It reminds me of a night at a concert, years ago, when a band on stage told a president to fuck off in front of thousands.

I remember the shock—how that protest rang through my chest louder than the amps.

I grew up idolizing that country, shaped by its culture, its wars, its promises. A Cold War kid chasing safety and order amid chaos. But now, I sit here, watching headlines flicker.

February 9, 2025. Another familiar figure back on screen. Last week, he swore we were exempt from new tariffs. Today, he announces we are back on the list.

No warning. No explanation.

Just like that, we are part of a new war. A quiet one. One that bleeds in paperwork, taxes, and sleepless nights.

And my brain . . .

Still burning.

Tears in Cancún

Cancún. Sunlight bounced off the tiled floor of the hotel. Tourists were laughing in the pool below. Inside, I sat with a printout of the interim Veterans Affairs report. My past, reduced to bullet points and bureaucratic language.

The weight of it hit me like a freight train. My body is a mangled mess of blast trauma, whiplash, and the daily wear and tear of being a combat infantry soldier. My neck still clicks when I turn too fast. My knees grind when I climb stairs. Some mornings, even my breath feels like it is carrying rubble.

But it was more than that. It was the lost years, the misdiagnosed symptoms, the missed treatments.

In that hotel room, I cried for everything I had lost.

My kids.

Lovers who came and went, never quite able to reach me in the ways I needed.

And a broken military health system that told me I was fine when I was not.

Almost fifteen years to the day since I left Canadian soil for my summer of war, I sat in a hotel room in Mexico, tears streaming down my face. Not from pain, but from the overwhelming gratitude that I survived.

I cried for the resilience of the human spirit.

How much it can endure.

How many storms it can weather in such a fleeting time.

Forty years of life. So short, yet so long.

My physical injuries are finally being recognized, which somehow allows me to hear them more clearly. For years, they were silenced. Just like so much of me was silenced.

As I sit and reflect on the true costs of war, I realize it was never about what happened "over there." The bullets, the bombs, the near misses—they left scars, yes. But the deeper wounds came later, in the silence. In the attempt to stitch a soul back together with trembling hands and no clear road map.

Coming home was not a return.

It was another battlefield.

No welcome parade.

Just a slow unraveling.

Sleepless nights.

Flashbacks mistaken for mood swings.

A thousand tiny losses: of trust, of memory, of direction, of self.

No one teaches you how to rebuild your life after war.

No one tells you that surviving the deployment is just the beginning.

I tried to piece everything back together with whatever I could find. Discipline. Distraction. Denial. But trauma does not stay buried. It finds ways to speak. In the body. In the relationships that collapse under the weight of unspoken grief. In the aching loneliness of being misunderstood by systems that claim to help but never truly see.

And yet, somehow, I am still here. Still piecing it all together.

Not perfectly.

Not quickly.

But honestly. And this time, with heart.

Repentance

I did not know I was broken, not at first. Not when I was charging through exercises in Meaford with a C9 on my shoulder, not when I was watching heat rise off the tarmac in Kandahar, not even when I buried the worst of what happened under alcohol, pills, rage, cannabis, and silence. Survival does not feel like sin when you are in it. It feels like momentum.

But war leaves its scent on everything. I brought it home in my pores, in my nervous system, in the way I could not sit still or say "I love you" without flinching. I did not know I was drowning until I started dragging others down with me.

There are things I did that haunt me, not because I meant to hurt anyone, but because I did not know how not to. I hurt the people I loved, the ones who needed me most. I gave my kids a hollowed-out version of their father because I did not know how to be full anymore. I let anger talk for me. I let numbness raise them.

To my daughters: I am sorry I could not be more present. The war did not end when I came home; it just changed theatres. I let it play out in my relationships, in the food I did not eat, in the mornings I could not get out of bed, in the stories I was too afraid to tell you.

But repentance does not come all at once. It is not a Sunday altar call. It comes in pieces. In the middle of the night, when your child will not stop crying and you don't know how to comfort them without scaring them. In the way you brace when someone touches your back. In the echo of an argument that sounds too much like your father's voice in your own mouth.

I used to think repentance was about shame. About grovelling. But now I know it is a resurrection. A reckoning. It is a holy "Fuck this" to the violence I inherited and repeated. It is not just regret. It is responsibility. It is telling the truth to yourself when there is no one left to lie to. It is grieving—not just for what was done to you, but for what you did because of it.

There are moments I will never get back. Faces I will never see again. Apologies that cannot be heard by the dead or the disappeared. But I offer them anyway, to the air, to the stars, to God, because repentance is about becoming someone who could not do again the things you once did.

Under the stars, after my final ketamine treatment, I felt it in my bones—the grief, the grace, the great unwinding. Tears rolled down my face as I stared at the Big Dipper, remembering the boy I was before all this. The last time I felt I was home was when I was with God before this lifetime even started. And in that moment, under the Big Dipper, I made a promise.

No more.

I will not pass it on.

I will not pretend I was not responsible.

I will not confuse pain with power again.

That is what repentance means to me now. A returning. A remembering. A refusal to let the past write the ending.

Never a Mother

I had forgotten about my TBI.

Or maybe I just stopped mentioning it, thinking it did not matter anymore, until my nervous system reminded me otherwise. Until the spiral started again.

Somehow, I ended up right back in the same abuse cycle I have been trapped in for most of my life. The formula never changes. Attack. Criticize. Blame. Then come the crocodile tears, the performance of concern. But it was never real care. It was manipulation. It was submission to emotional warfare. And I always fell for it.

I asked them to stop. I begged. I pleaded. I hung up. But then came the texts—the long, self-righteous paragraphs: *Why are you so mean to me?* The same script, every time.

And then, I was no longer forty.

I was seven.

My mother, charging down the hallway. A frying pan in her hand. The door rattling.

My body frozen.

My brain flooded with the memory—the sound, the panic, the paralysis. She never took responsibility. Instead, she punished and blamed. Her behavior was never about connection. It was about control.

Just like then, I found myself in a conversation that turned from confusion to chaos. A thirty-nine-minute call meant to be for reconnect-

285

ing ended with my blood pressure spiking and my brain injury flaring. Fight or flight took over. I was hit in the face by the sick familiarity of it.

I felt it in my body even though I didn't yet know its name: cortisol love. The rush in my chest when I mistake fear for connection. That dangerous cocktail of trauma bonding and false affection. I had seen it my whole life. In family. In lovers. In institutions. It is what happens when someone says "I care" but cannot stop hurting you.

This time, something inside me broke open. I said what I had never said aloud before: "You have never been a mother." I said it plainly, not out of spite, but as truth. She had been a manipulator, a moralizer, a shapeshifter who hid behind acts of service while poisoning every attempt at intimacy.

And instead of hearing me, instead of responding to the pain, she deflected. She pivoted to tone. She accused. She blamed. In that whole call, all I could hear was her rewriting the narrative, painting herself as the victim and me as the broken, dissociated son.

I tried to share how much pain I was carrying, how these patterns had shaped my brain, my body, my entire sense of safety. But she did not want healing. She wanted control.

I realized again how much she still manipulated me. I was stunned by the reach of it. I saw the pattern—I saw that she treated me exactly like the people she had warned me about. People who "don't care," who "only love conditionally."

The truth is, she never listened to understand. She listened to defend. And when that failed, she reached for the oldest weapon in her arsenal: shame.

And I almost believed it again.

Almost.

But this time, I caught it. I felt the spike in my skull, the pressure behind my eyes, the way my brain injury flared under the weight of her words. My body remembered for me. And this time, I listened.

CHAPTER 40

The Long Return

Washed in White Light

He was not wearing robes. Just white jeans and a white linen shirt, barefoot on the wet concrete.

The pool lay still beneath the bright light—not sacred in any traditional sense, but quiet, blue, waiting. There was silence like the kind that comes after you have wept your body clean.

I had already done the dying. In Panjwaii. In the years that followed, when the war kept living inside me. Therapy had stitched me back together. Psychedelics cracked me open. But this . . . this was different.

"Are you ready?" he asked, a smile on his young face.

I nodded and stepped into the pool. The water reached my ribs, cool against the heat, like stepping into a memory.

We stood there in silence. I placed my hand on his rib, and he placed his hand gently on my back. I held my nose. He nodded once and began the ritual.

As he lowered me into the water, the world faded, and everything turned white.

With my eyes closed under the surface, I saw Him, our Saviour. Just like that day in Afghanistan when He plucked me from the ambush. When I should have died.

But this time . . . there were no roaring guns. No sand in my face. No adrenaline in my skull. Just the lukewarm water. And the Divine.

It lasted only a few seconds, but in that moment, I felt it: wholeness. Not survival. Not fragmentation. Wholeness.

The Holy Ghost did not thunder. He came like warmth through my bones. Like breath in a body that had forgotten how to receive.

You are not what you did. You are not what was done to you. I never left.

When I rose, the white light hovered still, just above the pool, touching everything.

My shirt clung to my chest, soaked in water and something else I could not name.

The man in white jeans met my eyes and smiled, not like someone proud of what he had done, but like someone who had simply witnessed a return.

I stepped out of the pool and into the stillness. Not perfect. But free.

A towel was hanging on a hook. I wrapped it around my shoulders and stood in the shower stall, heart pounding with something other than fear.

Then, someone began to sing.

"Amazing Grace."

The same song that once crushed me under the weight of loss at funerals, ramp ceremonies, folded flags. The song that used to choke me with grief for the comrades who never made it home.

But this time . . . it was different.

The words did not land like a wound. They landed like a welcome.

The tears that fell were not for death. They were for life.

Gratitude spilled down my face—quiet, clean. Not forced. Not performative. Just real.

A new beginning.

As I looked around the room, wiping the tears away, I saw them—my new family. My soul tribe. People who, a few short weeks ago, had been strangers. Now, they were something else entirely.

Fellow seekers. Witnesses. Brothers and sisters, bound not by blood but by grace.

For the first time in years, I felt like I belonged.

Giving the Monkey a Seat

In the East, they say the monkey mind must be tamed with mindfulness.

In the West, we give it labels and throw meds at it.

Afghanistan: I gave it a C7 with sand grit in the chamber and told it to fight for meaning.

Canada: I gave it a keyboard and told it to write.

The monkey mind never leaves. It only changes roles.

And in healing? I gave it a seat beside me and said: "Speak. I am listening now."

Everything I Ever Needed: My Daughters

The house fills with their voices—laughter and bickering tangled together like a song only they know. One leans over a sketchbook, pencil scratching, while the other balances on a chair, legs swinging, words tumbling out too fast to catch.

At the stove, I flip pancakes, listening more than cooking. Plates hit the table, syrup floods across them, sticky fingers smear the page. A scolding comes, but the smile that follows gives it away.

The living room becomes a fortress of pillows and blankets, popcorn scattered across the couch, shrieks rising over the glow of a half-watched movie. Flashlights flicker beneath the covers, little constellations glowing as secrets are whispered into the night.

Later, the fortress collapses into quiet. We pile onto the couch, a tangle of limbs and blankets. Their heads rest heavy on my chest, small hands curling into mine. The television hums in the background, but what I feel most is the rise and fall of their breath, the warmth of them pressed against me, a peace that doesn't announce itself but seeps in slowly.

Outside, mats unroll across the damp grass. They wobble through tree pose, arms stretched wide, grinning as if balance is a treasure just discovered. I follow their lead, letting them play teacher. The ground is cool beneath us, the air sharp with the smell of cut grass. When we lie back on the earth, staring up at clouds—dragons, castles, hearts—the backyard becomes a temple, ordinary and holy all at once.

We load the car with towels and sandwiches, excitement spilling long before the shoreline comes into view. They charge into the waves without hesitation, squealing at the cold, laughter rising above the crash of water. Castles crumble against the tide, and I memorize the way the sun turns their wet hair gold.

The road winds toward waterfalls. Windows down, voices rising in made-up songs, hair whipping wild in the wind. They race ahead on the trail, eager to hear the roar before they see it. Mist clings to their faces as they stretch their arms wide, as if they could hold the whole cascade.

Halloween glows with lanterns on porches. Costumes rustle, buckets rattle, voices ring down the street: *"Trick or treat!"* Skeletons leap from bushes, shrieks collapse into laughter, strangers slip extra chocolate into their bags. At home, wrappers litter the floor, trades are made, and they drift off to sleep still glowing beneath the mask of the night.

On quiet afternoons, the backyard erupts in color. Buckets of dye line the table, rubber bands snap, white shirts twist into bundles of possibility. Splashes stain the grass, our hands, even our faces when dye flies too wildly. We laugh at the mess, knowing nothing will ever wash out of the fabric or from memory. When the shirts unfurl, they shimmer like galaxies, fireworks, accidental rainbows. The girls spin in circles, wearing their creations, fabric dripping, sunlight caught in the folds.

By the time the day winds down, their energy burns itself out. In the back seat, they collapse against each other, tangled hair and tired smiles, already dreaming. And in the quiet, I feel a truth no uniform or medal ever gave me: not the soldier, not the survivor—just Dad. And in that, everything I ever needed.

CHAPTER 41

Reintegration

The Long Road Home

Reintegration is a long, slow process. No one tells you how hard it is going to be, or how much of yourself you are going to lose or must rebuild just to function in the civilian world again.

Most of us in Combat Arms struggle with the transition. We come from a career built on structure, where time, movement, dress, and even the way you hold your hands at your sides are dictated. Then, suddenly, you are out. On your own. Expected to figure it all out without the systems you relied on for years.

I do not think people understand how much we do not fit in. Our humour? Dark. Twisted, even. It kept us sane over there, helped us bond, and helped us survive. Out here, it makes people uncomfortable. I have had clinicians tell me it is normal—that it is a coping mechanism, but in the real world, it gets you side-eyes or awkward silence.

And even the trivial things . . . they are not small. Like trying to schedule my day. Something that should be simple. I will set out with a list of things to do, reasonable tasks. But I will start one, then get distracted. Start another, then forget what I was doing. Before I know it, I have five or six things half done, nothing finished, and the day's over.

The house fills up with people returning from their lives, and I am just sitting there. Ruminating. Telling myself I failed again.

The worst part is knowing that I once thrived in chaos. I could navigate pressure, violence, and high-stakes situations with absolute clarity. But civilian life? Civilian life unravels me in a way war never could.

They cheered when we marched in, the bagpipes echoing off the Ortona building as we stepped through those Christmas-wrapped doors. The crowd clapped, cameras flashed. It was supposed to be a hero's welcome.

But I felt hollow. The uniform on my back was heavier than it had ever been, soaked in dust and ghosts no one else could see. I scanned the crowd and saw her—my daughter, no longer a baby, now walking. I had missed her first steps. Missed birthdays. Missed growing.

The crowd smiled, but I was somewhere else. My breath caught in my throat like a trigger half-pulled. People shook my hand and thanked me for my service. "Glad you're home." Home.

But I did not feel at home anywhere.

No one asked about the bodies. No one asked about the children we could not save. No one asked why I had not slept in days or why I flinched at the sound of a balloon popping. They did not ask because they did not want to know.

And I hated them for that.

Until, one night, sitting alone in the dim quiet of my room, the weight of it all pressing on my chest like body armour I could not take off, the words surfaced out of nowhere:

Father, forgive them, for they know not what they do.

Not a prayer. A survival instinct.

Because if I did not find a way to forgive my chain of command, the politicians, the civilians who said "Support the troops" but left us to rot, I would implode.

They did not know what it did to us. What it meant to come back to a world that had moved on. They did not know how we bled out quietly in the safety of Canadian suburbs.

They did not know.

And that's why Christ said it. Not to excuse it. Not to forget it. But to unhook himself from the hatred.

So, I started whispering it. On sleepless nights. At Remembrance Day ceremonies. When my own family said, "You just need to get over it."

Father, forgive them . . .

Because they didn't see what we saw.

And they never would.

Where I Learned Responsibility

They say the military teaches discipline, and that part is true. But discipline is not the same as responsibility. You can march in perfect step, polish your boots until they blind in the sun, fire your weapon with precision, and still avoid owning your life.

I learned responsibility the hard way. Not in the classroom. Not on the drill square. I found it in the aftermath, in the quiet after the gunfire stopped, in the silence when the adrenaline drained from my veins and left me hollow. In those months when no one knocked, no one called, and I realized: No one is coming. No one is going to save me.

The military drilled routine into me. It taught me how to carry weight that was not mine, to run on torn muscles and blistered feet, to laugh through bloodshot eyes after nights without sleep. But it never taught me what to do with the wreckage that followed.

That part came later.

It came when I had to face the ruins of my relationships, the unanswered phone calls, the child's drawing left on the counter, the silence I wore like armour and called strength. It came when I realized that blaming the chain of command, the mission, or even my upbringing, each of which carried its truth, would never set me free.

Responsibility is not about pretending the pain was fair or justified. It is about standing in front of the mirror and admitting: I am the one holding the weapon now. I am the one deciding who I become from here.

Because there is a war that begins after the deployment ends. A war for your own soul. For your own mind. And no sergeant, no padre, no shrink can fight it for you.

I did not choose what happened to me. But I choose what I do with it. That choice, that ownership, is the first act of healing.

And in that silence, with the mirror as my witness, responsibility begins.

Enough to Begin

It did not happen all at once. I did not suddenly wake up one day and call it abuse. But something shifted the day I whispered it to myself: *This is not love; this is survival.* That sentence cracked something open.

For years, my body had carried the wreckage of nights of sweat-soaked sheets, mornings that started already exhausted, the static of panic humming in my chest. I had mistaken the tension for normalcy, the collapse for rest. But naming it lit a match in the dark.

I began to see the patterns, not just in her, but in me. I was not broken. I was repeating. Reenacting. I was the boy who had been conditioned to meet other people's needs before his own. The soldier who had learned to shut up and suit up. The man who kept mistaking sugar-coated cruelty for connection.

Slowly, I started to map my nervous system, to track the tremors and shutdowns as if they were sacred signals. I said *no* for the first time. I walked out of the room when words cut too deep. I stopped explaining my pain to people who had no intention of hearing me.

That was the beginning of freedom, and freedom asked me to try things I never would have considered before.

Reiki was one of them. A therapist I found after my release suggested it. At first, I laughed at the idea, but curiosity outweighed cynicism.

The practitioner's room smelled faintly of lavender and resin. Clean, but not clinical. No fluorescent lights humming overhead. No framed degrees declaring expertise. Just a chair, a couch, and a woman who did not flinch when I said the word *Afghanistan*.

I lay back on the table. She hovered her hands above my chest, then my gut, like she was feeling for something invisible. Part of me wanted to bolt. Another part, the part that had nothing left to lose, stayed.

And then it happened. Not fireworks. Not a miracle. Just stillness. The static that had been my constant companion went quiet. My heart eased its pounding. My jaw unclenched. My fists softened. For once, my body was not a battlefield bracing for the next strike.

I did not tell anyone about that session. You don't exactly go back to the guys and say, "Hey, I think a woman waved the war out of me." But it was the first time I believed healing might not be something I had to carry alone. That it could arrive in unexpected forms—quiet, steady, unannounced.

It wasn't everything. But it was enough to begin. Enough to wake me up to the possibility that my body, my heart, and my life could belong to me again. Enough to show me that there was another way waiting, just beyond survival.

Discernment: A Path to Spiritual Growth

There comes a time on the healing path when you are asked to become loyal, not to a person, not to a system, not to the stories others tell about you, but to your innermost truth.

To the voice beneath the noise.

The heartbeat beneath the armour.

The breath that steadies beneath panic.

Spiritual growth is not always light and serenity. Sometimes it is standing alone in the wreckage of what you used to believe, the shattered glass of old certainties crunching beneath your feet, holding nothing but the quiet knowing that your heart is still beating in the right direction.

Discernment means walking away from what once felt like love if it coils around you like control. It means saying *no* when your body contracts, even if your mind is afraid. It means letting silence stretch like soil waiting for a seed, long enough for your soul to speak.

And when everyone else abandons your truth, when the people you tried to keep peace with turn their backs, you stay.

You stay with you.

Because spiritual growth is not about rising above your pain. It is about returning to the root of who you are and refusing to abandon yourself again.

That is discernment. That is growth.

Breath of the Soul

My awakening did not arrive like a bolt of lightning or a flash of white light. It came slowly, like breath returning to a body that had forgotten how to inhale without fear.

Through psychedelic-assisted integration, I met parts of myself I thought were long buried: the wounded child, the forgotten dreamer, the soldier who never came home.

And beneath them all, I found something deeper: my divine self. Still intact. Still pure.

The medicine did not heal me. It revealed me. It softened the hard edges. It turned down the static long enough for me to feel again.

To grieve.

To forgive.

To remember.

For years, I lived in fight-or-flight, scanning for danger even in silence, even in love. But slowly, I began to taste something I had not known since before the trauma:

A peace that felt like exhaling for the first time in years.

A body unbraced.

A heart unbarricaded.

A nervous system no longer mistaking home for war.

One morning, walking through pine woods after a rain, I noticed the air in my chest felt light. No clench. No armour. Just breath. And in that stillness, I discovered the most sacred thing of all: Reconnection.

With the boy who once believed in magic.

With the man who chose survival.

With the soul that never stopped singing, even under rubble.

This is the path of awakening— not rising above the pain, but descending into the body and finding God still there.

Morning light. Not outside, but within.

Karmic Reflection from the Ambush

The sand was warm that day, softer than it should have been beneath the weight of war. My body hit the ground before my mind could catch up.

One moment, we were advancing. The next: Crack. Thunder. Gunfire split the air, and time fractured. The farmers who had stood beside us were gone.

I was not a soul in that moment. I was a body surviving. I dug in, tasted grit between my teeth, heard the click of death snap inches from my shoulder, and my heart stopped to listen.

When the dust settled, something deeper stirred, not just around me, but inside me. A silence. A knowing. I had crossed into a place where karma keeps records, even if no one else does.

I do not regret protecting my team. I do not regret living. But the weight followed me home.

It changed the way I held a child, always too carefully, as if she might vanish in my arms. It changed how I looked at sunsets, the orange glow burning too much like tracer fire. And it froze me whenever someone asked, "Did you kill someone?"

What I carried was not punishment. It was a spiritual weight forged in fire, meant to be melted by meaning. I did not just fight for freedom. I fought to remember what it means to be human in a place that forgets.

But grief came home with me. At first, a quiet shadow. Then it hardened into anger.

The man I killed would not leave my dreams. Eventually, he followed me into daylight, into family dinners, birthday parties, Christmas morning. Turkey on the table. Wrapping paper across the floor. Pine and gravy thick in the air.

That Christmas with her parents should have been a gift.

I told myself I was happy to be alive if she was happy.

Her aunt handed me a beer. I hadn't had one in years. The cold glass stung my lip, and after a few swallows it hit me like a bottle.

By the time we left, I was slumped in the back seat, crying into my hands, the stale upholstery closing in.

Who was I now?

Somewhere in those years, I lost myself. I stopped being her partner and became her surrogate father, the one she manipulated into pregnancy, the one she shamed every day.

She told me I smelled bad. That I cried too much. That I was just like my father, a man she never met.

She didn't know how right she was, but not in the way she thought. He had come home from war broken. So had I.

Where he drank and raged, I swallowed the shame. I tried to keep us afloat. Even defended her when soldiers from my unit texted me to make her stop causing drama on base.

Home became worse than deployment. The fluorescent light in the kitchen felt harsher than the Afghan sun. Work was pressure. Home was war.

By 2012, I knew I needed help. It started with one sleeping pill. By the end of the year, I carried a whole zipper bag full. They rattled like bones when I walked.

Mefloquine still haunted my blood, and the pills dulled everything, food, laughter, even memory itself.

One morning, I woke from a nap to the sound of her and her sister complaining upstairs. Dishes clinked in the sink. Burnt coffee hung in the air. I walked to the kitchen, opened my hand, and showed her the bag of pills.

"You have no idea," I told her. "This is what it costs to keep going. You can thank me for your freedom."

She said nothing. And in that silence, I realized no one ever will.

The Devotee to Suffering

I used to think I was just a soldier. But looking back, I see it now: I was a Ray 6 soul in a uniform. Ray 6, according to "The Seven Rays and Their Masters" by Master Del Pe, is about the ray of devotion and idealism. I was devoted. Loyal to a fault. Willing to die for something I believed was good. A higher cause. A noble mission. That is the curse and calling of the Ray 6. You give your entire soul to a cause you believe will save others, even if it kills you.

This soul type had been shaped long before Afghanistan, by the archetype of the martyr. Raised in a house where love often looked like self-abandonment, I learned early that pain meant you cared. So, I became the one who always stayed, always fought, always gave more, even when it cost me everything. My loyalty was not just to the military or to Canada; it was to an ideal. A dream of justice. Of redemption. Of doing something that mattered.

But war does not care about your ideals.

In Kandahar, my heart had already attached itself to a small child, a girl I took a picture with on my last patrol. For me, she became a symbol of the mission, proof that maybe we could do something right. But watching her slip away tore a hole in my soul. I remember walking back to the forward operating base in silence, the weight of that one child heavier than the whole damn country. I was dying inside to be home with my daughter, and in that moment, this young girl became a stand-in for the love I could not reach.

Ray 6 souls are here to love with intensity. But we often give that love to the wrong things: leaders who lie, systems that use, relationships that mirror our wounding. My devotion turned into disillusionment when I realized the mission was not what I thought. I had been willing to give my life, but not for oil, not for politics, not for lies.

That was the beginning of my rebirth.

They say a Ray 6 learns by heartbreak. It is how we refine our devotion from blind loyalty to sacred purpose. The fall of Afghanistan broke me again. Not because of the politics, but because of the people, the interpreters, the children, the police officers we trained. I believed in them. And watching them be abandoned twisted the knife of moral injury even deeper. Their faces, their voices, still follow me.

Now I know devotion without discernment is dangerous.

I have had to learn how to love without losing myself. To stay committed without becoming consumed. That is the Ray 6 soul path. The lesson is not to stop loving, but to love wisely. To serve the light without needing to suffer. To lay down the martyr's cross and let the fire of sacrifice be transformed into the fire of creation. To rise from the ashes of blind devotion like a sunrise breaking through the night. To choose the kind of offering that uplifts both self and others.

As I walk the healing path, I still carry the same passion. The same flame. But I have stopped feeding it to causes that burn me out or betray my heart. My loyalty now belongs to the Divine, not to men with medals or partners who confuse control with care. I am learning emotional mastery, one breath at a time. Learning to expand from personal attachments into a deeper, more universal love.

In the end, the Ray 6 journey is not about dying for something. It is about living for what is real. It is about resurrection. It is about the dawn after the long night, the first light that proves life can begin again.

Suffering is not the proof of love. Integrity is.

CHAPTER 42

Homecoming to the Self

The summer of 2023 was not marked by one dramatic event. It was marked by a series of quiet ruptures and realizations that shifted the ground beneath me. For years, I had been living in cycles, in patterns of pain, reactivity, and survival. But somewhere between the long evenings of that summer and the still mornings when the air smelled of pine and rain, something in me began to change. It was not a bolt of lightning. It was a spark, small but steady, reminding me: *You are more than this body. More than this pain.*

Soul Awakening

It started simply, with breath.

One morning, I noticed I was no longer bracing as I inhaled. My chest expanded without fear. My ribs did not lock. My nervous system, which had been coiled tight for years, released just enough for me to feel space inside. And in that space, a whisper came: *I am more than this body. More than this pain.*

I carried that whisper into the days that followed. I heard it as I walked down forest trails, the crunch of gravel under my boots grounding me. I heard it when I lay in bed at night, listening to the ceiling fan hum while memories of Afghanistan still pulsed behind my eyelids. For the first time in years, I did not shut the voice down. I let it speak.

Soul Homecoming

I realized then that what I had been searching for all along was not a place; it was an essence.

Not the house I had lost. Not the relationships that had crumbled. Not even the uniform I had once worn like a second skin. What I longed for was the still point inside me that had survived all of it.

It felt like stepping into a room I had forgotten existed. Inside that room, I was already whole. Love was not something I had to bargain for or earn with sacrifice. Love was something to remember. I was not going anywhere new. I was coming home.

Completion of Initiation

The months before had nearly broken me. Grief had pressed into every rib. Rage had poured through me like poison. Nights had stretched long and unbearable, my mind rehearsing every failure, every betrayal.

But the summer refined me.

I did not walk out of the fire unscarred, but the scars became scripture. I learned to read them not as proof of damage but as evidence of survival. Each wound carried a key. A lesson. A passage deeper into my own humanity.

I understood then that initiation was never about comfort. It was about being stripped until only the essential remains. And in the aftermath, you do not crawl out empty-handed. You rise, holding what can never again be taken.

Embodying Christ's Peace

Peace began showing up in ways I had not expected.

In the way I spoke to strangers at the grocery store, offering softness instead of silence.

In the way I listened to my children, really listened, as though every word was holy.

In the way I stayed open when my body wanted to shut down, when my instincts screamed to armour up again.

Peace was no longer a concept I prayed for. It became a presence I carried.

To live with pierced hands and an open heart.

To sit across from those who had wounded me and still break bread.

To speak with the authority of compassion, not because I was untouched, but because I had been touched by everything and survived.

End of the Time Loop

For years, I had been stuck in loops, replaying old betrayals, reliving combat in my dreams, reenacting family patterns that kept me small. The reel spun endlessly: rage, retreat, collapse, repeat.

But that summer, I felt the loop break.

The karmic reel went quiet.

Time collapsed into Presence.

I stopped rehearsing the past. I stopped scanning for a future that had not yet arrived. For once, I stood inside the now, and it was enough.

"Yesterday is history, tomorrow is a mystery, today is a gift—
that's why it's called the present."

—Common proverb

Sacred Integration and Rest

At last, the exhale.

The warrior in me laid down his sword. The mystic in me returned to the garden, barefoot on grass still wet with dawn. I was no longer rushing toward the next battle, the next healing session, the next proving ground. I was simply here.

Being.

And in that stillness, I discovered the spark had never left. It had always been waiting, quietly alive beneath the rubble.

The summer of 2023 was not the end of my story, nor the end of my struggle. But it was a threshold. The moment I stopped running from myself. The moment I returned home.

Letter to My Father

You have shown me everything I needed to see.

You kidnapped us from our mother, and your family tried to cover it up. When I moved out, you told me you were disappointed in me.

But, sir, I have been disappointed in you my entire life.

You taught us nothing but how to fight and stir chaos. No life skills. No love. No safety. Everything I have learned, I had to learn on my own. And with my mom's help. She is a good woman.

You?

You are the devil in disguise.

You abused her. You abused my sisters.

And you never had the courage to own any of it.

You are not a man. You are a coward hiding behind intimidation and silence.

The next time I see you will be to piss on your grave.

CHAPTER 43

The Language of Scars

Scars

Anyone with a soul, anyone whose body has been tuned to survival, carries scars. I learned that long before anyone gave me the language for them. Some people bury their scars. Some numb them. But the wound is always there.

For years, I thought mine meant I was broken, that there was something wrong with me for not being able to move on the way others seemed to. But I see it differently now. The scars are not shameful. They are proof.

I am not wrong for what I carry. I am not broken. I lived through the unlivable, and somehow, I kept moving.

Grief in Disguise

There were the things people saw: combat, chaos, medals, a uniform that fit like armour. But beneath all that, my body kept score. I could not sleep through the night—always waking between 2:00 and 3:00 a.m.

Some days, I could not eat. Other days, I could not stop. Salt and sugar hit me like a car in a ditch.

Dizzy standing. Faint in crowds. Once, I went down hard on a grocery store floor, fluorescent lights burning my eyes.

My muscles screamed after the lightest workout. Sweat soaked me just from existing. My body was inflamed. My thoughts scattered. My memory flickered like a damaged film reel.

The coping wasn't clean. I survived like something feral: Over-exercising until silence filled my head. Violent outbursts to feel anything but fear.Driving like I wanted to die.

Pills. Porn. Songs that dragged me back to the war. Facebook memories that detonated like landmines.

I was addicted to intensity. To suffering. To the sound of helicopters and gunfire. I called it strength. It was grief in disguise.

And in the middle of it, ghosts who never loved me cleanly. The woman who said I never gave her a choice.

The man who bragged about me but never protected me. The family who called me names, then denied.

My inner protector still stands outside my bedroom door in Debert.

Boots planted on cold linoleum. Watching. Guarding. Even now, he does not rest.

The Last Soldier of This War

I did not have a road map for healing. No elder to turn to, no family legacy of wholeness to inherit. Just fragments of war, of childhood, of love lost, and pain passed down.

Rage and silence braided through my bloodline like DNA. Trauma was not the exception; it was the inheritance. But somewhere in the wreckage, I made a vow: I will not pass this on.

I became a cycle breaker. The one who faced the storm instead of burying it. The one who screamed the silent screams generations before me swallowed whole. The one who chose healing over hiding. It nearly killed me, but I did it so my children would not have to.

After Afghanistan, I saw it clearly: The pain in me was not new. It was ancient. Passed from father to son like a curse disguised as discipline.

The war did not just trigger my trauma; it cracked open the vault of generations.

I remember the slam of my father's fists on the kitchen table, the sour smoke of his cigarettes hanging in the air. That was war, too, long before Kandahar.

The military taught me to follow orders. Healing taught me to break them.

To break the silence, the denial, the generational numbness. I did not just survive war. I survived what created soldiers like me.

As a child, I thought surviving made you strong. Now I know healing makes you free.

I was not just recovering from battlefields abroad, I was recovering from a childhood of clenched fists and swallowed grief.

That is what being a cycle breaker means. You grieve what your parents never could. You learn to love in ways they never knew. You raise your children like you once wished to be raised.

My kids will never know what it is like to hide in their own skin. To be gaslit into silence. Because I chose to feel it all, so they would not have to. Because I chose to wake up, bleed out the poison, and try again.

Christ did not just die for our sins, He showed us how to resurrect.

In that way, I, too, died and was reborn. As a soldier. A father. A man.

As a cycle breaker walking through hell to make a path of light.

And if my children, or anyone who comes after me, ever lose their way, may they find these footprints and know the path was carved in love.

The Soul's Purpose: To Remember Itself

The soul descends into form to taste separation.
From Source,
From others,
From itself.
So it may remember its true nature:

LOVE.
UNITY.
DIVINITY.

Earth is the place of contrast. Through joy and through suffering, the soul discovers what it always was.

Each lifetime carries lessons: forgiveness, courage, compassion, trust, surrender. We return to heal the old, to close the loops, to finish what was left undone. Earth is a hard classroom, but its teachings lead to freedom.

We are here not only to learn but to give. To serve. To create. To embody the Divine in simple, human ways—through loving, grieving, listening, building, forgiving, and staying true. To . . .

Embody the Divine in Human Form

To live as your soul is to remember:
You are a spark of God, clothed in flesh.

This is not escape. The Divine does not bypass pain—it enters it.
Through prayer, stillness, movement, and breath.
Through the body itself.
Through joy that softens the edges, even through dance, until the body becomes a vessel instead of a wall.

Where there is shame, bring presence.
Where there is fear, offer love.
Where there is pain, answer with compassion.

The path is alignment, not perfection.
Ask often: What would Love do here?

"There are two ways to live your life: One is as though nothing is a miracle. The other is as though everything is a miracle."

—UNKNOWN

CHAPTER 44
Field Notes from Recovery

As part of a homework assignment in Julia Cameron's *The Artist's Way*, I woke up early to write these morning pages before the world stirs. These are some samples of days of fragile growth.

* * *

Mefloquine Poisoning and a PTSD Episode, 2023

Yesterd1ugh.

After a PTSD episode in the bath, I had a blood sugar crash around 5:30 p.m.

By 6:00, I felt sick. I checked my sugar: 4.3.

I drank a smoothie and got back in the bath, hoping I had caught the crash in time.

But as soon as I got out, I knew something was wrong.

Fog rolled in. My body did not feel like mine. I shuffled to the bed, trying to stay present. I checked my sugar again—it had spiked from the hot water, but it did not matter. My central nervous system was on full alert. I was drenched in sweat, even through the clean clothes I had just put on.

My partner told me I was "just anxious."

Another label.

That word, *anxious*, landed like an accusation.

Not a reflection. Not compassion. Just another layer of misunderstanding.

And I got defensive. Of course I did.

Because it is not just anxiety.

It is *mefloquine poisoning*.

It is *CPTSD*.

It is *TBI*.

It is the war still echoing through my nervous system every goddamn day.

* * *

Today's Episode: A Learning Opportunity, 2023

Even though today brought challenge, I met it with tools instead of shame. I did not spiral. I showed up. I *learned*.

- I started with **Tai Chi**, grounding my body and breath.
- I had the courage to **call for help**; I did not isolate.
- I turned to **writing**, giving my pain a voice instead of bottling it.
- I **ate**, even when I did not feel like it. Nourishment is self-respect.
- I tried something playful: **Legos**, rebuilding outside as I rebuild within.
- I made **hot water with lemon**, something simple, soothing, and alive.
- I **fed the dog and cat.** I showed up for life, for them, for me.

These are not trivial things. These are survival skills becoming *living skills*. This is healing in motion.

* * *

The Wait, 2023

I have an appointment at 10:00 a.m.

Still waiting on a ride from the driving service, again.

I am hoping they are not too late, as usual.

That always puts me in a state of anticipatory stress, watching the clock, bracing for the delay.

* * *

Therapy Today, 2023

Couples counselling at 1:00. I want to bring up something I have been holding inside:

I feel like my partner emotionally monitors me. It is constant: the sense that my tone, my moods, my body language are being watched, scanned, and interpreted—not with care but with *control*. It reminds me of other times.

Of bad people who did the same.

My father and his second wife used to strip our rooms military-style.

Drawers pulled out. Mattresses flipped. Private things violated in silence.

They called it "discipline."

But it was control. Shame. Power disguised as order.

That same feeling of being watched, invaded, and managed sits in my chest now when I sense her analyzing me.

It is not love.

It is surveillance.

And it brings back every layer of trauma I have tried to peel off.

* * *

Doctors, Mushrooms, and Fear Reconciliation, 2023

Yesterday, I saw the doctor at 4:00 p.m.

We ended up talking for over an hour and a half.

We covered a lot.

Starting with mushrooms and micro-dosing, how psilocybin might help with treatment-resistant trauma, and how it is already shifting things in some veterans I know.

Then she mentioned something new: fear reconciliation therapy.

It uses propranolol, a beta blocker, to disrupt the emotional intensity of traumatic memories while recalling them. It sounds strange, like science fiction, but also promising. The idea of changing how fear is imprinted in the brain? That is the kind of future medicine I wish I had ten years ago.

We also revisited my old blood work.

Looking for missed patterns, old signals the system never caught.

Trying to make sense of this body that still feels like it is burning through its own fuel too fast.

* * *

North Side, Father's Day, and Mefloquine Memories, 2024

I woke up with a jolt, the kind that yanks you out of sleep and drops you straight into the weight of another day on Earth.

Breakfast was already done. Most of the dishes were put away.

Our cat, Tommy, lay stretched across the couch—he is healing from a cut on his belly.

We are heading to the north side this morning—my partner has her ADHD assessment. I am proud of her. Getting answers matters.

We need yogurt and milk.

* * *

Groggy Morning, Dog Park Plans, 2024

The weather's off; rain is coming later this afternoon.

I am groggy. My legs ache like they have been moving all night, twitching with the ghosts of old battles.

I filled out the Disability Tax Credit forms yesterday. I am sending them today. They say eight weeks, so maybe August or September.

Around 10:00 a.m., I will take Steward to the dog park for an hour while my partner hits the gym. We are building routines.

Trying.

Trying to live.

I miss my daughters.

It is Father's Day weekend, and last night I got hit with a flashback out of nowhere. No warning, just the past crashing through the present like it always does.

"When we lose the right to be different,
we lose the privilege to be free."

—Charles Evans Hughes

CHAPTER 45

Starting to Understand Me

Saviour Complex

It took me four years after the fall of Afghanistan in 2021 to understand why I kept trying to rescue people even when they did not want to be rescued.

They call it a martyr complex. A saviour wound. After Kandahar fell, I felt it roaring inside me like wildfire. I watched the country collapse on my phone screen while sitting on a beach in Prince Edward Island. Every part of me wanted to jump back in. Strap on gear. Help someone. Save someone.

I could not save Afghanistan. But I could save the people around me. My partner. My sister. Strangers. Anyone.

It was reflex. Muscle memory from childhood, from war, from years of being the one who showed up when no one else did. I did not realize this compulsion was slowly killing me.

The fall of Afghanistan did not just reopen moral wounds. It revealed emotional ones. Afghanistan's collapse mirrored my own. I had sacrificed everything—my mind, my soul, my family—for a mission that no longer existed. In the aftermath, I kept trying to save people, hoping it would mean something. Hoping I would mean something.

Now, in the spring of 2025, I sit enrolled in an energy-healing course through the World Institute of Incurable Diseases in the Philippines. I am not here to save anyone anymore. I am here to understand why I kept giving myself away. Why my worth was tied to being useful. Why I kept bleeding for people who only came to take what I had left.

Afghanistan taught me I could not save a country. The years after taught me that I could not save people who did not want to be saved.

Alchemizing Pain into Presence

And yet, I know what this is. This is the alchemical path.

To grieve.

To rage.

To cry.

To turn pain into gold.

To let this life become an offering, not from martyrdom but from conscious, chosen service.

Whether I raise a child, create art, or love well in silence . . . I am here as a bridge.

Between soul and body.

Between heaven and earth.

Between the seen and unseen.

So that others, especially those who carry pain, can feel safe, seen, and sacred in my presence.

Now, I see it clearly. I was the one who needed saving all along.

Core Language and the Parts Within

In Internal Family Systems therapy (IFS), *core language* refers to the unconscious words and beliefs that echo from our most wounded parts.

Exiles

Exiles surface as whispers from the exiles the vulnerable, forgotten children of the psyche. Their messages run underneath everything, shaping how we see ourselves and how we move through the world.

For me, these messages often arrive before I realize what's happening. I slip into a PTSD memory and only catch it too late. My nervous system ignites, my mouth runs ahead of me, and words spill out—sharp, defensive. I try to ask for what I need, but it comes out like an attack. I watch as if from the outside, helpless.

I have been labeled since birth:

- The Flash
- Retarded
- Unstable. Unfit.

Different mouths, same message: *Something is wrong with you.* My identity was being written by someone else's hand long before the military inquiries ever began.

Firefighters

When exiles break through, *firefighters* rush in. They don't heal the pain—they smother it.

- **The Binge Eater**: After my first marriage ended, I lived alone and barely ate. One morning, I woke mid-bite, oatmeal in hand, chewing like my life depended on it—fast, panicked, as if the food might vanish. It felt like patrol rations in Afghanistan, or childhood nights sneaking food after my father's rage had finally quieted.
- **The Addict**: After years of pharmaceuticals, Veterans Affairs prescribed me ten grams of cannabis a day as a "miracle cure." It became another escape, another way to avoid the pain no one wanted to face.

- **The Perfectionist**: The military trained this part well. In the field, mistakes could mean death. Later, with PTSD, perfectionism became its own survival tactic. If I got everything right, maybe chaos wouldn't explode.
- **The Self-Harmer**: This part came in childhood. No safety, no escape. At twelve, I swallowed a bottle of Tylenol after my parents screamed for hours and then had sex, like releasing a volcano. Years later, it resurfaced in PTSD episodes. One ex even documented it:

"I have seen David strike himself on the head with wood, plastic, and a metal cane. I have seen him run full speed into walls. Evidence remained such as hematomas and contusions. I hope you see this as proof of the trauma he carries."

- **The Angry Outburster**: Before deployment, I was calm. After mefloquine, the screaming started inside first, then outside. As my pain was dismissed and my boundaries violated, anger became the only shield. It drove people away, but it was fighting to protect every broken part.
- **The Dissociator**: My most familiar firefighter. The military taught this one in trenches, on endless marches. When reality was too much, I disappeared into another world in my head. Later, dissociation became the only way to endure a life that felt unlivable.
- **The Saboteur**: Always waiting in the shadows, whispering that progress is dangerous, that I am unworthy of change.

Not all parts are destructive. Some carry wisdom, longing, or love:
- **The Inner Nurturer**: a protector teacher, creative, spiritual guide.
- **The Inner Child:** an exile innocent, playful, often wounded but still alive.

- **The Inner Lover**: an exile holder of sensuality, creativity, and pleasure.
- **The Warrior of Truth (The Loyal Soldier)**: a protector still standing guard in Afghanistan, smelling of sweat and dust, refusing to abandon the line.

The Self

IFS teaches that *the Self* is not a part. It is the core. The place of calm, clarity, and compassion that can hold everything else.

I have glimpsed this Self in therapy sessions, in medicine work, in rare moments of silence. It is the reminder that beneath the chaos of exiles, protectors and firefighters, there is something unbreakable. Something whole.

CHAPTER 46

Coming Home Through the Body

Energetic Acupuncture

I went for energetic acupuncture today. I was not expecting what happened. She started working on my root and sacral chakras, and within minutes, I was crying hard. Not just a tear here or there, but a deep, body-level grief that poured out of me for fifty minutes straight. I could not stop. It felt like the dam had finally cracked.

As she worked, I felt something I have not felt in years. Circulation in my hips. Warmth. Movement. Life. Since the ketamine, since the trauma, those parts of me have felt frozen, like they were miles away from the rest of me. Numb. Disconnected. Shut down.

But today something shifted. She unblocked something ancient, even primal. My hips woke up. My body started remembering. Not the memories themselves, but the feeling of aliveness that was buried beneath them. It was terrifying and beautiful all at once.

I left feeling cracked open, raw, but also a little more here. A little more in my body. And for the first time in a long time, that felt like a good thing.

The Ruptured Inner Child

There is a moment—I could not tell you the exact hour or day, but I know it happened. The rupture.

Not in my skull or in the desert sand. Not in the firefights or the body bags.

This one split me long before war ever touched my boots.

It did not roar. It did not bleed. It settled into my ribs like a stone, heavy and silent.

The rupture was quieter than an ambush. More cunning than the enemy.

And it struck when I was still a boy.

The inner child rupture is not always a scream. Sometimes, it is the silence when no one comes.

Sometimes, it is the look that says you are too much, or the absence that says you are not enough.

Sometimes, it is needing a hug and getting a slammed door.

I learned early that love came with conditions. That to be seen, I had to shrink. To be safe, I had to disappear.

So, I performed. I adapted. I armoured up.

Years later, in Panjwaii, the cracks showed. The rotors thundered overhead, kicking dust into the air. A boy crouched at the sound, arms over his head.

I didn't just see him. I felt him. The fear in my inner child's eyes reflected mine—ancient, trembling, alive again. The boy who had long ago stopped crying began to move inside me, like something thawing after a long winter.

After the war, when the noise quieted and the medals dulled, I met him again. The one I had left behind. And he was still waiting for someone to come back and choose him.

No one taught me how to hold that boy. No one warned me I would one day have to become the man he always needed.

But I am. Slowly. Painfully.

With every breath of forgiveness.

With every boundary set.

With every time I whisper to the broken child inside: You did not deserve what happened. You no longer have to carry it alone.

The world may have taught me to fight, but healing taught me to stay.

Stay with him.

Stay with myself.

And finally, after all these years, come home.

Healing Through the Chakras

Healing did not come in a flash of light or a final ceremony. It came in tremors—shivers in my psoas, tears I had not planned, moments when my daughter's laugh cracked something open in my chest.

Years after Afghanistan, I sat on my floor with a copy of *Eastern Body, Western Mind*, trying to make sense of why my nervous system was always either on fire or completely numb. Anodea Judith spoke a language that felt like it was written for people like me—soldiers with spiritual wounds, warriors with frozen hearts.

I learned the body keeps score in more than just flashbacks; it stores the whole damn war. My root chakra—the foundation—was shattered long before I deployed. Growing up in a house of sudden disappearances and shouted orders had already wired my body for alertness. Afghanistan just turned the volume up. Healing meant learning to feel safe in my own skin for the first time. Bare feet in the grass. Meals I cooked for myself. Letting the earth hold me when no one else could.

The sacral came next, allowing feeling again, not just surviving. Touch had become foreign, even threatening. I had to relearn how to be held, how to receive pleasure without shame. Trauma had confused love with threat. Slowly, through bodywork, breath, and presence, I began to thaw.

My solar plexus had always burned hot—driven, angry, adrenalized. In war, it served me. At home, it scorched everything I touched. Healing meant learning to soften, to move from domination to discernment. To have power without needing control.

The heart took the longest. I had built walls around it, thinking they were armour. But they were a prison. I remember the day I cried without knowing why. I was lying on a yoga mat, and the instructor barely whispered, "You're safe now," and something broke. In that rupture, I found room for my own grief. The kind of grief soldiers are not allowed to show. It was the beginning of forgiveness, not of war, but of myself.

The throat chakra reopened when I stopped trying to tell a tidy story. There is nothing clean about trauma. But there is power in naming it, even if your voice shakes. Especially when it does. I started writing. At first, it was just for me. Then, for the brothers I lost. Then, for my children, so they would know their father walked through fire and chose to heal.

The third eye had been with me the whole time. Visions during firefights, dreams that warned me, an inner compass I ignored because I was trained to obey, not to trust my intuition. But healing meant listening and honouring the sacred messages that came not from books or doctors, but from deep within.

The crown came in quiet moments. In the pause between breaths. In the tears during prayer. In knowing that I am more than what I survived. In knowing the soul cannot be destroyed, only buried, and mine was clawing its way back to the light.

Healing is not a finish line; it is a way of living. It is tending to each chakra like a wounded soldier, giving each part of me what war, trauma, and even childhood never did. Safety. Touch. Power. Love. Voice. Insight. Connection.

And for the first time in my life, I am not just surviving the war.

I am coming home.

Earth Angels

Somewhere along the way, in the thick of dust storms and trauma, I began to believe in Earth angels. Not the kind with wings or glowing halos, but the ones who showed up when I was broken, half gone, buried under shame and noise.

They did not always look divine. Sometimes, they wore uniforms. Sometimes, they were barefoot in a sunroom. Sometimes, they sat cross-legged in a quiet treatment room with soft music playing, palms glowing with intention, whispering words I did not understand but could feel in my bones.

There were the Reiki Masters. They did not poke, prod, or prescribe. They just held energy, space, silence. And somehow, that was enough to help me remember the parts of myself I had long before abandoned in Kandahar dust, in hospital beds, in courtrooms, in moments when I almost gave up. They saw me as more than a diagnosis. More than a rank. More than a wound.

There was the medic at Kandahar Airfield who did not flinch when I started shaking in the middle of an appointment, or the chaplain who handed me a Bible, knowing full well I did not believe in much anymore, but seeing something cracking open in me. And the Reiki Master who touched the space above my heart and said, "You are still here. You have always been here."

Earth angels are just people who remember how to love when the world forgets. Who see the soul under the uniform, under the trauma, under the diagnosis.

Looking back, I do not think I would have made it without them.

Angel Numbers: The Yoga of Numbers

The first time I noticed it, I was in a hospital room. The fluorescent lights buzzed overhead, and the monitor by my bed ticked out its rhythm. I turned my head to the clock on the wall: 4:44. My chest tightened. For a moment, the sterile room felt less empty, as if something unseen had just stepped in and sat with me.

Some people brush off repeating numbers as coincidence. But for me, especially after war, trauma, and the long unraveling of who I thought I was, they became guideposts. Little glimmers of pattern in the chaos.

I started noticing them everywhere: during therapy sessions when silence grew heavy, on long drives with the radio off, in the glow of a microwave clock after another sleepless night. Always the same—4:44. It happened so often that it stopped feeling random. These numbers were not chasing me. They were walking beside me.

At first, I wasn't sure what to make of it. But in a world where everything else felt unstable, the numbers gave me something to hold onto. They became anchors, patterns in the storm, whispers in the static. A presence without pressure, guidance without force.

Eventually, I discovered gematria, the ancient numerological tradition used in Hebrew and Greek scripture. Each letter carried a number, each word a hidden equation. Suddenly, I saw these moments differently. They were not accidents, but messages. A second layer of meaning, running beneath ordinary life.

In the book of Ezekiel, the prophet describes four living beings emerging from a great wheel, each with four faces and four wings, a vision of order and divine structure. That is 444: foundation, alignment, the presence of angels. Some say it appears when you are on the right path, even if that path is painful. When I saw it, I felt held.

I could be curled on the floor after a flashback, or numbed out on the couch after a session, when suddenly 4:44 would blink into view. It did not fix the pain. But it softened something. It reminded me I was not abandoned. Not entirely.

Later, I learned there are 44 months and 4 days between Jesus' baptism and the day God affirmed him before the crucifixion. Sacrifice, mission, and divine timing, all woven into one pattern. When 444 appeared, it felt like a whisper from beyond: *Stay the course. You are not lost.*

Then, there was 888.

Where 444 felt like structure and protection, 888 pulsed with warmth, victory, and love. In Hebrew, the word for love holds the value of 8. In Greek, the name Jesus totals 888. Not love once, but love multiplied and overflowing.

When I saw it, I felt more than surviving. I felt *seen*. Not by doctors, systems, or even people, but by something older, deeper. A swell would rise in my chest, loosening a place long locked down. Like grace was seeping into the cracks.

I remembered Psalm 19:1: "The heavens declare the glory of God." In gematria, the phrase adds up to 888. It felt like the sky itself was testifying. Not in sermons, but in signals. Not in dogma, but in patterns etched into the fabric of creation.

In recovery, I stopped seeing numbers as superstition and began to hear them as a kind of cosmic language. Not the whole story, but a thread through the dark. A breadcrumb trail of light. A reminder: *You are not forgotten.*

So, I keep going.

One number at a time.

One breath at a time.

Not chasing signs but receiving them. Not demanding proof but listening.

And in that listening, I live.

CHAPTER 47

Heal Every Aspect of Life

The HEAL Plan

By the time the HEAL Plan landed in my lap in 2025, I had already been buried by health care systems. The military system, the medical system, the mental health system—all of them had poked and prodded and labeled me, but none had seen me. None had felt the war still roaring in my cells or the way my soul had gone missing somewhere between Kandahar and my childhood.

It came on a flyer, in a bright green font that felt too hopeful. The HEAL Plan—a program offered by the World Institute for Incurable Diseases. How is that for irony? I laughed at the name at first. I was the incurable disease. Mefloquine poisoning, PTSD, traumatic brain injury, moral injury. Whatever label the system put on me.

But something about the phrasing stuck: Heal Every Aspect of Life.

They did not say *treat*. They did not say *manage*. They said *heal*, and they meant every part of me: physical, emotional, mental, even spiritual . . . and especially my past!

That was new.

I had tried everything else. Pills that numbed me. Weed clinics that blurred the pain into dissociation. Clinics in the woods run by narcissists hiding behind the language of healing. I had been desperate, abandoned, institutionalized, and medicated beyond recognition. Nothing could reach the parts of me that had died without bleeding.

But the HEAL Plan did not come with a prescription pad. It came with breathing, somatic movements, energy work, and something I did not even know I was missing—spiritual integrity. A kind of reanimation. I remember sitting through my first session thinking, *What the fuck is this?* But at the same time, I felt a strange softness begin to rise in me. Like my body was remembering itself.

So, when the World Institute for Incurable Diseases called the heal plan BEwell Science, perhaps the deeper longing—*to remember how to be soul again*—was an acknowledgment that wellness isn't merely biological. It's spiritual, relational, and deeply human: a return to the part of us that never needed curing.

There were no charts or five-point assessments. Just the breath. The body. The energy that had been locked in survival mode since I first put on the uniform. Since I first fired that Carl Gustaf. Since I first drove that LAV into a ditch in Gagetown and got called weak for crying through whiplash and shame. Since the blue door slammed behind me in Kandahar and I screamed at the high-as-fuck AUP officers, "We are all dying for your country!"

No one taught me how to feel after that. But here I was, learning it through stillness. Through slow movement. Through letting someone finally see the mess.

What shocked me most was not that it worked, but that it reached the parts nothing else could.

Where medicine had failed me, this plan said: You are more than your symptoms and story.

Where psychology once told me there was no hope, this plan said: You are sacred and wounded, and that is why you hurt.

Where the military turned my nervous system into a weapon, this plan helped me lay the weapon down.

I used to think healing would mean the war was over. But healing is how we stop fighting ourselves.

The HEAL Plan did not fix everything. But it gave me a language for what was broken, one that was not rooted in shame. It did not demand that I perform my pain or prove my injury. It met me where I had collapsed, and it gave me something rare in this world: a map home and compassion.

Even now, when the tremors return or the grief comes like a wave in the middle of the night, I go back to what it taught me—breath, presence, forgiveness. I go back to the man I found under all the wreckage.

The wisdom I started to gain from healing every aspect of my life is priceless. The experience brought hope—a new hope that kindled the light at the end of a tunnel and illuminated my path.

"He who has good health has hope,
And he who has hope can do everything."

—ARABIAN PROVERB

A Letter to the One Who Did Not Know

Dear younger me,

You were not weak for wanting to be loved. You were not naive for falling for the mask. You learned to find safety in chaos, and it kept you alive. But you do not have to earn love by bleeding anymore.

You do not have to fix anyone to be worthy.

The ones who truly see you will not punish your pain or weaponize your past. I know you are tired of fighting, of explaining, of proving that you are real. I see you. And I promise: Peace is not the absence of danger. It is the presence of truth. And your truth matters.

Love,

Me (finally free)

Letter to My Father

Dad,

There are things I used to want from you that I've finally stopped chasing. Approval. Understanding. A kind of love that didn't need to be earned through obedience, silence, or performance. For years, I mistook discipline for safety and control for love. I see now that you were only passing down what had been handed to you—the hard training of men who were never taught how to feel.

I used to think your anger was personal, that the weight you carried was aimed at me. But now I know it came from something older—from generations of soldiers and sons, each trying to outrun their own ghosts. You carried yours in your chest, like a radio transmitting orders from a war that never really ended.

I resented you for so long. For your silence, for your authority, for the way fear filled our home like smoke. But time and pain have softened me. I see now how much of you was shaped by service, by duty, by the need to hold it all together. I can see the young man inside you, trying to build stability out of chaos. I forgive that man. I forgive you.

I can't say the past doesn't still ache. It does. But I've learned that forgiveness isn't about pretending none of it mattered; it's about releasing myself from the gravity of it. I don't need you to change for me to heal. I only need to acknowledge that beneath the uniform, beneath the walls, there was once a father doing the best he could with what little he was given.

You taught me strength, even when it came through pain. You taught me endurance, even when it felt like punishment. And now, as I learn to soften—to breathe, to let love in without fear—I carry forward the best of what you gave me and lay the rest down.

I hope wherever you are, there's peace. I hope you know I've found some too.

Your son,

David

Letter to My Mother

Dear Mom,

I've spent most of my life trying to understand you,

the woman who held me and hurt me, who loved me in ways that sometimes felt like war.

You were barely holding yourself together back then. The house was chaos, fear, silence, broken glass, and the kind of exhaustion that seeps into the walls. I used to think you abandoned yourself, that you disappeared when I needed you most. But now I see you were just surviving. Just trying to make it through another day in a world that gave you no safety net.

You were a daughter before you were my mother.

You carried wounds that were never spoken, pain that turned into armour. I inherited some of that armour, the hardness, the vigilance, the way love can feel like walking on glass.

I used to carry so much anger toward you.

For not protecting me. For letting me become invisible. For teaching me to confuse love with endurance.

But the truth is, I see you now, not as the mother I wanted, but as the woman you were: scared, unhealed, human.

So, I forgive you. Not to erase what happened, but to free both of us from it.

I forgive the nights you disappeared into yourself, the mornings you were too tired to notice me, the words that cut because you didn't know how else to speak.

And I forgive myself for all the years I hated you for it.

I can love you now without needing you to change.

I can carry your story with compassion, not blame.

You gave me life, and from that life, I am learning to give myself what you could not.

That is my inheritance.

And that is my freedom.

Your son,

David

Conclusion

I set out to tell this story not to relive the past, but to reclaim it—from silence, from shame, from the lies I told myself to survive. What you have read here is not a war story. It is a soul story, a story of waking up: in the desert, in a hospital bed, in the ruins of a family, in the arms of my children, and in the stillness of my own breath.

I no longer carry a weapon. I carry memory and a responsibility to live with honour for those who did not make it home and for the man I am still becoming.

If you have been through fire, know this: You are not alone. There is life on the other side. Not perfect, but real. And it is worth living.

One morning, the light poured through the window, and everything stilled. It felt like a quiet reward, as if the world whispered that I was exactly where I needed to be. I paused. Breathed. Simply existed.

I thought about the tools and support that had come when I needed them most, and I did not take them for granted. There is something sacred in that kind of timing.

So, to whoever reads this one day: Thank you for the guidance, the grounding, the space to unravel and rebuild. I appreciate it more than I can say. And so, I leave you here, in the quiet, in the breath, in the light of a new morning.

Resources

This resources section was compiled in gratitude to the countless veterans, researchers, and advocates who refused to let the truth about mefloquine toxicity remain buried. Their courage in sharing lived experience, scientific insight, and clinical data has helped thousands find clarity, validation, and hope.

Special thanks to the **Quinism Foundation**, medical researchers in **neurotoxicology and vestibular science**, and all healthcare professionals working to distinguish mefloquine toxicity from PTSD and other service-related conditions.

May this guide serve as both education and empowerment for survivors and clinicians seeking understanding and compassionate care.

* * *

Fight, Flight, Freeze, or Fawn:
A Primer

Fight Response

Grounding:
- "I'm safe right now. My body is remembering danger that isn't here."
- "It's okay to feel angry. I don't have to act on it."
- "My nervous system is trying to protect me—I can thank it and still choose calm."

- "I can put down my armor for a moment. I'm allowed to rest."

Regulation:
- "I'm feeling triggered—this will pass."
- "I can be strong without being destructive."
- "This energy is nervous system, not truth."
- If anger is justified but needs boundaries: "I'll speak clearly after I calm down—not now."

Emotions:
- Anger
- Rage
- Confrontation

Body Feelings:
- Tight jaw
- Urge for violence
- Burning sensation in stomach or chest

Energy Level: High

Flight Response

Grounding:
- "I don't have to run—I'm safe in this moment."
- "My body wants distance, but I can give it calm instead."
- "I can pause and breathe before I decide what to do."
- "There's no danger here now. I can slow down."

Regulation:
- "I'm safe right now."
- "I can slow down."
- "It's okay to stay."
- "I can take a breath before I move."
- "My body thinks I'm in danger, but I'm not."

Emotions:
- Anxiety
- Panic
- Avoidance

Body Feelings:
- Excessive movement (fidgeting, pacing, leg shaking)
- Numbness or disconnection from body

Energy Level: High

Freeze Response

Grounding:
- "It's okay that I feel frozen."
- "Nothing's wrong with me—my body is protecting me."
- "I can start by noticing one thing around me."
- "I'm safe enough to take a small breath."

Regulation:
- "I can move one finger or take one gentle stretch."
- "I don't need to rush my way out."
- "Stillness can shift when it's ready."

Emotions:
- Dissociation
- Dread
- Emotional shutdown

Body Feelings:
- Pale or clammy skin
- Heaviness, cold limbs
- Stiffness or immobility
- Pounding heart (paradox: frozen outside, racing inside)

Energy Level: Low

Fawning

Grounding:
- "It's okay to have my own needs."
- "I don't have to earn safety by pleasing."
- "My worth isn't tied to anyone's approval."
- "I can pause before I say yes."

Regulation:
- "Breathe—I can check in with myself first."
- "I can listen to my body before I respond."
- "It's safe to take a moment before helping."
- "I can say no kindly and stay connected."

Sensations:
- **Emotions**: Confusion, suppressed anger, resentment
- **Body Feelings**: Tense posture, clenched hands or jaw, over-smiling
- **Energy Level**: High on the surface but low underneath.

Mefloquine Toxicity

Initial Exposure or Accumulation

- **First dose**: Some people experience symptoms after just one pill.
- **Cumulative dosing**: The drug accumulates in fatty tissues and the brain. Symptoms may appear or worsen over time.

Changes in Dosing

- **Loading dose**: A high initial dose (sometimes given to soldiers or travelers) can provoke acute symptoms.
- **Missed or irregular doses**: Inconsistent intake can confuse the brain, making symptoms more likely.

Stress or Trauma

- **Combat or deployment stress**, family separation, or trauma (physical or emotional) can destabilize the nervous system and interact with mefloquine's effects.
- **Mefloquine may amplify normal stress responses** into paranoia, rage, or panic.

Concurrent Illness or Injury

- **Heatstroke, dehydration, infections, TBIs**, and other injuries can increase the likelihood of mefloquine neurotoxicity manifesting.
- **Fever and inflammation** may change how the drug crosses the blood–brain barrier.

Alcohol and Other Drugs

- Alcohol and certain medications (like antidepressants, benzodiazepines, or stimulants) can interact dangerously with mefloquine, increasing the risk of:
  - » Seizures
  - » Hallucinations
  - » Suicidal ideation

Sleep Deprivation

- Mefloquine often causes intense, **vivid dreams**, nightmares, and insomnia. Chronic sleep loss can rapidly lead to:
  - » Disorientation
  - » Flashbacks
  - » Psychotic breaks

Sensory and Environmental Triggers

- For veterans of mefloquine toxicity, **loud noises**, **crowds**, or **bright lights** may retrigger neurological symptoms, even long after stopping the drug.
- This is sometimes called **kindling**—the brain becomes sensitized and overreacts to stimuli.

Genetic and Biological Sensitivity

- Some people have a genetic vulnerability to quinoline-based neurotoxins, including those with:
  - » A history of **seizures**, **mental illness**, or **TBI**
  - » **Low body weight** (higher concentration in brain tissue)

If you've already taken mefloquine and are experiencing strange symptoms—especially those that resemble PTSD, psychosis, or vestibular issues (dizziness, balance problems)—it's important to know:

These symptoms are **not imaginary**. *Mefloquine neurotoxicity can be permanent.*

* * *

Tracking Mefloquine Toxicity Symptoms

1. Start a Symptom and Trigger Journal

Create a log to track:
- Date and time
- What you were doing before symptoms started
- What you ate, drank, or took (meds, supplements)
- Who you were with; what was happening
- Your emotional and physical state
- Symptoms that followed (e.g., dizziness, rage, panic, flashback)

After 1–2 weeks, you may notice patterns.

2. Watch for Early Warning Signs

Triggers usually cause subtle shifts before a full flare. Look for:
- Brain fog or disorientation
- Nausea or vertigo
- Chest pressure
- Sudden emotional changes (rage, fear, dissociation)
- A sudden need to escape or hide

These **prodromal symptoms** can signal that a trigger is present.

3. Notice Repetition

If a similar symptom always follows a certain situation or stimulus, that's a likely trigger. For example:
- Crowds → vertigo and panic
- Loud, sudden noises → dissociation or rage
- Argument with a loved one → collapse or despair
- Carrying heavy gear → dizziness and flashbacks to patrols

Repetition means it's not random—your nervous system is reacting to a stored association.

4. Differentiate Internal vs. External Triggers

Internal	External
Fatigue or hunger	Loud noise
Hormonal shifts	Bright lights
Shame or intrusive thoughts	Crowds, certain smells
Flashbacks	Specific places or people

Identifying **whether the trigger comes from within or outside** can help you build specific strategies to manage it.

5. Use Controlled Exposure

If safe, test a suspected trigger in a **gentle, controlled way** (like sound recordings, lights, certain foods), and observe your reaction over the next 1–48 hours. This helps confirm whether it's a true trigger or coincidental.

Do this only if you have grounding tools and are not in a vulnerable state.

6. Use Body Awareness and Somatic Tracking

Your body knows before your mind does. Tune in to:

- Tight jaw
- Shallow breathing
- Change in body temp or sweat
- Shaky limbs

Those are pre-trigger cues. Sometimes the trigger isn't conscious—it's **stored in your nervous system or brain stem** (as in trauma or brain injury).

7. Correlate With Known Mefloquine Symptoms

Mefloquine triggers often affect:

- Balance (vestibular system)
- Visual/auditory processing
- Emotions like fear, rage, or hopelessness
- Sleep/dream cycles
- GI upset and sensory sensitivity

If symptoms flare with exposure to motion, light, sound, or stress, that's likely a **toxic brain loop** being activated.

* * *

Common Mefloquine Triggers, Grouped by Type

How to use this list:
- Highlight or check off any that resonate strongly.
- Start logging your **last three flare-ups** and see which ones appeared right before.
- Use grounding, pacing, and boundaries around **repeat offenders**.

Sensory Triggers

- Loud, sudden noises (e.g. slamming doors, explosions, barking dogs)
- Bright or flashing lights (especially overhead fluorescents or strobe lights)
- Crowds or busy visual environments (supermarkets, parades, malls)
- Motion (elevators, escalators, driving, boat rides)
- Certain smells (diesel, smoke, decay, sweat, cleaning agents)
- Sudden temperature changes (heat, especially, can worsen symptoms)
- Vestibular overload (rapid head turns, scanning rooms, walking on uneven ground)

Physical/Medical Triggers

- Lack of sleep
- Low blood sugar
- Alcohol or cannabis
- Caffeine
- Dehydration
- Exercise that strains the neck or core (affects vagus or brain stem)
- Infections (even minor ones can cause symptom flare)

- Hormonal shifts (e.g., cortisol spike, menstrual cycle)

Emotional Triggers

- Confrontation or arguments
- Feeling trapped or judged
- Memories of deployment or trauma
- Being asked to "calm down" or being otherwise invalidated
- Sudden intimacy or affection (can feel overwhelming or threatening)
- Feelings of abandonment or rejection

Environmental Triggers

- Returning to military bases or hospitals
- Hearing military lingo or commands
- Media coverage of war or veteran's issues
- National holidays (e.g., Remembrance Day, July 1, November 11)
- Places with high echo/reverb (gyms, churches, large halls)

Cognitive Triggers

- Overthinking, analyzing, or perfectionism
- Racing thoughts, compulsive loops
- Flashbacks or intrusive images
- Loss of time or disorientation
- Sudden urge to "do something" or flee

Relational Triggers

- Feeling not believed (about illness or symptoms)
- Toxic, dismissive, or controlling dynamics
- Being ignored or ghosted
- Witnessing others deny their trauma while you're suffering
- Trying to parent, perform, or lead while internally breaking down

* * *

Why Driving Triggers Mefloquine Symptoms

1. Vestibular and Visual Overload

- Mefloquine damages brain regions involved in **balance, motion perception, and spatial orientation**, especially the **vestibular system** and brain stem.
- While driving, your brain must process rapidly changing **visual fields**, **movement**, and **depth perception**, all of which can overstimulate a compromised system.
- Result: **vertigo, nausea, tunnel vision, sensory confusion, or panic**.

2. TBI-Linked Motion Sensitivity

- Many mefloquine survivors also have undiagnosed or mild TBI.
- The **inner ear, brain stem**, and **cervical spine** (neck) all interact during driving. Bumps, turns, and eye tracking can create:
  - » Headaches
  - » Brain fog or disorientation
  - » Feeling "drunk" or "tilted" even while upright
  - » "Rubber band" visual effect (delayed eye tracking)

3. Spatial Disorientation or Derealization

- The **sense of self in space** can become distorted. You might feel like:
  - » The road is moving, but you're not
  - » The car is floating or not fully under control
  - » You're watching yourself drive, but not "in your body" (dissociation)

- These symptoms are **neurological**, not just anxiety-based. Mefloquine affects the **temporal and parietal lobes**, where body–space awareness is processed.

4. PTSD or Combat Associations

- Driving in urban environments or rural back roads may trigger **combat memories**, such as:
  - » IEDs and ambushes (especially from Afghan roads)
  - » Scanning for threats or sudden noises
  - » The act of being hypervigilant behind the wheel, which can reawaken dormant fight-or-flight circuitry

5. Sudden Triggers While Driving

- Flashbacks or panic attacks while driving can be dangerous. Common sudden activators include:
  - » Diesel smells, military vehicles, emergency sirens
  - » Roadkill or construction rubble
  - » Getting lost or turned around, which provokes spatial panic
  - » Passengers' talking, especially if emotionally charged

* * *

Common Symptoms Reported While Driving

- Dizziness or unsteadiness
- Feelings of unreality/detachment
- Sudden nausea or sweating
- Visual "flickering" or light sensitivity
- Panic, rage, or a desire to flee the vehicle
- Freezing, forgetting where you're going, missing exits
- "White-knuckling" the steering wheel in survival mode

Tips to Manage or Reduce Driving Triggers

- **Drive during calm times** (low traffic, low sensory input)
- **Wear polarized sunglasses or dark lenses** to reduce visual overload
- **Listen to calming music**
- **Avoid driving long distances alone** until you're stable
- **Plan your route in advance**; use GPS to reduce cognitive load
- **Ground your body**: sit on a weighted blanket or sheepskin, and press your feet firmly into the floor
- **Keep hydration and protein snacks in the car** (blood sugar dips = symptom spikes)

* * *

Common Overlapping Triggers Between PTSD and Mefloquine Toxicity

Sensory Triggers

- Loud, sudden noises (e.g., fireworks, gunshots, slamming doors)
- Bright or flashing lights (strobe effects, vehicle lights at night)
- Overcrowded environments (malls, transit stations, concerts)
- Sudden temperature or pressure changes
- Certain smells (diesel, blood, burning, cleaning agents)
- Tactile overload (tight gear, wet clothing, scratchy uniforms)

Neurological Triggers

- Sleep deprivation or fragmented sleep
- Nightmares or night terrors
- Disorientation from motion (driving, flying, elevators)

- Overstimulating environments (too much visual or auditory input)
- Vestibular overload (balance-related disorientation)

Both conditions result in hyperreactive or destabilized brain stem responses to sensory input.

Situational Triggers

- News about war or conflict
- Anniversaries of traumatic events
- Military ceremonies, parades, or uniforms
- Being in a crowd or stuck in traffic
- Authority figures or hierarchical power structures
- Hospital visits, especially psych wards

Combat-Specific Triggers

- Driving on rural or potholed roads (mimics IED conditions)
- Backfiring cars or helicopters overhead
- Military lingo or commands
- People shouting or yelling behind you
- Metallic sounds or slamming hatches

Relational Triggers

- Being misunderstood, doubted, or dismissed
- Feeling trapped in a conversation or emotionally cornered
- Sudden emotional intimacy or vulnerability
- Loss of control in a relationship
- Accusations or blame, especially around past trauma

Moral Injury and Identity Triggers

- Hypocrisy or betrayal by leadership
- Seeing others suffer while feeling powerless

- Children in danger or distress
- Being called a hero when you feel broken
- Hearing people justify war or deny its effects

Why They Overlap

- Mefloquine can **chemically influence the same brain regions** impacted by PTSD: amygdala (fear center), brain stem (startle response), temporal lobes (memory), and vestibular system (balance/safety).
- This overlap makes **PTSD triggers feel more physical** and **mefloquine toxicity feel more emotional**, blurring the line between the two.

Trigger: Witnessing Others Deny Their Trauma While You're Suffering

Why it hits so hard:

- It evokes **invalidation**: your own pain feels **dismissed, minimized**, or **taboo**, especially if others are pretending they're fine.
- It activates **shame, self-doubt**, or **rage**: "Why am I still broken when they're 'normal'?"
- It can fracture unit or community trust: "I thought we were in this together."
- It taps into **moral injury**—the deep, soul-level conflict that arises when people ignore, rationalize, or gaslight the reality of shared suffering.

Mefloquine-specific triggers:

- Many veterans were told their symptoms were **"just stress"** or **"PTSD"** when they were in fact caused by **brain damage from a neurotoxic drug**.

- Watching others deny this reality—whether knowingly or not—compounds the injury.
- Survivors often feel **isolated**, **betrayed**, and even **gaslit** by their peers, medical professionals, or chain of command.

The nervous system impact:

This trigger can send you into:
- **Fight** (anger, arguments)
- **Flight** (shutting down emotionally or fleeing connection)
- **Freeze** (numbness, brain fog)
- **Fawn** (people-pleasing or silencing your own truth to keep peace)

Symptoms you might notice:

- Tight chest, difficulty breathing
- Ruminations like "Am I crazy?" or "Am I weak?"
- Emotional collapse or emotional overreaction
- Desire to isolate
- Sudden mistrust or resentment toward peers or family

Sweating as a Symptom and a Response to Triggers

Why Sweating Happens

In PTSD:

- Triggered by **fight-or-flight activation**: The sympathetic nervous system kicks in.
- Your body prepares for danger—increasing **heart rate**, **blood pressure**, and **sweat** to cool you off in case of combat or flight.
- This can happen even **without conscious fear**, especially during:
  » Nightmares or flashbacks
  » Sudden reminders of trauma
  » Emotional overwhelm

In mefloquine toxicity:

- Mefloquine disrupts the **autonomic nervous system**, leading to:
  » **Thermoregulatory dysfunction** (you sweat too much or not enough)
  » **Panic-like episodes** without external cause
  » **Brain stem dysregulation**, especially near the hypothalamus (your heat regulation center)

In both cases, sweating can be **an early warning sign** that your nervous system is dysregulating—even before panic, rage, or dissociation shows up.

Types of Sweating to Track

Type	Description	Possible Cause
Cold sweats	Damp skin with chills	Fear, anxiety, flashbacks
Soaked clothing	Sudden and heavy sweat	Panic, heat dysregulation, autonomic storm
Night sweats	Waking up drenched	Mefloquine damage, nightmares, cortisol spikes
Facial or back sweating	Localized bursts	Sensory overload or TBI-related dysfunction

When Sweating May Be a Trigger Signal

- Right before **emotional flooding**, rage, or disorientation
- After exposure to a known or subtle **trigger** (e.g., loud noise, military talk, intense light)
- When repressed memories or **moral injury** themes are stirred
- During or after **driving**, especially with vestibular sensitivity

What to Do When It Happens

- **Don't ignore it**; treat it like an "early flare warning"
- Move to a **cool, low-stimulation environment**
- Do a **vagus nerve reset** (cold splash, neck tilt, long exhale)
- Sip **cool electrolyte water**
- Ground with weight, scent, or gentle pressure
- Track in a journal: *What just happened? Where was I? What was I thinking or hearing?*

Further Readings

For Veterans with mefloquine toxicity often exhibit symptoms that **mimic PTSD**, leading to misdiagnoses and prolonged undetected neurotoxicity:

- Livezey, J., Oliver, T., & Cantilena, L. (2016). *Prolonged neuropsychiatric symptoms in a military service member exposed to mefloquine.* Drug Safety—Case Reports, 3, 7. https://doi.org/10.1007/s40800-016-0030-z
- Kime, P. (2016, August 11). *Malaria drug causes brain damage that mimics PTSD: Case study.* Military Times. Retrieved from https://www.militarytimes.com/news/your-military/2016/08/11/malaria-drug-causes-brain-damage-that-mimics-ptsd-case-study/

Chronic CNS toxicity syndrome, complicating PTSD diagnoses:

- McCarthy, S. (2015). *Malaria prevention, mefloquine neurotoxicity, neuropsychiatric illness and risk-benefit analysis in the Australian Defence Force.* Journal of Parasitology Research, 2015, article ID 287651.

Quinoline-based drugs (including mefloquine) induce a chronic neurological condition called **quinism**, frequently confused with PTSD/TBI due to overlapping symptoms like dizziness, sleep disruption, and emotional disturbance:

- Ringqvist, Å., Bech, P., Glenthøj, B., & Petersen, E. (2015). *Acute and long-term psychiatric side effects of mefloquine: A follow-up on*

Danish adverse event reports. Travel Medicine and Infectious Disease, 13(1), 80–88. https://doi.org/10.1016/j.tmaid.2014.10.021

Quinism Foundation—Chronic Neurotoxicity from Quinoline Drugs:

- Nevin, R. L. (2014). *Idiosyncratic quinoline central nervous system toxicity.* PMCID PMC4095041. https://www.ncbi.nlm.nih.gov/pmc/articles/PMC4095041/

Mefloquine can also cause sweating because it can disrupt the autonomic nervous system, causing thermoregulatory dysfunction and panic-like episodes:

- Canada. Department of National Defence. Surgeon General Branch. (2017, June 1). *Surgeon General Task Force Report on Mefloquine* [PDF]. **https://www.canada.ca/content/dam/dnd-mdn/migration/assets/FORCES_Internet/docs/en/about-reports-pubs-health/surgeon-general-report-mefloquine.pdf**
- U.S. Food & Drug Administration. (2013, July 29). *FDA Drug Safety Communication: FDA approves label changes for antimalarial drug mefloquine hydrochloride due to risk of serious psychiatric and nerve side effects* [PDF]. Retrieved from https://www.fda.gov/media/86285/download
- National Academies of Sciences, Engineering, and Medicine; Health and Medicine Division; Committee to Review Long-Term Health Effects of Antimalarial Drugs; Board on Population Health and Public Health Practice. (2020, February 25). *Assessment of long-term health effects of antimalarial drugs when used for prophylaxis.* Washington (DC): National Academies Press (US). Chapter 4: Mefloquine. Retrieved from https://www.ncbi.nlm.nih.gov/books/NBK556592

Case Study—PTSD vs. Mefloquine Toxicity: A U.S. servicemember initially diagnosed with severe PTSD (anger, nightmares, memory loss, gait issues) was later identified as suffering from **mefloquine-induced brain stem toxicity** after deployment in 2009:

- Livezey, J., Oliver, T., & Cantilena, L. (2016). Prolonged neuropsychiatric symptoms in a military service member exposed to mefloquine. *Drug Safety – Case Reports*, *3*, 7. https://doi.org/10.1007/s40800-016-0030-z

Guide to Grounding Yourself

Grounding yourself means bringing your awareness back to the present moment: out of racing thoughts, flashbacks, or emotional overwhelm and into the safety and reality of *here and now*.

It's the process of reconnecting your mind to your body, your breath, and your surroundings so you can feel stable, centered, and in control again.

Grounding is not about pretending you are okay. It is about learning methods that can help you weather the storm, and about learning that you are still worth saving, even in the middle of the chaos.

Whenever you experience symptoms, take these steps.

Use self-talk.

- I have an injury. I am not a bad person.
- These thoughts, urges, and emotions are just symptoms. They are not who I am.
- I am safe. Right here. Right now. I am not back there.
- I can handle it when things go wrong. I already have. Look at all the times I made it through. I'm still here.
- This shall pass. It always does, even when it does not feel like it will.

Breathe.

In through your nose. Hold. Out through your mouth. Again. Again.

Choose to relax.

Drop your shoulders. Loosen your jaw. Find your breath.

Put on soothing music.

Let the rhythm regulate your nervous system. Let it soften the static.

Change your posture.

If you are sitting, stand. If you are standing, sit. Move something. Reconnect.

Do something stimulating.

Freezing water. Texture. Movement. Sound. Come back. Come home.

Remind yourself that this is temporary.

You do not have to fix everything. Just survive this moment.

What to Do When I Spiral and Shut Down (Advice for Caregivers and Loved Ones)

1. Do Not Try to Fix It

Just be nearby. I will not be able to hear advice or logic in that state. It is not personal; I am in survival mode.

2. Prioritize Calm, Not Conversation

Stay grounded in yourself. A gentle tone and few words are better than trying to reach me through noise. Try: "I see this is hard. I am here."

3. Give Me Space with Presence

Stay in the room or nearby, but do not hover. Let me come back on my own time. It helps to know you are close, even in silence.

4. No Sudden Moves, No Demands

Keep your energy soft. No pressure to talk, fix, or perform. Do not try to force eye contact or affection. Just safety.

5. Set a Gentle Anchor

Leave a grounding object nearby—a blanket, a glass of water, something warm. Soft music or nature sounds are sometimes okay. Let me find my way back.

6. Trust That I Will Return

Even if I am unrecognizable for a while, I am still in here. Your steady, nonjudgmental presence is the bridge I will eventually crawl back over.

About the Author

David Wiseman is a Canadian veteran, writer, and father whose life has spanned the worlds of combat and recovery. As a former infantry soldier with the Royal Canadian Regiment, he deployed to Kandahar, Afghanistan, in 2010. His experiences with trauma, traumatic brain injury, and mefloquine toxicity shaped a decade-long journey through PTSD, loss, and transformation.

Drawing from those years of silence and survival, Wiseman began writing to understand how the wars we inherit, both at home and abroad, continue to shape us. His work explores the intersections of intergenerational trauma, masculinity, and the long road of healing after violence.

His debut book, *From the Sands of Kandahar*, traces his path from a childhood shadowed by military life to the deserts of Afghanistan and into the deeper terrain of recovery and redemption. Told with raw honesty and cinematic detail, it is a memoir about the human cost of service, the courage to confront one's past, and the quiet act of rebuilding a life.

Wiseman lives in Atlantic Canada, where he continues to write and to support others navigating trauma, intimate partner violence, and the search for meaning after war. He enjoys painting, being in nature, and spending time with his pets.

Review

"With refreshing candor, David Wiseman immerses the reader in his remarkable triumph over unimaginable adversity. Abused and neglected in the most malevolent ways in childhood, he had no blueprint to navigate relationships. In the military, obedience, hardship, and survival were well-known protagonists. His six-month tour in Afghanistan was his final descent into hell. From deadly Taliban ambushes to unnerving patrols in bazaars where even children were potential threats, fear was his constant companion. The same fear that permeated his childhood met him on the sands of Kandahar. Unwavering fortitude has since guided him in his ascent to healing body, mind, and spirit."
—**Dr. Sandra T. de Blois,** PhD
Professional Counsellor and Trauma Expert

"In *From the Sands of Kandahar,* readers will learn how David Wiseman grew up in a challenging and difficult household. They will follow him through his training with the Canadian military and his experiences as a soldier in the War of Afghanistan, where he lived through things that nobody should have to experience. When he came home to Canada, another war began as he struggled to adjust to civilian life and be a loving husband and father. Despite physical and mental health issues, Dave learned to take control of his life and get the help and treatment he needed to achieve a good quality of life and be an inspiration to his family and friends. Now he helps other veterans cope with the consequences of war. Dave's message: Regardless of life circumstances, you can change your story and become the author of your best life. What does not break you will make you a strong soul in life. Never give up. This is a must-read book and a great gift anytime for anyone who is struggling in life."

—Mr. Glenn Roil,
Executive Chairman, Senior Advisor, and Co-Founder, Mental Health Foundation of Canada
Member, Government of NL Mental Health Care and Treatment Review Board
President and Chairman of the Board, Canada Without Poverty

"From the Sands of Kandahar is not only a gripping account of military service in Afghanistan—it's a profound exploration of trauma, healing, and the invisible burdens carried across generations. David Wiseman's memoir is courageous in its honesty as it illuminates the psychological toll of war and the long, often painful path towards recovery.

"What makes this memoir especially powerful is how it highlights the severe consequences of generational trauma. David's memoir doesn't just chronicle one man's trauma and PTSD; it reveals how trauma can ripple through generations, shaping identities, relationships, and coping mechanisms. David's willingness to confront this legacy head on is both brave and necessary.

"In sharing his story, Wiseman has created more than a memoir—he's offered a road map for healing, a call for compassion, and a reminder that the scars of war are not always visible. His voice is one of resilience, and his journey through the healing process is a beacon for those seeking new paths to recovery. David is a fighter: not only did he choose to enlist in the middle of a war and amid childhood trauma, he then chose to keep fighting for himself through his healing process. David's story shows us that healing doesn't always happen overnight. It can take years, multiple efforts, and different types of resources. Eventually he realized that sometimes the best healing doesn't come from outside but from within. "To David, I say thank you. Thank you for your service, your honesty, and your courageousness to share.

"'The Lord is close to the brokenhearted and saves those who are crushed in spirit.' (Psalm 34:18)"

—**David Muise,**
Director of Business Development, Nuvista Psychedelic Medicine

"From the Sands of Kandahar is a raw, deeply personal memoir by Canadian veteran David Wiseman, tracing his journey from a turbulent childhood marked by domestic violence to his 2010 deployment in Afghanistan and the long, painful path of healing that followed.

"The memoir follows Wiseman's enlistment in the Royal Canadian Regiment, where he sought structure, belonging, and redemption. Instead, he found trauma that layered upon trauma. He eventually learned that a childhood filled with fear, silence, and abuse had prepared his nervous system for combat.

"From the Sands of Kandahar is not just a war memoir—it's a testimonial of survival and transformation. It exposes the hidden costs of military service, the silence of trauma, and the courage it takes to rebuild a soul. Wiseman's story ends not in despair but in reclamation."

—**Simon B. MacInnis,** Ocdt. Retired

"The RCR motto 'Never Pass a Fault' was intended as a call not for criticism, but for action: report an issue, and, in a perfect world, resolve it. *In From the Sands of Kandahar,* David Wiseman breaks the deafening silence and lack of recognition around mefloquine toxicity, known as quinism. By relaying his experiences in the military at multiple levels, crossing continents and commands, Wiseman illuminates a broken link

within the chain of currency unspent in the care of our injured soldiers who are suffering and enduring hardships despite the systems meant to support them. A read worth sharing. Spread the awareness! Pro Patria!"
—**Bruce Given**, CD, Sgt. Retired
Fellow RCR, author, and veterans' advocate
Edmonton, AB

"This memoir had me riveted to the pages, unable to read it fast enough. This is a raw brutally honest story of a traumatized boy to a dysfunctional man, a dysfunctional young man to a soldier.... to Mefloquine. It's heartbreaking, and as a mother, I am left just wanting to try and fix everything, wanting him to be free of all the demons and atrocities he faced his entire life, only to find out he has been poisoned.... Mefloquine Poisoned.

"Dave honestly writes in a fashion that makes the reader feel a part of the scenes unfolding. You are left feeling dry in your throat from fear, panic and dust, and the smells that this author brings to your senses almost leave you tasting blood and gunpowder.

"As I read, I felt deafened by the noise of war and chaos that his words brought to the reader. There are scenes in this book I wish I had never read, but that's because of the things he saw and shared with the reader.

"I met Dave Wiseman at my 9th Annual Veterans Mefloquine Conference. Dave spoke at the conference and shared one small passage from his book, and his words stunned us all. I knew this book would be impactful after hearing him read that excerpt at the conference, because I witnessed another veteran walk up and thank Dave for 'opening up his soul.'

"For anyone who has ever served, and especially all the veterans and their families impacted by the horror of Mefloquine, this book is a must-read.

"My hope is that as he shares so honestly about his life, other families who do not understand the veteran who returned home after Mefloquine, just might find this book a window to understanding.

"I recommend this book, and truly as it is written and played out in the pages, I can't help but think....wow this would make one hell of a movie."

—Marj Matchee,
Founder of The Annual Veterans Mefloquine Rally/Conference

Photo Gallery

Here are some photos from my days in Afghanistan.